Magic in Practice

Those who say it can't be done
should not interrupt the person doing it.

Ancient Chinese proverb

Personal Development Plans: A Special Offer to all Readers

After reading this book, health professionals are invited to log on to www.magicinpractice.com to complete an online test.

The Society of Medical NLP will issue successful participants with an official learning record, equivalent to six hours of advanced communication skills study, for inclusion in their personal development plans. This represents a full day's training in Medical NLP. Society of Medical NLP trainings have been accepted in the UK for Postgraduate Education Allowance (PGEA) and Personal Development Plans (PDP) since 1998, and Continuing Professional Development (CPD), since 2007. See www.magicinpractice.com for further details.

Magic in Practice

Introducing Medical NLP: The Art and Science of Language in Healing and Health

by Garner Thomson

with

Dr Khalid Khan

Introduction by

Dr Richard Bandler

Co-creator and Developer of Neuro-Linguistic Programming

Hammersmith Press
London, UK

First published in 2008 by Hammersmith Press Limited,
496 Fulham Palace Road, London SW6 6JD, UK
www.hammersmithpress.co.uk

Disclaimer
Please note that all information in this book is provided for educational purposes only and should not be construed as, nor replace, medical or psychiatric advice. If you are suffering from a physical or psychological problem, please seek the advice of the appropriately qualified health professional. If you wish to use Medical NLP in the treatment of others, either adjunctively or alone, you are required to undergo the appropriate training. See www.medicalnlp.com for details.

British Library Cataloguing in Publication Data: A CIP record of this book is available from the British Library.

ISBN 978-1-905140-19-0

Commissioning editor: Georgina Bentliff
Designed by Julie Bennett
Copyediting by Carrie Walker
Typesetting by Phoenix Photosetting, Chatham, Kent
Production by Helen Whitehorn, Pathmedia
Printed and bound by MPG Books, Bodmin, Cornwall

Contents

Acknowledgements

Many people have contributed to this book in a variety of ways – but none more so than Dr Richard Bandler, without whom it, quite literally, would have been inconceivable. His insight, intellectual honesty and wisdom have combined to create one of the most significant epistemological developments in the past century. Apart from his work, which continues to inspire our own, we are hugely grateful for the support and encouragement he has given to the foundation and development of The Society of Medical NLP. The number of doctors, students and allied health professionals who have had the opportunity to experience the power and potential of this extraordinary technology and to pass on the benefits to their patients is growing, and will, we hope, continue to do so as the years go by.

We thank those many doctors, students and allied health professionals who have entrusted us with their training, and we applaud their courage in seeking to explore beyond the edges of their known maps. The discoveries and experiences they report back to us are a constant source of inspiration and delight.

Our appreciation goes to those researchers whose work we cite in this book. While they have inspired us in our search for explanations for the theories of NLP, and the mysteries of the body-mind system, human relationships and health, we emphasise that any interpretation placed upon their work is that of the authors of this book, and should in no way be taken as support or endorsement for our theories and findings. Our thanks, too, to those writers and thinkers who granted our requests to quote their words or reproduce their diagrams. To those who did not, or were, for any reason, unable to respond, we would appreciate it if they contacted us so we can include credits in later editions.

A particular mention must go to our publisher, Georgina Bentliff, who believed in this book from the very beginning and whose faith and encouragement never failed.

Finally, we would like to extend our gratitude to our patients – undoubtedly, the greatest teachers of all.

IMPORTANT NOTE

Introduction

Dr Richard Bandler

Co-creator and Developer of NLP

All I can say is: *it's about time*. This is the kind of book I hoped one of my students would write. What Garner Thomson has done, with Dr Khalid Khan, is to take my work further and, with great precision, present tools for health-care professionals, while at the same time offering all those in NLP a solid understanding of how the technology of NLP works in the brain.

I have for years been very good at modelling successful healers, but have fallen short on providing the science. I have used Magnetic Resonance Imaging since it was available to understand the mysteries of the brain. Now, these gentlemen have gone so much farther. I say thank you – and recommend that any Neuro-Linguistic Programmer read this over and over and over.

It seems obvious to me that the more we know about the brain and how it works well, the better off we will be. And the two most important applications of my work will always be education and health. My work has been accepted by psychologists and therapists. Over the years, I have trained thousands of doctors, teachers and health-care professionals. The American Dental Society claimed that NLP had the only cure for dental phobia. However, I doubt that myself: I believe there are as many ways for the brain to learn better behaviour as there is imagination in the world.

What this book represents is a startling step forward in filling in details and applying technology. Rigorous, yet easy to understand, this is a presentation of powerful patterns of human learning. I believe that, 50 years from now, you will find it on every health-care professional's bookshelf. So be one of those exceptional people who lead the pack and get it there now.

I am proud to have been the inspiration for such an elegant and wonderful book. Having read it just once, I am now going to go back through it again. You should do the same.

The only other thing I can say is: Thank you!

About the Authors

Garner Thomson, NLP Master Practitioner and Trainer, and founder and training director of the Society of Medical NLP, is the creator of the Medical NLP programme taught to doctors, allied health professionals and medical students since 1996. Trained in NLP by Dr Richard Bandler, and with a background in psychology, communications, Ericksonian hypnotherapy and trans-cultural and integrative health-care approaches, he also runs a busy Medical NLP and Hypnotherapy practice, writes and lectures widely, and appears on radio and television, both as presenter and guest.

Dr Khalid Khan is a primary care physician and registered pharmacist. A GP trainer, tutor at King's College London School of Medicine and St George's University of London, he also practises as a medical acupuncturist, is a Fellow of the Chinese Medical Institute and Register (CMIR) and is an advisor to the International Journal of Acupuncture. Author of the popular Mnemonics for Medical Students and a Master Practitioner in both NLP and Medical NLP, Dr Khan is co-founder and primary care advisor to the Society of Medical NLP.

What to Expect from this Book

Magic in Practice comprises 19 chapters arranged in two parts. The first explains the rationale of Medical NLP; the second outlines the realisation of its proprietary three-part consultation process. Our intention in the latter section is not to suggest an alternative to any existing model, but rather to provide a 'map' that can help the practitioner to integrate Medical NLP principles and techniques into whatever approach he currently employs. By recognising and addressing the psychosocial, as well as the biomedical, elements of the patient's experience, the practitioner can begin to meet at least some of the demands of medical reformists and patients themselves: to practise 'whole-person' healing.

A substantial number of references have been included, mainly of a kind that seldom passes across the desk of busy medical practitioners. Our intention has been twofold: to disabuse those who claim "no evidence" for anything that is not officially approved for general use in their field (particularly the 'irrelevance' of the 'human' aspect of the consultation), and to justify many of the empirical observations and conclusions made with such prescience by NLP's ground-breakers as long ago as 1975.

Magic in Practice – now the official handbook of The Society of Medical NLP's licence trainings – has evolved out of the same spirit of curiosity and experimentation that gave rise to NLP. When practitioners learn (or re-learn) to trust their own instincts and observations, as well as the uniqueness of each patient, surprisingly, the complex, chronic and confusing often start to make sense.

Understanding the purpose and outcomes of each phase of the Medical NLP Consultation Process allows the busy practitioner to navigate through these complex patient encounters and even, if necessary, to 'bookmark' the stage arrived at for resumption and completion at another time.

Although each chapter is largely self-contained, the reader will benefit from following the sequence in which they have been laid out. Some of the skill-sets made explicit in the final chapters require practice and assimilation in order for them to be applied with the three qualities of an effective Medical NLP practitioner: confidence, behavioural flexibility and positive expectancy. In practice, however, the health professional can use the process easily to reorientate himself if, at any point, he feels he might be losing his way.

The first part of the book addresses a number of issues we regard as important to the health and well-being of both patient and practitioner. These include the consultation itself as a solution-oriented, rather than a purely problem-solving, process; the role in all dysfunctions of limbic arousal; avoiding practitioner burnout; the impact of language on healing and health; the processes by which meaning and experience are constructed; and three valuable 'thinking tools' by which we can clarify complex situations and reduce the risk of making premature or inaccurate decisions.

The second part of *Magic in Practice* is devoted to the three phases of the Medical NLP Consultation Process: Engagement, Alignment and Reorientation.

Engagement provides easily applied, specific techniques for gaining immediate 'resonance' and concordance with the patient; managing crucial 'first impressions'; and reducing the risk of misunderstanding and litigation.

Alignment involves applying a 'broadband' awareness of both consciously and unconsciously expressed communication; accessing and stabilising the as yet unrecognised resources the patient brings to the consultation; and, safely and productively entering and understanding the patient's model of his world. This approach opens the practitioner to one of the most potentially transformative ideas of the book – that the patient's symptoms are not problems in themselves, simply to be eradicated when life-threatening risk has been eliminated and the 'cause' remains indeterminate. Sometimes, they may be seen as unconscious forms of symbolic communication which, when the underlying distress is resolved, diminish or disappear. This is discussed in detail in Chapter 11.

Many techniques aimed at restoring balance to the patient can be applied indirectly or conversationally.

Reorientation makes explicit the mechanisms that underlie the techniques, both so their function can be easily understood, and in order that the practitioner may develop bespoke approaches to meeting each patient's unique needs.

Processes employed during the reorientation phase include: developing outcomes; understanding time and its effect on illness and health; using indirect hypnotic language; applying metrics for clinical effectiveness; and, creating and installing new strategies and behaviours that the patient can carry into the future.

Although the Medical NLP Consultation Process falls into three distinct phases, practitioners may find it necessary to cycle back to certain points to gain information or test hypotheses. This is how the model should be used. Understanding the function of each phase allows the practitioner flexibility without him losing his way.

The final chapter draws all the elements together to provide the practitioner with a framework within which he can develop and apply interventions that answer the key question we believe should act as an organising principle in all consultations: *what does this person need in order to live a full, healthy and effective life?*

Notes on style

- After much debate, we have decided to use the traditional pronouns "he" and "him" to refer to both patient and practitioner, rather than more cumbersome alternatives such as "he or she", or even the fabrication "s/he". The decision was made in the interests of stylist coherence alone, and we apologise in advance for any offence this might cause.
- Also in the interests of smoother reading, the first-person plural, "we" (when used to refer to the authors) may apply to one or the other, or both.
- Although in his practice, one of the authors prefers to use the words "client" and "clients", we have agreed to refer to "patient" and "patients" throughout. "Practitioner" is used to describe both medical and non-medical health professionals.

- We use double quotation marks (“ ”) for direct quotations, and single marks (‘ ’) either to denote a secondary quote within a quote (“He always says, ‘Have a good day’”) or to signal that the word should be approached with caution.
- We use hyphens to unite two or more processes or concepts to suggest they should be regarded as a whole (for example, “body-mind”, “patient-as-whole-person”), and sometimes to denote a slightly different meaning (“dis-ease”, for example, being used to suggest a systemic imbalance causing discomfort, while “disease” retains its traditional meaning of an illness or dysfunction with a known cause).
- When using the word, ‘functional’ according to its medical definition, we put it in single quotes (our reasoning being that it has acquired questionable overtones of mental or emotional causation, and should therefore be regarded with caution); when it is intended to mean “operational”, “useful” or “practical”, we use it without quotes.

Overview

Any sufficiently advanced technology is indistinguishable from magic

Arthur C. Clarke[1]

Why, in the most scientifically, economically and socially advanced time in the history of our species, do we seem to be suffering from more depression, anxiety and psychophysical problems than ever before? Medicine has defeated most of the infectious diseases that shortened our lives 100 years ago; we are living many more years, with greater access to health care. And yet, between 25% and 50% of the problems for which patients now seek help have no evident pathological cause[2].

Despite the almost daily promises of medical "cures" and "breakthroughs" in the media, the list of "functional" or "somatoform" disorders is long and seems to be growing. At the moment, it includes chronic medically unexplained pain, irritable bowel syndrome, chronic fatigue syndrome, non-ulcer dyspepsia, headaches, premenstrual syndrome, Temporomandibular Joint Disorder (TMJ), a wide range of autoimmune dysfunctions, and environmental illnesses, such as electromagnetic hypersensitivity, and allergies.

Add to that, the 'emotional' disorders, such as depression, anxiety, phobias, Obsessive Compulsive Disorder and Post-Traumatic Stress Disorder, and we can see why the health services are in danger of being overwhelmed and patient dissatisfaction is growing.

The changing face of disease

Part of the problem may be simply explained: the molecular, biomedical, cause-and-effect model that proved so spectacularly successful in defeating the microbe is failing to address the more complex psychosocial factors that are equally responsible for failing health.

Cartesian Dualism, the separation of 'mind' from body, still affects medical training and research. The hunt for 'causality' has shifted from germ to gene, and while the prognosis for a number of fairly rare genetic disorders is improving, no gene is likely to be found for each of the scores of medically unexplained dysfunctions with which practitioners and patients wrestle every day of their lives.

Failure to find the cause (what is "the" cause of depression? what is "the" cause of cancer?) means in practice that the focus of treatment falls on the symptom. Therefore, our dependence on the trillion-dollar pharmaceutical industry is growing, and is matched only by the hopes invested in technological innovation as the rescuer of humanity in what is perceived as an ongoing battle with the 'disease' of life.

The problem of 'mind'

The implication of all diagnoses of 'functional' or 'somatoform' disorders may be that they are all, or partly, "in the mind". And 'mind' is not widely considered a matter of concern for the average medical professional. Current treatment guidelines offer two main options: psychotropic (mind-altering) medication, and outsourcing the problem to a "talking cure" professional (where these are available). Either way, the integrity of the patient-as-a-whole is compromised, and Cartesian Dualism is reinforced.

The delivery problem

The problem increases when we look at the "delivery" of health care, as opposed to its application. For various reasons, some of them political, we have entered a period of cost-effectiveness, "quality-adjusted life years", evidence-based medicine and increasing bureaucracy.

As care becomes increasingly standardised – by the National Institute for Health and Clinical Excellence and Primary Care Trusts in the United Kingdom, and insurance companies in the United States – the personal is giving way to the impersonal, compassion is surrendering to science, and practitioners, patients and the economy are all paying the price. Doctors are increasingly required to practise medicine according to a set of guidelines, or face highly punitive consequences. Patients' unhappiness with the care they receive is, in turn, reflected in the growing trend towards litigation.

It should be no surprise, then, that so many physicians retreat behind the barricades of professional detachment, from where they practise an essentially defensive form of medicine that places the effectiveness of the patient's treatment on the other side of a mountain of bureaucratic obligations, legal concerns, official guidelines, targets and restrictions on finances, resources and time. And no surprise that so many patients are responding negatively towards what they regard as a lack of concern, interest and sufficient information by emigrating towards "alternative" healthcare, or to the offices of their legal advisors with an intention to sue.

A crisis in the making?

Some commentators fear that medicine is approaching crisis point. The relational gap between patient and health provider is widening, with increasing dependence on technicians and specialists for diagnosis, and heavily drug-oriented approaches to treatment. According to several reviews, iatrogenic illness (caused by medical treatment) is now regarded as the third leading cause of death among Americans[3], while in Britain, the number of medical accidents and deaths, including those caused by misdiagnosis and adverse reactions to medication, is conservatively estimated to be more than 1 million a year[4].

Health professionals, too, are victims of the situation. A large body of evidence exists that shows many doctors suffer high levels of stress as a result of their work, impairing both their health and their ability to provide quality care to their patients. The main sources of work-related stress and burnout among doctors, in both primary and secondary care, have been identified as workload and the resultant effect on their personal lives, organisational changes, poor management, insufficient resources, constant exposure to the suffering of their patients, mistakes, complaints and litigation[5].

It is our contention that both patient and practitioner can benefit from an expanded model of health care – the patient by being seen and treated as a 'whole person', and the practitioner by having a choice of non-invasive, non-pharmacological tools and principles that, in the consultation partnership, can help to meet that need.

Whole-person healing

In many ways, this is an idea whose time has come. The Centre for Advancement of Health in Washington DC[6] is one of several influential organisations currently lobbying for changes in the approach to health care. Those organisations and a growing number of individual campaigners are broadly in agreement that:

1. Attitudes, thoughts, feelings and behaviours must be recognised as important aspects of healing and health;
2. The mind and body flourish or perish together. Therefore patients should not be sent to one 'repair shop' for sick thoughts and feelings, and another for sick bodies;
3. Scientific evidence is overwhelming that how and where we live, who we are, and how we think, feel and cope can powerfully affect our health and well-being. To ignore this is irresponsible; and,
4. Patient care must shift to treating the whole person. This will result in healthier individuals, healthier communities and healthier nations[7].

Noble as these sentiments are, it is not enough simply to urge the health professional to begin practising whole-person health care. What exactly is "holistic patient management", and how might it be practically pursued in the context of the medical consultation? Indeed, although we have come to know a lot about disease, what exactly is "health"? These are just some of the questions this book seeks to answer.

Health as process

Our first presupposition is that health is more than an absence of disease. Rather, it exists along the 'sweet spot' between order and chaos. Our body-mind system is in a state of constant, dynamic interaction with both the internal and external environment, which itself is changing rapidly. The degree to which we are able respond to these changes and can restore body-mind systemic balance reflects both our current health and our ability to heal.

One purpose of this book is to unravel (as far as is possible at this stage in our knowledge) those elusive qualities that make up a "positive relationship" between doctor and patient – and to share with our colleagues in the health-care professions some of the principles and techniques that we, and many of the doctors and medical students who have undergone our trainings, have found to help facilitate the healing process.

The development of NLP

"Neuro-Linguistic Programming", as its name suggests, refers to language (words, as well as other symbol systems, such as physical posture, gestures and related non-verbal forms of communication) as a function of the nervous system and its transformation into 'subjective experience'. Put more simply, it focuses on the way we use our five senses to create a 'map' of 'reality', which we then use to navigate our way through the world. It is a basic premise of NLP that the quality of our maps dictates the quality of our lives.

In our opinion, NLP ranks as one of the most significant epistemological developments of our time. It developed – and continues to develop – out of Dr Richard Bandler's curiosity about the nature of subjective experience, especially that of individuals whose performance is outstanding in their fields. While most scientific research begins with investigation into how problems and deficiencies develop, Dr Bandler's question has always been, *how do people achieve excellence*?

His first subjects were a group of therapists, unrelated in their approaches, but who were nonetheless achieving results well beyond those of their peers. These included Dr Milton Erickson, a medical doctor and clinical hypnotist, Virginia Satir, now widely regarded as the founder of family therapy, Gestalt therapist Fritz Perls and noted body-worker Moshe Feldenkrais. Bandler observed certain commonalities in their work. Interestingly, none of the subjects of his study appeared consciously aware of these patterns, and they had never met each other, and even when they later came together, they were reportedly unimpressed by one another.

Bandler and his colleague, John Grinder, began to experiment. By identifying each sequence of their subjects' approach, testing it on themselves and other eager volunteers, and refining the processes, they found that the effects could be replicated. Furthermore, these capabilities could easily be taught to others, with similar results. These experiments led to one of the key presuppositions that has come to underpin NLP: *Subjective experience has a structure.* Following on from that is the corollary: *Change the structure, and the subjective experience will also change.*

It was widely believed at that time that, apart from drugs, interpretation and insight were the only means whereby effective emotional and behavioural change could be achieved, and that only with considerable effort and time. But Bandler continued to demonstrate, on a range of patients, including long-stay schizophrenic and psychotic patients, that changing the map could have a dramatic and immediate effect.

In the introduction to his first book, *The Structure of Magic*, published in 1975, he wrote:

> *The basic principle here is that people end up in pain, not because the world is not rich enough to allow them to satisfy their needs, but because their representation of the world is impoverished.*[8]

Two other key principles emerged from Bandler's essentially pragmatic approach. The first was that human beings act largely according to various permutations of automated, or patterned, responses, and the second that each person has a signature way of 'coding' his experience by the use of his five senses.

Medical NLP and health

Medical NLP – the application of the principles and techniques of NLP to the specific needs of health professionals and their patients – is an internationally recognised and licensed model that formally integrates non-invasive, non-pharmacological and clinically effective approaches with the existing principles and techniques of the consultation process*.

Supported by extensive research and clinical experience, it offers, for the first time, explicit principles and techniques applicable to a wide range of complex, chronic conditions that have symptoms, but no readily identifiable cause. In holding as a goal the physical and psychological coherence of the patient, and integrating seamlessly with any aspect of health care, it functions as a practical and continually evolving "salutogenic" model of "whole-person" healing and health in the spirit of that envisioned and advocated by Aaron Antonovsky[9].

One of the central messages of *Magic in Practice* is that a fundamental component of an effective consultation is an equal and proactive contract between doctor and patient. The relationship functions as a therapeutic agent in itself.

Many practitioners will admit to being mystified by the fact that two patients with apparently identical symptoms will respond entirely differently to the same treatment. And many patients can recall encountering a physician, who, somehow, by some indefinable means unrelated to any specific treatment, just "made" them "feel better". If pressed, both will agree that some factor, other than conventional medical treatment, is responsible for facilitating healing. The doctor may attribute this to the patient's "attitude", the patient to the doctor's "bedside manner".

The underlying dynamic undoubtedly depends on effective communication. To focus our students' attention on the true process and purpose of communication, we draw attention to the origins of the word. It is derived from the Indo-European collective, *Ko,* meaning "share", and *Mei*, meaning "change". Communication in Medical NLP, therefore, is a *Ko Mei* process - a *coming together in order to effect change.*

We would like to emphasise, too, that practitioners of NLP and Medical NLP are not *de facto* 'therapists'. As Dr Bandler repeatedly

* All training and certification by The Society of Medical NLP is recognised and licensed by Dr Richard Bandler, the co-creator and developer of NLP, and his Society of NLP. It has also been approved in the United Kingdom since 1998 as suitable for PGEA (now Personal Development Plans), and, since 2007, by the Royal Colleges, for Continuing Professional Development (CPD).

asserts, practitioners strive to help their clients (or patients) re-learn more resourceful physical and/or psychological behaviours. Therefore, a knowledge of, or adherence to, a particular school of 'psychology' or a specific medical specialisation is not necessary for effective intervention.

What is not in doubt is the fact that the *quality* of the relationship between doctor and patient is at least as important as the treatment itself. Historical evidence exists that a number of treatments now discarded as "unscientific" demonstrated a 50–70% cure rate when they were still regarded as mainstream[10]. More recent research, specifically in the area of 'emotional' disorders (increasingly falling within the provenance of general medicine), suggests that as little as 15% of effectiveness results from the therapeutic procedure alone[11].

Physicians who have been in practice for more than a few decades will not be surprised by this. For much of the first part of the 20th century, the relational quality between doctor and patient was emphasised in medical training and explicit in practice, even as science was advancing the knowledge and expertise of the health practitioner. This commitment to partnering human values with technological innovation was reflected in Britain's Royal College of General Practitioners' adoption in 1952 of the motto *Cum Scientia Caritas* (Science with Compassionate Care).

To this end, *Magic in Practice* presents key NLP techniques applied in the specific context of health care, as well as new approaches developed in real-world situations out of the principles of observation, information-gathering, hypothesis-creation and testing.

Although the principles and techniques presented here are not intended to replace medical consultation and appropriate treatment, they will be of interest to doctors in both primary and secondary care, as well as nurses, psychologists, counsellors and therapists – anyone, in fact, interested in developing a more integrative and effective approach to patient care.

Why "Magic"?

Since NLP's emergence in the mid-1970s, "magic" has been a word often associated with its practice. Where it functions as a "meta-psychology", it focuses on structure and process (how we create and maintain our model of 'reality'), rather than losing itself in detail and speculation.

It demands behavioural flexibility on the part of the practitioner to accommodate the uniqueness of each individual's patterns, and provides the systematic means of generating techniques specifically tailored to the needs of each patient or client.

The speed with which an elegantly designed and applied intervention can result in change can often challenge and mystify. The mystery is intensified when we consider that the primary tools of these interventions are non-pharmacological, non-invasive, and non-toxic, something that cannot be said for virtually any other treatment in the field of medical care.

More than 30 years ago, the idea that neurological processes could be impacted and re-routed by non-invasive processes was largely speculative. Bandler was one of the first researchers to apply neural scanning by Magnetic Resonance Imaging (MRI) technology to explore the impact of NLP on brain function. Since then, as we will show in this book, neuroscience and psychology have evolved dramatically, to cast even more light into the "black box" of brain and behaviour. We now know – and ignore at our own peril and that of our patients – that the brain constantly moves in and out of complex, interrelating dynamic equilibria, responding to the context or 'meaning' of its experience[12], is actively damaged by 'negative' data[13] and can even alter its physical architecture[14]. It follows then that communication within the practitioner-patient relationship is an important source of data for the meaning-making brain and the body with which it functions as an integrated whole.

Words can literally affect us for better or worse. It is surprising, then, that so little time and attention is paid to the quality and precision (what NLP calls the "elegance") of the language we use. Substantial research supports the assertion that *how* a respected health professional says something can directly affect the patient's physical and psychological well-being at least as much as *what* he says[15].

Communication works both ways. Not only can clinical outcomes be affected for better or worse by the quality of the patient-physician relationship, but, in the event of medical accident, the patient's decision to litigate has been shown in several studies to be based substantially more on the doctor's "attitude" and the quality of the relationship between doctor and patient than on the accident itself[16].

We believe that at least part of the apparent "magic" of Medical NLP derives not from any mystical properties of the methodology, but from the narrowness of the paradigm it is seeking to expand. To take Arthur C. Clarke's Third Law further, it is not difficult to demonstrate that virtually any health technology would appear superior to one that regards the individual as merely:

1. a biomechanical 'object' whose thinking processes have little impact on his health or well-being;
2. a product of purely Newtonian cause-and-effect processes;
3. a closed system, largely uninfluenced by other 'closed systems';
4. equal in every way to every other individual, benefiting from standardised treatments;
5. an organism that produces symptoms which require suppression or removal without any significant regard to the reason or reasons for the appearance of those symptoms; and,
6. 'fixable' by the application of purely mechanistic rules in much the same way as a watchmaker fixes a watch.

The placebo effect: the neurophysiology of care

Any change for the better that is unexplained by scientifically approved treatment is often labelled by the medical establishment as a placebo response. We are not unduly perturbed by this. So prevalent is the response at all levels of research and treatment that we are utterly confident in the declaration that *something important is happening that deserves to be recognised and, wherever possible, incorporated into practical healthcare.*

Furthermore, we believe that a greater awareness of this apparently inbuilt psychophysiological capability can renew hope for millions of people whose complex chronic conditions remain inadequately addressed by Western scientific knowledge. By this, we are not proposing a reintroduction of dummy pills and sham treatments, but rather consideration of the psychological and biochemical substrates that underlie the human bodymind system to self-regulate under certain conditions, the mechanisms of which are just beginning to be understood.

The problem faced by medical orthodoxy, as pointed out by Gershom Zajicek in a seminal paper in *The Cancer Journal*, is that nothing in pharmacokinetic theory accounts for the placebo effect. "(Therefore) in order to keep the theory consistent, the placebo effect is regarded as random error or noise which can be ignored," he says[17].

Regrettably, the word, "placebo" (derived from the mediaeval prayer, *Placebo Domino*, "I shall please the Lord") has acquired pejorative overtones, suggesting deception, weakness, and scientific irrelevancy. But this is a semantic rather than a scientifically grounded shift. As we will point out throughout this book, the word for a thing is not the thing itself. We should not confuse naming or defining with understanding or experiencing. *We do not make something invalid merely by labelling it as such.*

Indeed, so pervasive – and sometimes so dramatic – is the placebo response that some scientists have suggested reclassifying it. Suggestions include "the healing response", "remembered wellness", the "human effect" and the "meaning response", none of which suggests irrelevance or spuriousness.

Research into the effect is widespread. Taken together, the studies suggest that the placebo response is a product of a complex interaction of various processes that fall into three main classifications: "expectancy", "meaning" and "conditioning"[18]. Briefly, this suggests that both practitioner and patient expect a positive outcome, and that the patient is able to understand and attribute meaning to his experience. Conditioning refers to the adoption and perfection of new, health-related behaviours and responses, as well as to the linking of a specific stimulus to a new and healthful response.

It would be difficult to study, or even identify, the placebo response, except within the context of relationships – those of the patient and his world-view; the patient and his understanding; and, crucially importantly, the patient with his practitioner. All treatment outcomes are, in large part, a result of relationships, and relationships are made or broken by communication. We therefore respectfully offer this book for the consideration of all practitioners, regardless of school or specialisation, who believe there should be 'something more' to health care than standardised interpretations and treatments. Conditioning, expectancy and meaning are all processes that can be modelled, developed and transmitted through the principles and techniques of Medical NLP.

Whatever we choose to call it, there is more to healing and health than a drug, a surgical procedure or psychological counselling. As we will show, there is an increasing body of research that suggests that the success of many currently accepted procedures (up to 75% in one recent review of 19 depression therapy studies[19]) is unrelated to the physical treatment itself. Whether we call it the placebo response, the human effect or the healing response, it is both 'real' and a valuable component of good medicine. In the words of Dr W Grant Thompson, a noted consultant on clinical trials and author of *The Placebo Effect and Health*:

> *Whatever the view, (it) exists, and understanding it is important to modern medicine. Wise doctors know that it is a factor in every treatment and an essential part of their daily work.*[20]

We (the authors) do not claim to have definitive answers; we certainly have many questions still unanswered that continue to spark our curiosity. But, even at this stage, we can point to a substantial body of theory and research currently excluded from "evidence-based" medical decision-making. It is also interesting to note how much of this now supports the observation and reasoning that prompted Bandler and his colleagues to develop NLP more than 30 years ago. We also present explicit principles and techniques that we and our Medical NLP-trained colleagues have found useful in our practices, together with anecdotes and case studies to illustrate their practical application (certain details, of course, having been changed to maintain confidentiality).

We encourage you to develop curiosity and behavioural flexibility, to explore these principles for yourself and to reclaim the status of the practitioner as co-creator of his patients' health by actively enhancing and administering what Michael Balint referred to as the most powerful of all drugs – the practitioner himself[21].

Or, as a senior consultant remarked at the end of one of our trainings, "If all this is the placebo effect, I want to be the best placebo I possibly can."

Part I: Rationale

1

Towards Healing and Health: a solution-oriented approach

Problem-solving is an energy-intensive approach that focuses on deficiencies in the hope of identifying and removing them. Solution-orientation explores and develops options, choices and possibilities with a view to reorientating the individual or group towards flexibility and growth.

Problem-solving is reactive, remedial and piecemeal. Solution-orientation is active, generative and holistic.

Problem-solving looks at people as a collection of 'parts'. Solution-orientation sees the person-as-whole.

Many of the current problems in health care derive from a reductionist, mechanistic view of humans and human nature that is several centuries old. Still largely committed to both the cause-and-effect model and the enduring myth of Cartesian Dualism, the separation of humans into mutually exclusive domains of body and mind, mainstream medicine has little power over the rising tide of complex, chronic, inexplicable dysfunctions that can result in lifetimes of debility and pain.

People are living longer, mainly because of science's massive advances in the areas of infectious and acute medicine, but they are not necessarily enjoying a consistently better quality of life. The nature of the problems we now face is changing. Disease itself is changing. But we – health providers and patients – are not.

Today, a doctor may go through his entire career without ever encountering a case of smallpox, diphtheria or epiglottitis, but he will almost certainly feel overwhelmed by the sheer weight of the conditions that now characterise the majority of the problems patients present. In Britain, the Royal Society of General Practitioners has been reported as estimating that around 50% of the problems seen by general practitioners are social, 25% psychological, and approximately half of the remaining 25% are psychosomatic[22]. In practice, physicians report that most of the remaining 12.5% of "organic" disorders seen involve at least some aspects of the psychosocial dysfunctions mentioned above.

The cause-and-effect model, when routinely applied to some complex, chronic conditions, is contributing to a massive epidemic of new problems. Over-dependence on the "magic bullet" approach contributes to tunnel vision, iatrogenic illness and reduction in treatment options for the practitioner. The complex, multi-factorial nature of illness and the inherent biological diversity of human beings are in serious danger of being ignored in the pursuit of a "perfect science"[23,24].

Meanwhile, misdiagnosed and under treated anxiety disorders alone cost the United States' economy $54 billion a year, with much of the economic burden resulting from patients seeking – and receiving – treatment for the physical symptoms of the dysfunctions[25]. In England, the total cost of mental health problems has been estimated by the Sainsbury Centre for Mental Health at £77.4 billion, including £12.5 billion in care, £23.1 billion in lost output, and £41.8-billion in 'hidden' costs[26].

Despite the best intentions of its practitioners, medical practice is morphing from the provision of "health care" into costly, and often inadequate, attempts to manage or contain dis-ease.

Evidence for solutions

The rise of evidence-based medicine (EBM) – the standardisation of treatments based on randomised controlled trials (RCTs) – as the only acceptable basis for health care is also giving rise to problems. Its application, to the exclusion of human qualities such as instinct, experience and common sense, diminishes artistry and compassion, both qualities long accepted as significant adjuncts to the practitioner's application of best available scientific knowledge.

Treatments not easily validated by RCTs are largely ignored – despite the fact that much of our historical success in defeating disease has arisen from trial and error, based on bold hypotheses, rather than from *in vitro* RCTs. Many treatments still in use, and unlikely soon to be abandoned, derive from 'another kind' of evidence. These include antibiotics, insulin, tracheostomy (to relieve tracheal obstructions), the draining of abscesses, vaccination and even the use of aspirin.

Some scientists – even those from within the ranks of EBM – are beginning to suggest that certain classes of evidence, other than that provided by RCTs, warrant acceptance. Professor Paul Glasziou, Director of the Centre for Evidence-Based Medicine at the University of Oxford, together with three colleagues, has developed a simple and elegant algebraic formula for measuring what they call the "signal (treatment effect) to noise (natural outcome) ratio". A high signal-to-noise ratio, they say, reflects a strong treatment effect, even in the presence of confounding factors, such as the natural progression of a disease[27].

We (the authors) continue to argue that an outcome that satisfies an individual patient's needs (and does no harm) should be the prime objective of every consultation. Many studies now emerging help give direction and substance to the Medical NLP proposition that whole-person health is both possible and applicable – with some adjustment to our current viewpoint. Some of these suggest that:

- 'health' does not necessarily follow from the removal of the symptom;
- many 'dysfunctions' are, in fact, adaptive responses that have helped us survive and flourish as a species;
- a purely medical response to some of these may actually damage the individual's overall ability to resist and progress towards healing and health;
- our bodies, brains, and especially our immune systems, need to be challenged in order to function effectively. Removing challenge may impair our ability to respond and survive;
- while one gene may predispose the carrier to a particular disease, many of the factors that influence gene expression – whether some conditions develop or not – lie within the way we live our lives, the attitudes we hold, the meaning we attribute to our situation and the relationships upon which we can, or cannot, rely;

- physical symptoms can often not only 'communicate' emotional or social distress, but can also provide the astute practitioner with highly specific guidance on how he can assist the patient to restore balance to his life;
- the *relationship* between practitioner and patient is an important (sometimes the *most* important) factor that precipitates healing;
- the practitioner's communication – verbal and non-verbal – can bypass conscious processing and directly and measurably affect the functioning of the patient's neurological system ... for better or worse.

Most practitioners may well feel overwhelmed in the face of the implications raised by all this and, quite understandably, revert to the first-line response of attempted symptom removal. However, a simple shift of perspective, from a purely problem-solving to a solution-oriented approach, helps us to make sense of it all.

More than 30 years ago, when Dr Richard Bandler posed the paradigm-shifting question, *If knowing how people get ill doesn't always help them recover, how do people get better?* he opened the way for the development of the methodology now known as Neuro-Linguistic Programming. This also alerted some leaders in other fields – humanistic, systemic and family psychology, sports and business, in particular – to the possibility that energy previously spent trying to remedy apparently intractable problems could be more profitably directed at exploring outcomes and solutions.

This generative (as opposed to remedial) approach has since been strongly supported by research. Expectation alone – the anticipation, of both health professional and patient, that something good and positive will result from treatment – has been demonstrated to have a powerful, positive effect on clinical outcomes[28,29,30].

Solutions: more than the removal of a problem

When medicine's essentially problem-solving approach fails to remedy a complaint, or constellation of complaints, a subtle transfer of responsibility to the patient takes place. Labels, such as "functional", "psychogenic", "somatoform", "psychosomatic" and "medically unexplained" may carry implications of some degree of mental or emotional imbalance. Now, the label (and the patient) becomes the problem.

A problem-oriented approach easily confuses the removal or sedation of the symptom with its cure – but, as anyone who has been treated with antidepressants will confirm, "not being depressed" is seldom the same thing as "being happy".

According to the problem-oriented model, illness, in all its forms, is the result of some deficit or other, whether it is the failure of the individual to pursue sensible dietary advice, an immune system that ignores a cancer cell, or a brain that ceases to balance its uptake of serotonin. Problem-oriented medicine looks for "proximal" causes and largely ignores factors such as the evolutionary or adaptive nature of the illness, the unconscious 'meaning' or value the dysfunction might have to that specific individual, and the entire psychological, social and spiritual landscape within which the patient and his problem exist.

An expanded view

A solution-oriented approach recognises the need for an expanded view of both illness and health. Although many organisations and individual practitioners recognise the need for a more 'holistic' approach, few suggest how this might be achieved. Some attempt to accomplish this by randomly incorporating or recommending 'complementary' techniques, such as homeopathy, acupuncture and aromatherapy.

But although any of these may well add value for the patient, their piecemeal incorporation does not equate with a whole-person view of the patient. The Medical NLP approach presented in this book aims to help widen the practitioner's perspective to include, along with his biomedical profile:

- the uniqueness of each patient;
- the emotional and psychological aspects of his situation;
- the 'meaning' of his illness, both personally and adaptively;
- the social context within which his problem has arisen;
- the as yet untapped resources he brings to the consultation.

With this in mind, the practitioner is better equipped to explore with the patient his needs, resources and endogenous potential for change.

The need for options

All patients seeking help from a health professional for any problem whatsoever are stuck and stressed. The problem has not yet resolved itself (if it is self-limiting), or all previous attempted actions and remedies have failed. The inbuilt capacity for self-regulation (shared by all living systems) has been compromised. This either causes, or is a factor in, almost every major illness to which people fall prey[31].

Flexibility, responsiveness, adaptability – these biological necessities must all be restored if health is to be improved and maintained. Medical NLP regards the human being as a biological system operating within a succession of larger systems (psychological, social, spiritual and evolutionary). To help an individual create options at any of these levels is to increase the flexibility of his functioning as an integrated whole.

Practitioners themselves also benefit from having more options – especially those which have the potential to help their patients in the moment, without unnecessary recourse to drugs or outsourcing the problem to costly and time-consuming "talking" therapies.

Seeking opportunities

The possibility of something positive emerging from the challenge of illness and dysfunction is surprisingly appealing to many patients. It is easy to understand how compelling (and sometimes how useful) such a belief might be when they are faced with the fear and chaos that can accompany chronic, inexplicable dysfunction and dis-ease.

Some writers and psychologists, including Joseph Campbell and Carl Jung, have suggested that the metaphor of the individual's journey through crisis, challenge and renewal is embedded in our cultural DNA. Certainly, the structure known as "The Hero's Journey" is encountered throughout all story-telling societies, including in their fairytales, movies, soap operas and computer games*.

But whether you and your patients choose to regard the consultation process as part of a symbolic journey or a partnership based on developing more choices, it is an opportunity to bring order out of chaos. To accomplish this, both need to explore the possibilities (other than the moderation or removal of the symptom) that can emerge when a previously stable situation suddenly destabilises, and we embark on the complex, intriguing and challenging process of change.

The qualities of change

Change can be easy, instantaneous and lasting. Curiously, as family therapist Virginia Satir often observed, it is also something that many people fear more than anything else. Experience shows that this fear is almost always based on the belief that gain can only arise out of pain, and on not knowing how – or even that – a specific change can take place.

The opposing belief, that change can be relatively effortless, runs counter to the received 'wisdom' that suggests it should be a slow and painful process – or, as the old joke has it:

> *Q: How many psychiatrists does it take to change a light bulb?*
> *A: Only one – but it'll be a long, difficult and expensive process – and the light bulb has really got to **want** to change …*

Certainly, change does not need to be hard work. As they were exploring the structure of the patterns they were observing, Bandler and his colleagues began to question the belief that change is always incremental and

* The structure of The Hero's Journey involves a call to action (the crisis) and the protagonist's response to the call (seeking options, opportunities and guidance in an effort to resolve the crisis). A series of challenges and setbacks lead to a decisive – though often risky and frightening – final act, in a bid to gain healing, redemption or reward. The hero then returns to his own world, renewed, healed or somehow transformed. For a moving and inspiring contemporary non-fiction account that reflects this process in the context of healing and health, see *Choosing to Heal: Surviving the Breast Cancer System* (2007), by Janet Edwards (London: Watkins).

takes place over an extended period of time. Bandler's suspicion, derived from the speed with which people learned to fear the object of a phobia, was that the brain was capable of rapid, or even "one-pass", learning. Success with his now famous Fast Phobia Cure (also known as Visual-Kinesthetic Dissociation) bore this out. Since then, hundreds of thousands of people have benefited from this insight alone, in its wide range of applications.

This contrasts with slower, not necessarily equally effective, processes, including systematic desensitisation, which gradually exposes the subject to the source of the phobic response, and flooding, which seeks to overwhelm the sufferer in a bid to "blow out" the neurological circuits holding the responses in place. Critics of these approaches (including ourselves) believe the first is too slow and, at best, only partly successful. The second carries a high risk that the subject may be unable to process the flooding, and be re-traumatised by the 'cure'.

Bandler's approach by-passes both objections. "It's easier to cure a phobia in ten minutes than in five years," he says:

> *I didn't realise that the speed with which you do things makes them last … I taught people the phobia cure. They'd do part of it one week, part of it the next, and part of it the week after. Then, they'd come to me and say: 'It doesn't work!' If, however, you do it in five minutes, and repeat it until it happens very fast, the brain understands. That's part of how the brain learns … I discovered that the human mind does not learn slowly.*[32]

Although, on the face of it, this might seem like a version of desensitisation, it differs in three other important respects: success depends on the effective dissociation of the subject from the experience, disruption of the process the sufferer has been unconsciously using in order to repeat the phobic response, and the creation of a solution frame.

We will deal with the first two "differences that make a difference" in later chapters, but the third – developing outcome frames – is critical to the Medical NLP solution-oriented approach.

The requirements of change

In order to make change possible, the subject needs to:

1. *want* to change;
2. understand that he or she *can* change;
3. know *how* to change; and,
4. notice *that* change has taken, or is taking, place.

Medical NLP regards the "resistant" patient as a myth. Perceived resistance usually stems from either a failure of the practitioner to uncover as yet unmet needs, or too little time being spent on trying to effect the change.

Sometimes, the fear of changing is overwhelming, and this in turn we believe is based on the patient not understanding that change is possible and not perceiving that both he and the physician have resources that have yet to be tapped. It is the practitioner's responsibility to reduce the patient's anxiety level, identify unmet needs and orientate the patient towards accepting the possibility of change. These will be discussed in detail later, but it can often be as simple as a form of verbal martial art:

Patient: *I don't feel any better, and I've tried everything…*
Practitioner: *Everything? So, when do you get time to sleep?*
Patient: *Well, I mean I've tried a lot of things, and nothing has worked.*
Practitioner: *…yet.*
Patient: *Well, I can't see how this is going to help.*
Practitioner *(smiling): …yet.*
Patient *(smiles): Okay … "yet".*

Strategies such as this require good engagement and rapport with the patient. As you progress through this book, you will encounter (and, we trust, test and incorporate into daily practice) a number of principles and techniques to help increase motivation, change unresourceful beliefs and behaviours, and act directly in a wide range of chronic and 'functional' disorders. Meanwhile, an important theme of this book, and the basis of any truly solution-oriented approach to medicine, is this: *the patient needs to know* ***how*** *to get (and remain) well.*

In working within the Medical NLP systemic model, the practitioner evaluates and may intervene at all levels of the patient's experience: physical, mental, psychological, social and spiritual. Since these operate as a Gestalt (an interactive system), and each Gestalt is unique to the individual, improvement or healing needs to be a bespoke process that the patient understands, and one which does not cause unnecessary concern or discomfort as it proceeds.

While a solution-oriented approach to consultation does not preclude the medico-legal requirements of due diligence, appropriate investigation and best practice, undue focus on the problems has been shown sometimes to increase, rather than reduce, patients' distress. Consider the following: when investigating pain, most physicians are taught to ask a series of direct clinical questions as part of the decision-tree process known as the differential diagnosis. Questions, where cardiac problems are suspected, may include:

- Is it a crushing pain?
- Does it radiate into your left arm?
- Does it get worse if you exert yourself?

Practitioners generally admit this is a problem-oriented approach, but consider it a necessary evil. At the same time, many suspect that even the mere suggestion of pain may in fact worsen patients' reporting, or their subjective experience, of pain. This turns out to be true, in certain cases at least[33].

In contrast, effective questioning can contribute substantially to the success of treatment. For example, the more general question, "What's it like?" may elicit specific details about the problem without exposing the patient to excessive and potentially harmful synonyms for suffering. In many cases, the patient will provide specific information about location, onset, severity, aggravating factors, etc – most, if not all, the information needed – without any prompting or further suggestion. If necessary, further gentle probing can fill in the details necessary for a full and appropriate diagnosis.

And, when the time comes to reorientate the patient towards improvement, the question, "What will you be doing, and how will you feel, when this problem you've been having has been resolved?" is just one of the tools of the solution-oriented practitioner. The way the human brain is wired requires the patient to direct his attention away from his present, problematic, state, towards a future-oriented solution-state, *in order for him to be able to provide an answer.* Quite literally, the practitioner has begun to alter the firing of the neurons in the patient's brain. Purely conversationally, he is performing 'microsurgery', with language as his tools. (More detailed suggestions for solution-oriented information-gathering appear in Chapter 9, featuring the Medical NLP Clinical Questioning Matrix.)

Knowing where to go

Solution-orientation is almost non-existent among existing consultation models. We have reviewed more than 15 frameworks, from the Calgary-Cambridge Comprehensive Clinical Method[34] to Usherwood's extensive model[35], and have found only two that suggest, in part, that the patient's role may fruitfully extend beyond the end-point of merely understanding and following treatment advice.

The model advanced in this book supplements existing models with a number of elements, all of which have been demonstrated positively to influence the outcome of the healing relationship. These include: a proactive and equal partnership between doctor and patient[36]; recognition of and matching to the patient's unique world-view; the development of an increased sense of self-efficacy through manageable strategies[37]; a clear blueprint for further action; a shared expectation that progress is to some degree or other possible[28,29]; and, an agreed system whereby progress can be measured.

Furthermore, focusing on solutions rather than problems (developing health and healthy behaviours in place of removing 'sicknesses') helps the patient (and, in many cases, the physician) "unstick" from a stuck situation, and begin to reduce frustration and stress. This, in turn, opens up room for hope and belief to enter the arena – both of these are now known to influence positively a number of health-supporting processes, including the functioning of the immune system, cellular activity and even the expression of DNA[38].

Our proposition here is simply that if, as virtually every doctor believes, there exists the problem of "psychosomatic illness", we must accept and pursue as a solution "psychosomatic healing and health".

EXERCISES

Begin to reframe problems in terms of possible solutions. By asking the right questions, you can orientate yourself, your patients, family and friends towards choices and options, as well as help to create a future beyond the problem-state.

Some suggestions for solution-oriented questions include: "What will you be doing, (how will you be thinking, feeling, speaking, etc.) when you have moved past this point?"; "What will be different or better when you are healthy again (have achieved your goal, etc.)?"; "What have you not been able to do that you will really enjoy doing when this problem is solved?"; and, "What will you have learned from this experience?"

Notice any differences in your own, or your subject's, response.

Keep notes of any particularly effective patterns you create.

2

Stress and Allostatic Load: the hidden factor in all disease

A story we heard some time ago featured a gifted young medical student strolling along the banks of a river with his professor when they heard the cries of a drowning man. Being young and fit, the student leapt in and dragged the man to safety. A few metres further along, to their surprise, they spotted another man, swept up in the current and screaming for help. Again the student plunged in to the rescue. Only minutes later, the same thing happened. The now drenched and exhausted student dragged the victim to safety, and gasped, "I don't know how many times I can keep doing this." The professor pondered for a moment and then said gently, "Perhaps you should run ahead and stop whoever's pushing them in..."

With between a third and a half of all patients who seek medical attention suffering from symptoms that have no identifiable pathology or cause[39,40,41], the time has come to move upstream and take another look at the factor or factors that all of them have in common.

"Stress" has been labelled a "global epidemic" by the World Health Organisation on the basis of studies showing that it can disrupt the functioning of almost every organ and system in the body, and is implicated to some degree in all cognitive and emotional dysfunctions. And yet, despite evidence for the role of stress in human illness, no effective, comprehensive model or guidelines exist to give practitioners the tools and understanding to curb its effects.

The reductionist approach to illness has led inevitably to organising presenting symptoms into sometimes arbitrary syndromes, which creates an illusion of discrete conditions, each of which has (or should have) a specific cause. Treatment here tends to be proximate, aiming to provide symptomatic relief, usually by pharmacological means.

In this chapter, we propose revisiting the deeply complicated and controversial subject of stress with a view to redefining its purpose and function. We are not suggesting that all illnesses can be 'cured' simply by 'managing' stress, but we, and many of our colleagues, can report considerable success in helping patients gain control over, or recover from, many chronic disorders using the working model we outline below and the approaches discussed elsewhere in this book.

In many ways, the history of the problems we face in diagnosing and treating stress parallels the history of the word itself. Linguistic Relativity*, General Semantics and Neuro-Linguistic Programming all suggest that "stress", like most other diagnostic terms, seeks to describe a process as if it were a concrete object or thing (as in "I caught a cold", or "My memory is bad", as if colds and memories have a physical reality separate from the process of 'cold-ing'† or 'remembering'†).

Most European languages share this tendency to "reify", that is, to favour nouns over verbs. In NLP, this process is known as nominalisation – reducing an experience, construct, concept or process to an object – and it can have a limiting effect on how we perceive and approach many emotional and physical problems. In medicine, this can lead to favouring biomedical explanations for ill-health over the processes they involve, ignoring social and psychological factors. This, in turn, can result in excessive pharmacological and surgical treatments[42].

Psychologist Walter Cannon suggested nearly 100 years ago that stress could overwhelm the body's capacity for self-regulation, resulting in a breakdown of the body's integrity. The idea was largely ignored for

* Also known as the Sapir-Whorf Hypothesis, it suggests that the structure of our language affects the way we think.

† The lack of verb forms for many conditions means we sometimes have to invent them in order to help patients restore movement and process to their experience.

several decades, until Hans Selye, then a young medical student, noticed that all the patients he observed being treated for infectious diseases shared certain symptoms apparently unrelated to the conditions being treated. His observations were dismissed by the senior physicians he took them to as irrelevant to the diseases they had diagnosed and were treating.

Only in the 1930s could Selye, now a qualified endocrinologist at McGill University, pursue his research into what he had begun to suspect was a "generalised response" to the stress of systemic overload – a theory supported by further research which demonstrated that the same set of symptoms could be induced by virtually any stressors he applied to his subjects. Despite continuing hostility from the medical profession, now firmly wedded to the belief that every symptom or disease should have a specific cause, Selye published his theory of a General Adaptation Syndrome in 1936[43].

Since then, stress and its effects have driven hundreds of studies that unequivocally link it to most chronic disorders. But medical science's failure to develop an effective broad-spectrum approach has caused it to be co-opted by the 'complementary' therapies, where "stress management" has become a multi-billion-dollar industry.

Why do we experience stress?

In evolutionary terms, it's easy to see that the fight-or-flight response is, as its name suggests, adaptive. Whether you're stepping into your morning shower, driving to work in the morning rush hour or facing a tiger that's escaped from the zoo, your brain is working at near light-speed to monitor for potential threats, mobilise your resources and prompt you to action.

Responding to millions of years of natural selection, your brain 'remembers' the dangers of confronting a predator without full preparation. The protective regions of your brain are ancient and quick-tempered. They mistrust the slower calculating speed of the more 'reasonable' frontal cortex. The quarter-second or so that it takes to assess a situation rationally may mean the difference between life and death, so if the alarm is strident enough, it hijacks activity away from rational thought and trusts entirely to a primaeval, entirely automated, response.

Simply put, when this happens, the hypothalamus fires the alarm to the adrenal glands, triggering thousands of simultaneous responses. Your adrenals flood your system with epinephrine (adrenaline), pushing your heart rate up, sending blood to your muscles and organs, and flooding your lungs and brain with oxygen. Glucose is released and fatty acids mobilised as a quick source of energy. Fibrinogen is released as the vessels near the surface of your skin contract, both actions intended to reduce bleeding and increase the clotting ability of your blood in the event of injury. Endorphins – your body's natural opiates – lock into their receptors, blocking the sensations of pain. Nature doesn't want you to get hurt, but it also doesn't intend you to quit if the enemy draws first blood.

This is the classic fight-or-flight response. You are poised to move, either towards or away from a predator. You are hyper-alert, hyper-responsive. Time may seem to slow down as your synapses go into overdrive. Your vision alters, ready to detect any movement that may signal danger. The response is almost instantaneous and its purpose is to *prompt you into action* in order to keep you alive*.

When the challenge has passed, your body-mind enters its second phase. Your body has suffered enormous chemical challenge, and it begins to generate other chemicals to neutralise the effect and to start repairs. One of the chief players here is cortisol. This steroid hormone, derived from cholesterol, has multiple functions: among other things, it exerts an anti-inflammatory action, helps the body restore your depleted energy sources, prompts the delivery of white blood cells to any site of injury and, crucially, combines with other functions to fix the ordeal into your long-term memory for future reference.

This effect, reproducible under laboratory conditions, is known as stress-enhanced memory[44] and, from this point on, your brain's recall centres will seek to match the pattern of the threat you've survived to those situations you will encounter (or even imagine you'll encounter) in the future. This is why we tend to remember exactly where we were and what we were doing when we encountered massive shock, such as the

* Note that the majority of symptoms experienced by patients suffering from many 'functional' disorders are easily explained as natural, evolutionary responses to perceived threat. We find that patients are often deeply reassured when their beating hearts, tingling fingers and churning stomachs are explained in this way.

September 11th bombing of the Twin Towers in New York. This is also how phobias and Post-Traumatic Stress Disorders are seeded by traumatic events.

All this is well and good; we would not have survived as a species had the system not been looking after us so efficiently. Like our prehistoric and animal ancestors, we are pretty well equipped to deal with acute stress.

The problem today

The problem today is twofold. Our fight-or-flight response is still alive and well and responding to perceived threats. However, it cannot easily distinguish between the stresses of the modern world and real life-and-death confrontations of the kind played out on the savannahs of our past between predator and prey.

The stress response is biphasic – that is, the system meets short-term stress by increasing certain responses, including immunological functions. Sustained stress, unresolved trauma and failure to adapt can, however, all seriously impair cognitive functions, downregulate immune responses and, eventually, create cellular and metabolic damage. In short, the very processes designed to save our lives in the short term become corrosive and damaging to both body and mind[45].

But, of course, not everyone is equally vulnerable to stress, and what follows are some suggestions as to why this might be so.

Some definitions

To avoid confusion, we have adopted certain terms that we will use from here on. The words "stress" and "stressors" will refer to challenging events and experiences originating from outside the patient's body. These may include incoming infections, the loss of a job or a loved one, or a daily drive to work on an overcrowded freeway.

Aside from the "fight-or-flight response", the interplay of physiological and psychological responses that comprise the patient's autonomic reaction to challenge or perceived danger will be referred to in several different ways, including "sympathetic arousal" or "limbic arousal".

The self-regulating mechanism that seeks to restore order after systemic shock or challenge is often referred to as "homeostasis", a word that suggests the body has a set internal state to which it must return to maintain balance and health. Instead of this, we have borrowed the more recently coined word, "allostasis", defined as a process of achieving stability through psychological, physical or behavioural flexibility[46]. A growing body of research suggests that health is a product of dynamic equilibrium – the ability to respond to challenge – rather than an absence of imbalance*. This corresponds with Richard Bandler's assertion that effectively applied NLP should *increase* the choices available to the subject, rather than simply remove the problem-response.

Finally, "allostatic load" and "systemic overload" refer to the point at which the patient is unable to process stress and maintain allostasis, and physical and/or psychological dysfunction occurs. Allostatic load may result not only from external stressors, but also from lifestyle, personal experience, meaning, unmet emotional needs, understanding and attitude.

A more viable approach

From the above, it becomes apparent that increasing the individual's ability to achieve and maintain allostasis is a more viable approach to 'functional' disorders. We caution against medicating symptoms of allostatic load in all but the most serious situations. Incautiously removing either the stressors or the symptoms of stress may actually reduce the ability fully to engage with and enjoy life, and disable the processes on which our physical and emotional survival depends. To put it another way, *we need stress.* And, under the right conditions, we even enjoy it.

The question persists, what makes the difference between the person who succumbs to stress and the one who not only survives, but may even thrive? Part of the answer may be genetic, although no conclusive

* The metaphor we sometimes use to explain allostasis to patients is that of riding a bicycle or learning to walk, both of which involve a constant interplay of losing and recovering balance. Without surrendering to the constant loss, and immediate recovery, of balance, we cannot move forward.

evidence has yet appeared to support this premise. The rest may, in fact, lie deep in our evolutionary past.

Research from two very different fields – ethology, the scientific study of animal behaviour, and thermodynamics – opens a promising new direction, one we have found extremely useful in practical applications with patients suffering from a wide range of 'functional' disorders.

Connections with our animal past

Animal studies show that encounters with predators in the wild trigger much the same physiological response as humans experience when faced with an acute stress: a surge in stress chemicals accompanied by a rush of endorphins, presumably to deaden the pain of being torn apart. This is followed by immobility – the freeze alternative to fight or flight.

However, should the attack be aborted and the prey escape, something interesting occurs. Delivered from an untimely death, the animal stays frozen for a while, and then appears to be seized by a series of tremors. Sometimes these mimic the act of running away; at other times they seem more like uncontrollable muscle spasms. But they are always the consequence of a narrow escape. After a few moments, the animal will right itself and make its escape. As far as we know, it does not develop ulcers* or end up on a psychiatrist's couch. Ethologists now agree that the animal maintains allostasis by *dissipating*, or discharging, his stress.

The significance of dissipation as a factor in allostasis also derives from the work of Russian-born, Nobel Prize-winner Ilya Prigogine, who argued that the Second Law of Thermodynamics – that increasing disorder and entropy are the inevitable result of expending energy – did not always hold true. Instead of collapsing into disorder, many systems move

* Referring to this phenomenon, Stanford University's Robert M. Sapolsky, a professor of biology and neurology, has written an entertaining and scholarly book on the effects of chronic stress on health called *Why Zebras Don't Get Ulcers* (3rd edn, 2004, New York: Owl Books). We also recommend Peter A. Levine's rather more populist book, *Waking the Tiger* (1997, Berkeley, CA: North Atlantic Books), which explores our human response to perceived threat.

towards *increasing* order. Prigogine pointed out that science had thus far been focusing on closed systems, all of which tend towards an equilibrium state of maximum entropy.

Open systems (those which take in energy in whatever form from outside themselves), however, maintain equilibrium when they are able effectively to dissipate entropy. Allostasis, then, may be seen as being maintained, not in spite of entropy, but because of it. Failure to dissipate will inevitably result in increasing chaos and dysfunction.

This led Prigogine to another extraordinary discovery: that energetic challenge (let's call this "stress" for the moment) drives the system effectively enough until it reaches a point of maximum tolerance (called the bifurcation point), where the system either collapses in disorder or dissipates enough entropy to 'escape' (literally, a non-linear, quantum leap) to a higher level of organisation.

Further research has found that this model applies, not just to chemical systems, Prigogine's original focus, but also to traffic flow, companies, plants, animals and human beings. In the case of human beings, our ideas, inventions, philosophy, even our brains, become more complex with use. Immune function is just one example of this process in action; the body is challenged by a pathogen and responds by reassembling its resources in order to meet a similar challenge in the future. The system does not become 'a little bit resistant', or 'gradually more resistant', but can escape to a level of more complex organisation at which it operates until encountering the next challenge.

The important point to remember is that, as "open, adaptive, dissipative structures", we function well in unstable environments and in the face of challenge, as long as (1) we retain the flexibility to respond, and (2) we have the capacity to dissipate entropy when it approaches the bifurcation point. In other words, we have evolved to self-regulate and develop as a result of stress – *given the right circumstances.*

Indeed, powerful new evidence of health as a constantly emerging property of challenge is appearing in a number of studies. Routine obstruction of this evolutionary response – say, by overmedication of all symptoms of allostatic load – may, in the long run, act against our natural capacity to adapt and evolve[47].

Figure 2.1 illustrates the biphasic nature of stress, together with bifurcation and escape to a new order.

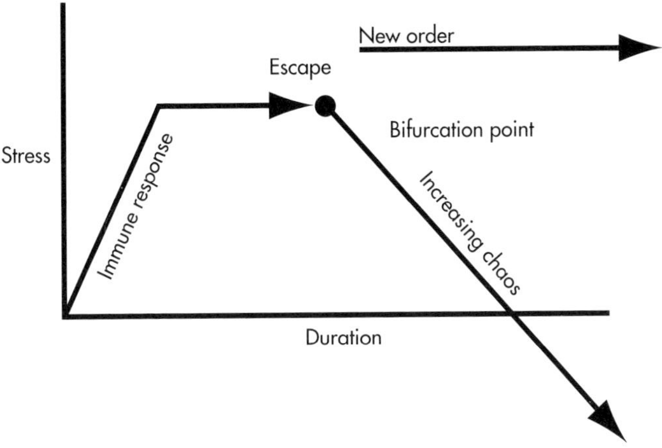

Fig 2.1 The biphasic nature of stress, bifurcation and escape to new order. The immune response improves in response to immediate challenge. But, when chronic stress approaches the bifurcation point, the subject either descends into increasing chaos, or "escapes" to a new and higher level of neurological organisation. Escape depends on effective dissipation of the excessive input of energy.

Most patients seeking help from a medical professional do so near or after the bifurcation point. Symptoms are indications that the system is struggling to dissipate entropy and move to a new, more flexible or resistant, order.

Whatever the specific cause or causes may be, this response, a loss of neurophysiological coherence, is readily observed by monitoring the subject's Heart Rate Variability (HRV). Simply put, HRV, commonly used as a diagnostic tool in cardiology and obstetrics, provides a reliable measure of the functioning of the autonomic nervous system, which in turn reflects the overall psychophysical status of the subject. HRV, one of the technologies we have adopted in Medical NLP, may be seen as a real-time measure of allostasis, the loss of which can be damaging or even fatal[48].

The myth of 'somatisation'

During any consultation, the patient and practitioner seek to bridge a gulf of subjective meaning. The events the patient notices and tries to describe are "symptoms"; the doctor, meanwhile, is largely looking for "signs" – usually described as "objective indications" of disease or disorder. In some cases, the disease is readily identifiable – say, jaundice – because the signs are evident. Where the practitioner favours signs to the exclusion of symptoms, problems can arise.

In the absence of readily observable signs, due diligence and medico-legal concerns usually mean that the patient will be referred on to one or more specialists for further consultations and tests. Where no pathology is identified, the patient is at risk of being stigmatised as "somatising", suffering from a "psychosomatic", "somatoform" or "conversion" disorder, "functional illness" or "hypochondriasis".

None of these nominalised terms is particularly helpful, because none of them provides insight into the problem. Moreover, they tend to exclude the patient's experience, the context within which his problem arises. Patients are quick to detect the underlying suggestion that what is ailing them is "all in the mind". If they do not medicate the patient, many doctors are quick to outsource the problem to psychologists, psychiatrists or counsellors (where available), reinforcing the picture of troublesome neurotics wasting the medical profession's valuable time.

Medical NLP regards "somatisation", with its overtones of neuroticism, as a myth. Not only do imbalances within the body-mind system express themselves somatically, both as some kind of physical felt sense and in changes in cellular function or structure, but we cannot have *any* experience without some physical movement or manifestation.

As "open adaptive systems", we humans are constantly processing billions of bits of data, both exteroceptive (from outside the body) and enteroceptive (from within), most of which are filtered out of our conscious awareness by mechanisms we will discuss in Chapter 5. When these processes pass a certain threshold, they surface as somatic events, which are then subjected to descriptions, inferences and evaluations, by both the 'experts' reviewing the condition and the patient suffering from its effects. However, we should not confuse the descriptions and inferences we use as convenient forms of classification with the event itself. The diagnosis is not the disease. The symptom is not the problem. The problem is the problem, and the symptom is the signal that the problem has not yet been recognised and resolved.

Closing unclosed 'loops'

In everyday experience, we are painfully aware of the stressful effects of 'unfinished business'. Uncompleted tasks remain in our conscious awareness, or just below, adding to the daily pressure of getting other jobs done.

This process was identified and studied by Russian psychologist Bluma Zeigarnik, who noticed that waiters tended to remember pending orders in exquisite detail, but immediately forgot them once those orders were filled. Now known as the Zeigarnik Effect, its function, it is believed, is to create 'psychic tension' to drive us to complete an action[49]. In Gestalt terms, we are hardwired to seek "closure".

Many otherwise mysterious 'functional' disorders are now also thought to result from 'unfinished business' – that is, emotional or physical assaults on the system that were not effectively resolved at the time. Somatic memory – that is, the 'psychic tension' held in the body's sensory, autonomic and somatic systems – seeks resolution, sometimes many years later[50]. One possible manifestation of this – observed in fields as disparate as cardiology and ophthalmology – is known as the Anniversary Effect. Close inspection of patient records often reveals that some people return for consultations on or around the date of what turns out to be the anniversary of a particularly traumatic experience[51].

Rather than investigate or revivify past traumas, it is our experience in a number of cases that some of the approaches we write about later create a context within which patients can safely and painlessly reintegrate and complete the experience, thus freeing themselves from the prison created – or perceived as created – by their history (see Chapter 18).

To restore allostasis and increase our capacity for healing and health, open loops need to be closed, whether by working through a backlog of unmade telephone calls, or by symbolically reclaiming the power that was stripped from us by overwhelming events from the past. We cannot, of course, change what happened in the past, but we *can* change the way we have been consciously or unconsciously responding to it.

3

Avoiding Compassion Fatigue: the dark side of empathy

Stress and its impact on health and well-being do not begin and end with the patient. If patients can be at extreme risk from stress, health professionals of all specialisations can be doubly so. Physical and emotional well-being are dependent not just on the practitioner's capacity to achieve and maintain allostasis in his own life, but also on how resistant he may be to the daily, invisible risk of 'infection' by his patients' distress.

Patients expect the practitioners they consult to care about their problems. Doctors and other health professionals are encouraged – at least in their training – to display "empathy" towards their patients. By understanding and sharing another person's feelings and ideas, it is widely believed we deepen our ability to help. This is undoubtedly true. Empathy is a valuable tool for any health professional, and one deeply valued by patients. But unless it is understood and managed, it comes at a price.

We can be reasonably confident that empathy is necessary for the survival of our species. The ability to share feelings and experiences vicariously allows us to work together for the greater good of the group. Conversely, the apparent inability of some people to care about the impact of their negative actions on others usually fills us with profound revulsion, as if some deep and sacred law has been violated.

Many training programmes suggest that empathy is a learned skill. In fact, as many researchers are now beginning to suspect, we cannot *not* be empathetic, supposing we are free of any 'psychopathic' disorders that, for reasons not yet understood, prevent us from even comprehending, much less experiencing, any of the emotions normally elicited by witnessing someone else's pain. We have all experienced wincing in sympathy when we see someone else stumble or trip. Even though we might laugh at the comedian who slips on a banana skin, we do so as a release of tension caused by seeing someone 'like us' suffer ignominy or pain. It is a natural, automatic response.

Medical students are given conflicting messages during training: be empathetic, but remain dispassionate when dealing with patients' pain and discomfort. Under pressure, many physicians take the second route, and understandably so. A surgeon or a doctor who has problems with blood or open wounds is of no use to the patient. But it is important for health professionals to know that, while we might learn to conceal our feelings (even from ourselves), millions of years of evolution have ensured that the response is wired into our neurology.

For example, when you see someone else's hand being pricked by a needle, the motor neurons in the same area on your own equivalent hand freeze as if you have received the needle-prick yourself. Using Transcranial Magnetic Stimulation (TMS) for their studies, researchers have been able to establish that the "social dimension" of pain extends to basic, sensorimotor levels of neural processing[52]. "Somatic empathy" – our body's automatic response to the neurological state of another person[53] – is there, whether we notice it or not.

The empathic 'mirror'

The discovery in the 1990s of a group of cells called "mirror neurons" offers some explanation for how we translate exteroceptive information into internal, 'psychosomatic' experience. This brain-to-brain communication system synchronises neural firing patterns so that the observer 'feels' someone else's experience as if it is happening to him. Mirror neurons probably also allow us to learn by observing, and neuroscientist V. S. Ramachandran has suggested they may have been the driving force of the "great leap forward" in human cultural evolution 50,000 years ago[54].

With the advent of language, the problem becomes more complicated. When the subject uses limited descriptions of his experience – often nominalised words such as "depression", "anxiety", "relationship", "anger" – the listener is required to plumb the depths of his own experience to attach meaning.

Known as a "Transderivational Search" (TDS), this has its dangers. Unless we fill in the deleted part of the patient's communication, we are repeatedly re-entering and re-experiencing our own past experiences, and paying the price for reactivating the cascade of neurochemicals associated with pain and distress. We may 'understand' what the patient is going through, and we may 'feel for' him. We may think of ourselves, and be thought of, as 'good people'. However, we not only reduce our ability to fully help the patient extricate himself from his problem, but also suffer the corrosive effects of the patient's distress.

Psychologist Daniel Stern warns of the risks of being "captured" by another person's nervous system[55]; the result of this is what Elaine Hatfield and her colleagues at the University of Hawaii call "emotional contagion"[56]. Hatfield's theory – in line with NLP's earlier observation that physiology informs feeling, and vice versa – suggests that the listener's unconscious mimicry of the speaker's posture, facial expressions, tonality, breathing, etc, may 'infect' the listener with the speaker's emotions*. She goes on to suggest that "emotional contagion" is an unavoidable consequence of human interaction.

Although we fully agree with the first part of Hatfield's conclusions, we question the second. Taking on the subject's experience 'as if' it is our own is an example of association, well known in NLP. Put another way, we leave our own subjective experience (dissociate) and 'step into' the patient's (associate). Even though this is an imaginal act, neuroscience can now demonstrate that there is little functional difference between a physical and an imagined action. We can even weaken or strengthen our muscles by simple mental rehearsal[57]. Our ability deliberately to associate into and dissociate from a patient's experience is the key to achieving engagement and emotional resonance, without suffering negative effects.

* Richard Bandler often tells of observing psychiatrists sliding deeper into depression as they listen 'empathetically' to their patients' problems. Could this be one reason why psychiatrists for so long had the highest suicide rate of all health professionals?

This capacity, as we will later demonstrate, can also be harnessed to therapeutic effect.

Medical NLP recognises three 'points of view' that allow us effectively to manage our relationships with others (Table 3.1). However, failure to control these positions and the time we spend in them can lead to a number of undesirable consequences. (Please note that we may often observe mismanagement of these positions among patients. For example, someone who takes responsibility for spousal abuse because "I make him mad" may be stuck in Position 2.)

Table 3.1 Perceptual positions

Perspective	*Description*	*Positive effect*	*Negative effect*
1. Self	Associated into one's own body, engaged in subjective processing of data, feelings, behaviours	Allows us to apply learning and experience that the other may lack	To the exclusion of 2 or 3: single-mindedness, refusal to consider information that does not match own schema, 'selfishness', etc.
2. Other	Dissociated from self, associated into the other, sensing or imagining his feelings, responses, etc.	Open to other possibilities, increased understanding and empathy, increased social and emotional connectedness	To the exclusion of 1 and 3: Overinvolvement in the other's problems, loss of ego boundaries, physical and emotional overidentification, "co-dependence", emotional contagion, burnout
3. Observer	Objective, 'as if' from physically and emotionally detached viewpoint	Yields information about the relationship between 1 and 2, open-mindedness, avoids bias and premature cognitive closure, reduces overemotionalism	To the exclusion of 1 and 2: Detached, uninvolved, uncaring, 'cold', machine-like

And, as we acquire flexibility in managing these aspects of our relationships with patients, we also learn how to avoid the defence mechanisms adopted by some health professionals to cope with daily exposure to illness, pain and fear – withdrawal, dissociation and alienation from the 'human connection' on which effective consultation should be based (permanently in Position 3).

CHAPTER 3

When entropy prevails

Various authors have proposed different names for the negative risks practitioners face, including "burnout", "compassion fatigue", "vicarious traumatisation" and "secondary traumatisation". We do not propose to discuss the differences between each of these models; it is enough to recognise that the signs and symptoms of allostatic load among practitioners are similar to those of patients. These signs and symptoms are both communications of, and attempts to resolve, imbalance. *How* these are experienced and expressed may depend on the particular strategy or strategies the subject unconsciously adopts.

Table 3.2 demonstrates the effects of three behavioural responses to mounting allostatic load: Displacement, Obstruction and Distraction. We assume these coping strategies are learned during childhood, when they might have served a purpose. As we mature, however, they tend to become less socially acceptable and more detrimental to health and well-being.

Whether some effects, such as anxiety and aggression, result from sympathetic arousal, and others, including withdrawal and depression, from parasympathetic arousal, is still a subject of some contention among researchers. However, it is safe to assume that some or all these responses occur when the balance of the autonomic nervous system is disturbed. We expect new applications of technologies such as Heart Rate Variability

Table 3.2 Responses to allostatic load

Response	*Effect*
Displacement:	
Attempts to dissipate energy	Aggression, excitability, anxiety, crying, talking, physical activity, compulsive behaviour, etc.
Obstruction:	
Attempts to prevent energy entering the system	Withdrawal, depression, loss of energy and appetite, etc.
Distraction:	
Attempts to divert from feelings of disease	Dissociation, excessive use of food, alcohol, sex. Smoking and substance abuse, absorption in passive entertainment, such as television, etc.

(HRV) will yield answers to these questions with the passage of time. Rather than facilitating the flow of energy, these strategies all have the potential for spiralling down into more serious dysfunctions and disease.

The stress-proof individual

Some people, however, undoubtedly have the ability to engage fully with the day-to-day challenges of work and life while somehow remaining impervious to stress and its effects. Although this may be partly genetic, research indicates that the ability to flourish in the face of challenge (in terms of the model outlined in the previous chapter, effectively to maintain allostasis) is marked by certain qualities usually ignored in orthodox medicine.

Hans Selye's largely reductionist approach (that the stress response is purely physiological) has been substantially modified by the discovery that *perception* of stress can both trigger and regulate allostatic load. Known as *psychological modulators*, these fall into five main categories: social support/connectedness, a sense of control, predictability, outlook (optimistic vs. pessimistic) and the ability to dissipate frustration. All five are open to modification by the principles and techniques featured later in this book.

Although exploring how these psychosocial variables may be affecting patients with medically unexplained disorders could provide the practitioner with valuable insights, we urge you to use the following information and Figure 3.1 to audit the psychological modulators that may be affecting your own allostatic load.

Note: Read the sections that follow, then record a score from 1 (meaning 'a little') to 5 (meaning 'a lot') on each corresponding segment of Figure 3.1. When you have finished, connect the dots to make a six-pointed shape which will provide a clear visual representation of your strengths and weaknesses.

Social support and connectedness

Researchers investigating strikingly low rates of myocardial infarction reported in the 1940s from the little Pennsylvanian town of Roseto, where

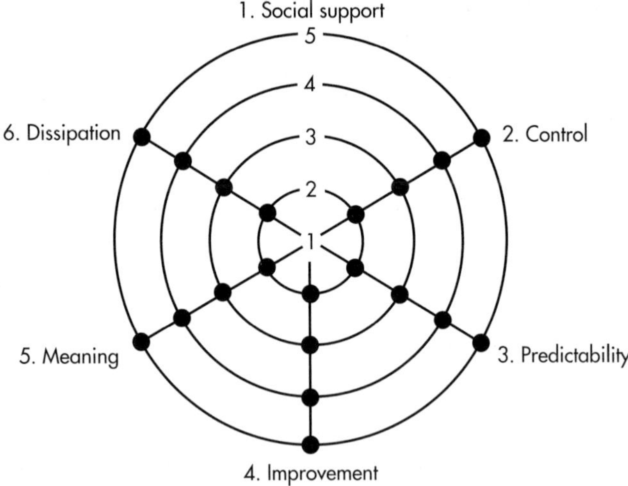

Fig 3.1 Life balance audit

they expected to find a fit, tobacco- and alcohol-free community enjoying all the benefits of clean-living. When they arrived, they found as many smokers, drinkers and couch potatoes as in the rest of the country, where heart disease was on the rise. The difference between Roseto and other similar towns, the researchers discovered, was a particularly cohesive social structure. Somehow, the closeness Rosetans enjoyed inoculated them against cardiac problems.

Predictably, as the community became steadily more 'Americanised', the protection disappeared. A 50-year longitudinal study, published in 1992, categorically established that social support and connectedness had provided a powerfully salutogenic (health-promoting) effect on the heart[58].

Nor was this a random fluctuation affecting a small, isolated community. A number of studies have confirmed that host resistance to a wide range of illnesses is affected by the social context in which you live and the support you feel you receive. A key factor in social integration has been identified as having someone to confide in, help with financial issues and offer practical support, such as baby-sitting, when you need it, and with whom you can discuss problems and share solutions[59].

Some of the established benefits of social support and connectedness include: extended lifespan (double that of people with low social ties)[60]; improved recovery from heart attack (three times better for those with high social ties)[61]; reduced progression from HIV to Aids[62]; and even protection from the common cold[63].

Question 1 is: How much support do I get from family and friends?

A sense of control

Feeling you are in control of your work and personal life is one of the best predictors of a long and healthy life. Conversely, feeling victimised by unpredictable forces outside of your control can be a killer. One large-scale study has revealed that people who feel they have little or no control over their lives have a 30% increased likelihood of dying prematurely than those who score highest in tests measuring a sense of power and control[64]. Whether we look at rats or humans, the effect is the same. Where predictability and control are low, and environmental or occupational stress is high, the risk of cardiovascular and metabolic disease soars.

Happily for our survival in a stressful world, the converse is true. Not only can health improve as control is restored, but even *knowing* that we have choices can significantly offset the effects of even major life-challenges[65], reduce our experience of pain and need for medication[66] and measurably increase longevity, even in later life[67].

Question 2 is: How much control do I have in my life?

Predictability

Our ability to predict events, such as pain and stressful situations, helps arm us against their effects. Habituation – the regularity with which stressful events occur – also helps us cope. Studies of urban populations in Britain who faced regular nightly air raids during World War 2 showed a greater level of resilience to stress diseases than their counterparts in the suburbs, where bombing was substantially more erratic.

Once again, perception is the key to how we respond. If our worldview is one of being at the mercy of random events – most of which are negative – allostatic load is inevitable. If we enjoy surprises (and there are many who do), the emotional response to the resultant surge in stress chemicals and endorphins is likely to be interpreted as excitement.

It must be emphasised that predictability, like control, can have its downside. Just as a misplaced sense of control over issues that are beyond our influence can be counter-productive, so can too much predictability. Studies of work-related stress have repeatedly shown that highly repetitive (read: boring) tasks can result in high levels of job dissatisfaction, absenteeism and blood pressure. Less predictable work interspersed with the production-line activities reverses the effects[68].

Question 3 is: How well do I cope with unexpected events?

Expectation of improvement

Blind 'hope', as advanced by many self-help books, may have little impact on disease outcome, and exhorting someone to remain hopeful in difficult circumstances can prove taxing and lead to depression and self-blame. However, realism, coupled with the anticipation of improvement, however small, can moderate the stress chemicals that an otherwise serious or critical situation can trigger.

A landmark study, referred to by Robert Sapolsky in his highly readable book on stress and coping, *Why Zebras Don't Get Ulcers*[69], demonstrated that parents whose children had been diagnosed with cancer showed only a moderate rise in their glucocorticoid levels when told there was a 25% risk of death. The reason for this, the study concluded, was that odds of 75% of survival were perceived as miraculously high. As Sapolsky observes, it is not so much the 'reality' of the situation that affects our response, but the meaning we ascribe to it.

Question 4 is: How much do I expect my situation to improve?

Meaning, purpose and spirituality

The way we evaluate past, and anticipate future, events can influence many aspects of our experience, including our health and well-being. Large-scale and longitudinal studies, such as those carried out at Harvard University and Harvard School of Public Health, have demonstrated that explanatory styles – whether we apply an optimistic or a pessimistic spin to the meaning of our experience – are strong indicators of our future health status[70,71].

Meaning is governed by many variables. Meta-analyses show that those people who are strongly committed to a religious belief and practice are nearly a third more likely to survive serious illness than those who hold no religious belief[72]. A common factor of those with strong religious beliefs is an acceptance of events, positive or negative, as "God's will".

Studies such as these arouse much controversy in scientific circles. The most frequently encountered argument against a "faith effect" is that religious people tend to follow healthier lifestyles and/or enjoy greater social integration than their non-religious counterparts. However, the 2000 study cited above (by Michael McCullough and colleagues) established that the highly engaged 'believers' lived significantly longer, even after the researchers accounted statistically for health behaviour, physical and mental health, race, gender and social support.

Discussing spirituality with their patients is something most practitioners avoid. And yet, holding some larger organising belief in which we are a smaller, yet nonetheless, important, part proves to be a significant part in achieving and maintaining allostasis.

We (the authors) do not intend to equate "spirituality" with "religion", and we advise health professionals to be equally cautious. What we are more interested in, and what appears to have a greater impact on health, is a belief that the patient's life has some purpose or meaning as a part of a greater whole. This may express itself as a deep commitment to an organised religion, or as an important goal or mission, such as "being there for the children".

We are greatly inspired by the experiences of Austrian psychiatrist Viktor Frankl, who was arrested by the Nazis in 1942 and deported with his family to Theresienstadt, a notorious concentration camp set up by the Germans near Prague. During the following three years, incarcerated in the death camps of Auschwitz, Dachau and Turkheim, Frankl lost his parents, his brother and his wife, Tilly. Frankl himself survived, despite nearly succumbing to typhoid fever during the last months of the war.

His seminal work, *Man's Search for Meaning*[73], recounts both his experiences and conslusions. Frankl spent his time at the very edge of annihilation observing his fellow prisoners, searching out the distinctions between those who survived and those who succumbed without struggle. His observations suggested that those who looked for and found a sense of meaning in their lives – in other words, who believed they still *had a mission to be fulfilled* – and were *free to choose their responses* to whatever happened to them, were best equipped to transcend their circumstances and flourish, no matter how terrible those circumstances might be.

These two beliefs – in a mission or purpose, and the ability to choose our responses – are central to Medical NLP's therapeutic approach. Many of the principles and techniques later presented are aimed at achieving these ends.

Question 5 is in two parts. The first part to consider (but not mark) is: What do you find helps you to cope when you have a problem or challenge? The second, which should be scored on the audit, is: How much does this help?

Dissipation

We draw a distinction between dissipation and displacement (yelling, crying, punching a wall, etc.), none of which has been shown effectively to reduce chronic allostatic load, and may even worsen it.

As Table 3.2 above indicates, displacement is usually counterproductive – physically, psychologically and socially. Dissipation, on the other hand, may be incorporated into an ongoing programme, designed to counter-balance, or even downregulate, the fight-or-flight response. Some examples may be: regular* exercise, especially light aerobic workouts, yoga, martial arts and meditation (see Appendix A). However, when making a lifestyle change to facilitate allostasis by dissipation, it is important to select an activity you find satisfying. The positive effects are directly related to perceiving your programme as enjoyable. If it is not, find something else.

* By "regular", we mean at least four times a week for aerobic exercise and at least once a day for yoga, meditation, T'ai chi etc.

Question 6 is: How much 'downtime' do I allow myself (this should involve at least one regular practice selected from the suggestions above)?

Now, unless you are a DC Comic™ superhero, you will have found areas of deficiency in your life balance audit. This is valuable information, and we suggest you make a note of any area or areas open to improvement to use as material for later exercises.

EXERCISES

1. Practise "mirroring" the posture, breathing patterns and pitch, rhythm and tonality of speech of a partner, and notice how this changes your internal "state". This is the effect of being in Position 2 in Table 3.1 above. (Only do this with the agreement of your partner, or where you can be sure you can do it without drawing attention to yourself. Until you are proficient in mirroring, you need to be discreet to avoid giving offence.)
2. Now, step back into Position 1. Make sure you are fully associated, seeing through your own eyes, hearing through your own ears and feeling with your own body.
3. Imagine floating out of your body and up into an 'observer' position. Notice the reduction or absence of emotions. Practise watching your interaction with your partner as if you were a neutral observer. Suspend comment or judgement.
4. Now, step back into Position 1. Make sure you are fully associated, seeing through your own eyes, hearing through your own ears and feeling with your own body.

Practise these four steps as often as possible, until you can move easily and safely in and out each position at will.

Important note: Always end the exercise by re-associating into your own 'self'. From this point on, make sure you are back in Position 1 after seeing each patient, and especially at the end of the day.

4

Words that Harm, Words that Heal: Neurolinguistics in the consultation process

Words were originally magic, and to this day words have retained much of their ancient magical power[74]

Sigmund Freud

Imagine for a moment that you, as a health professional, are given a tool that if used *correctly* could:

1. account for more than 50% of a successful clinical outcome – even using treatments that have been discarded as "ineffective";
2. significantly reduce the need for painkillers, antihypertensives and anxiolytics; and,
3. cut the risk of litigation by up to 60% – even if a medical error has occurred.

Would you use it?

Now, imagine you have a tool that if used *incorrectly* could:

1. *increase* your patient's experience of pain and *delay* healing;
2. *trigger attacks* in diseases such as asthma; and,

3. more than double your chance of being sued in the event of medical error.

Would you use it?

As you've probably guessed, it's one and the same tool. The good news is that it's a tool you already have. In fact, it came free in the genetic package you received at birth, along with the colour of your eyes and the size of your feet. The bad news is: it didn't come with an instruction manual.

We're talking about language and its effects, what Professor Stephen Pinker calls that "extraordinary collection of hisses and hums and squeaks and pops"[75] that not only carry packets of information, simple and complex, but also binds us to others of our species. Language, if some linguists are correct, is an innate capability in our species. We are born hardwired to communicate, to rapidly acquire the syntax (the rules) of our native tongue, and thereby connect with those around us in order to have them meet our needs. If we fail to bond, or lose those connections important to us, we may sicken and die[76].

The challenge of communication

The suggestion that language can affect our health is the fundamental proposition of Medical NLP, and we are aware that it will be deeply challenging to some. To others, especially those at the receiving end of clumsy or malevolent communication, there's a visceral recognition that it's true. Two incidents come to mind.

> ***Case history:*** *The 82-year-old mother of a friend had just been passed "in pretty good condition" by the young doctor who had examined her. As she got ready to leave with her husband, a sprightly four years her senior, the physician patted her arm and said, "But, I want you to hold on to your husband's arm whenever you go out. You're pretty fragile, and if you don't you'll trip and fall and break a hip."*
>
> *On the way out, her husband offered her his arm. The lady pulled away and said sharply, "I haven't needed to hang on to you in 50 years of marriage, and I'm not going to start now." As she stepped out of the front door of the clinic, she tripped and fell – and broke a hip.*

The story is true, And, unfortunately, so are many we hear from patients who have had similarly accidental, but negative, encounters with careless communicators.

Some years ago, when Aids first made its appearance in the West, statistics indicated that mean survival from diagnosis to full-blown disease was roughly 2.5 years.

> ***Case history:*** *Two patients, both of whom were HIV-positive but uncharacteristically asymptomatic, were examined by the same consultant, a newly fledged 'expert' in this new and mysterious disease.*
>
> *"Technically", he said, "you've passed the deadline. According to the statistics, you shouldn't even be alive now."*
>
> *Within two weeks, both were dead. Nobody in the immediate vicinity was remotely surprised. After all, everyone knew a diagnosis of Aids was a death sentence. The only anomaly was that their symptoms had taken so long to develop.*

One man, had he known about these cases at the time, might possibly also have been unsurprised – although for entirely different reasons.

John Bargh is an American psychologist, a gifted, respected and unorthodox researcher in the field of language and influence. One of his experiments stands as a warning to all those professionals entrusted with the health and well-being of others.

Bargh gave two groups of subjects a collection of five-word sets with the instructions that they were to make grammatical four-word sentences out of each set. An example of these Scrambled Sentence Tests might include the words: *apple*, *give*, *an*, *me*, *red*. The correct sentence would be "*give me an apple*", the word, *red* being redundant. One of Bargh's groups, however, was given sets that included words that might be associated with old age and its symptoms – *grey*, *wrinkled*, *tired*, etc – but never explicitly in that context.

The results were astonishing. The group exposed unconsciously to 'age' words were observed to move more slowly than before and reported that they were lacking energy and enthusiasm. The words they were exposed to literally made them temporarily older[77].

Bargh and his colleagues have repeated the exercise in many different forms, always with the same results. The conclusions are inescapable: we unconsciously extract meaning from the words to which we are exposed and react according to the perceived meaning. This is known as priming.

Let's try a little experiment. Complete each step *before* moving on to the next.

Step 1
Stand, feet shoulder-width apart, with your right arm and forefinger extended directly in front of you.

Without moving your feet, turn your upper body around to your right, following your pointed finger, as far as you can comfortably go. Find a mark that will let you know where your limit was. Return to the front and drop your arm to your side.

Now move on.

Step 2
Close your eyes, and in your imagination only, repeat the exercise without actually moving your body. Mentally follow your pointing finger around, right up to the point you last reached, and then *some considerable distance past.*

Pause for a moment before continuing.

Step 3
Now, open your eyes, extend your arm and forefinger again, and turn your body around to the right as far as you can, and notice this time how far your new limit has been re-set to.

The exercise is simple but enlightening. Although demonstrations like this often feature in business and self-development seminars as "proof" of the "power of the mind", the real wonder is in the mechanisms that underlie the phenomenon. "Priming", the ability of the brain to recognise and respond to words and images smuggled in beneath the subject's perceptual radar is one of the great curiosities of psychological and neurological research.

If you found you could easily reach beyond your earlier attempt, you were effectively primed – in other words, your brain was set up by words alone to perform differently ... and, your muscles, tendons and joints unquestioningly obliged. The words and phrases used to trigger this effect were presuppositional – that is, they assumed, without overtly stating, that your second performance would be an improvement on the first: *comfortably go, far, new limit, re-set* etc.

Nor should we be too embarrassed at the ease with which the effect is achieved. It simply means we're human.

Hypnotists, salespeople and parents who use their offspring's full names to signal Something Very Serious is About to Happen have all understood the power of priming for many years. Bargh and his colleague, Ohio State University psychologist Tanya Chartrand, estimate that around 95% of all behaviour is automated, and have repeatedly demonstrated how easy it is to influence subjects to respond to certain unconsciously delivered cues, such as touching their elbows or scratching their noses[75].

But pointing or touching your nose is entirely different from emotions, and emotions are distinct from physical health, are they not?

Well, not exactly.

Mending the body-mind split

Throughout the nineteenth and twentieth centuries, the division between mind and body was unquestioned in scientific thought. Then, in 1985, Georgetown University School of Medicine psychopharmacologist Candace Pert published a ground-breaking paper, co-authored by Michael Ruff. It revealed the existence of an interactive "psychosomatic network" buzzing with informational substances – peptides, hormones and neurotransmitters – which acted in concert to maintain or impair the health and integrity of the individual[78]. Pert, since credited as the discoverer of the opiate receptor, went on to extend her research into the multiple psychophysiological feedback loops mediated by what she has dubbed "the molecules of emotion". Furthermore, she found receptors for these molecules were not confined to the brain, but were distributed over almost every cell in the body.

Pert's discoveries were hugely challenging to the establishment. She endured criticism, marginalisation and even an attempt to hijack her research. But she held fast and has since been proved correct. Her findings were largely responsible for transforming the newly emerging field of psychoneuroimmunology, the study of the relationship between the brain and health, from a little known area of research into a fully fledged science. No longer could it be credibly argued either that the brain was merely a troublesome appendage to a mechanical body, or that the body was little more than a convenient perch for the patient's neck-top computer.

One problem, though, persisted in the field: if psychoneuroimmunology could demonstrate the interaction of brain on body and body on brain, how did the brain acquire the information to trigger the process? Operating outside the mainstream medical paradigm, thinkers, including Alfred Korzybski, Milton Erickson and Richard Bandler and colleagues, had long concluded that communication was the key – permutations of the many ways in which we impart and process information, between each other and within ourselves. Since then, psychologists have largely concurred, but their evidence is often dismissed as "soft" by their medical counterparts or, more commonly, is simply ignored.

Enter Dr Richard Davidson and his team of researchers from the University of Wisconsin-Madison. Armed with the newly developed "hard" research tool of functional Magnetic Resonance Imaging (fMRI), which provides a convenient real-time 'window' on brain functions, they set out to discover whether 'emotion' was registered by the brain. They found more than this. Not only were specific areas of the brain seen to light up, but the body responded – just as Pert and her colleagues had been suggesting.

Davidson and his team monitored the responses of a group of asthmatics as they were exposed to three different categories of word: asthma-related words such as "wheeze", negative, but functionally unrelated words, such as "loneliness", and neutral words such as "curtains". At the same time, the subjects were given known allergens – dust-mite or ragweed extracts – to inhale. When the asthma-related words were encountered, not only did significant areas of the brain – the anterior cingulate cortex and the insula – show increased activity, but the volunteers promptly suffered asthma attacks.

The team, who have since embarked on large-scale studies, believe they have found hard evidence that certain emotions can cause flare-ups of the disease. This is something doctors have known empirically for some time. But, and this is the important point, the 'emotion' inducing the asthma attacks was transmitted by one or other of those "hisses and hums and squeaks and pops". *The subjects had been physically harmed by a word*[79].

The risk of negative priming

Even if none of the above research had been carried out, most people have an intuitive understanding, based on everyday experience, of the relationship between language and the "gut response". Think of how you feel when the boy racer on the freeway cuts you off in the fast lane, then winds down the window and yells obscenities at you. Or remember a heated argument with a spouse or a friend, or being reprimanded by your boss. Just words – except they have the power to light up the brain and set in motion a complex chain of neurochemical events, causing your palms to sweat and your guts to wrench, and which now have to be metabolised before your body can return to its default 'normal' state.

One of the concerns which the phenomenon opens up involves the possibility of negative and unintentional priming by means of the increasing number of patient questionnaires being introduced to 'assess' a wide variety of conditions, including pain, depression, anxiety and Obsessive Compulsive Disorder. Davidson's team elicited an asthma attack with a single condition-specific word. What is happening inside the patient who is required to work his way through anything from 10 to more than 100 words related to illness, discomfort and pain without being invited to offer his own words to describe his unique experience?

The quality of words is important, too, Richard Bandler often cautions. "Your voice bathes the listener's entire body with the waveform," he says. "What you say and how you say it has a direct impact on his nervous system." Pert's recent research seems to bear this out. Words (like music), she says, affect the "psychosomatic network" by causing certain ion channels to either open or close, thus regulating how a particular neural network works. "You're literally thinking with your body," she adds. "The words … because sound is vibrating your receptors … actually (affect) the neural networks forming in your brain."[80]

Wherever application of the molecular, cause-and-effect model has failed to bring the patient relief, we need to look more deeply into what else we can do. Since "stress" is undeniably a factor in all 'functional' disorders, we have it within our powers to (1) reduce sympathetic arousal, (2) help the patient to learn to recover allostasis, not by blocking the symptoms of imbalance, but by helping him to raise the bar on his own physical-emotional resilience, and (3) wherever possible, alter the structure and process of his illness-behaviour. The medium, always, is the word.

Our ability as a species to influence and be influenced by language is an important contributory factor to restoring and maintaining health. The fact that we are enormously suggestible can and should be exploited – although, of course, with due and diligent care.

Changing thoughts, changing minds

Any discussion about language and suggestibility would be incomplete without reference to two significant subjects: hypnosis and brainwashing.

Even after two centuries of effective application, hypnosis remains a controversial topic in mainstream medicine. This is a shame. We (the authors) strongly believe that, in order to practise in the best possible interests of the patient, all health practitioners should understand hypnosis and hypnotic phenomena and regard them as unavoidable components of their daily consultations.

Hypnosis – if, by that, we mean states of increased suggestibility – occurs naturally, whether or not the practitioner has developed the sensory acuity to notice it. As we discuss in Chapter 16, spontaneous trance states can be utilised adjunctively in the treatment process. Meanwhile, practitioners need to be aware of the potential risks attached to unrecognised trance and trance phenomena when they occur during the consultation process.

Milton Erickson defined hypnosis in terms of a progressive narrowing of attention. The inference here is that the subject's ability to create new patterns of experience and function depends on eliminating the "noise" of competing sensory data in favour of the "signal" of the hypnotic injunction. He entertained certain presuppositions by which he operated and, as a result of which, many thousands of patients benefited.

Among these was the existence of an "unconscious" mind. As a medical doctor and psychiatrist, he was fully aware that this was a metaphor – a convenient term for all the physical and psychological functions that operate below the level of immediate conscious awareness. Erickson also believed these 'other-than-conscious' functions exhibit intelligence (although not necessarily the deductive intelligence of the 'conscious' mind), metaphoric and analogical processing (much of his work was carried out obliquely, through stories and anecdotes), and also – in some cases – an almost child-like literal responsiveness to what it perceives as a 'command'.

In terms of outcome, there appears to be little distinction between hypnosis and priming, except that the latter occurs without the induction of 'formal' trance or through the medium of well-crafted suggestions. Either way, it is possible to deliver influential and potentially negative messages to the patient's unconscious – *whether or not they are intended by the speaker.*

Forcible or surreptitious "thought-changing" is popularly regarded as brainwashing. Commonly associated with extreme political groups and cults, heightened suggestibility is also known to be induced by trauma, fear and confusion. The late Margaret Thaler Singer and Janja Lalich identified a number of key prerequisites to successful thought-changing.

Simply put, thoughts, values, behaviour, allegiances and beliefs may be substantially altered in conditions where the subject is deprived of his or her own clothing, familiar foods, timetable and sense of control. The effect is magnified when the victim is exposed to, but often excluded by, a highly specialised language, is required to submit to the 'wisdom' of a superior "sacred" science, is discouraged from asking questions or making objections, and is constantly aware that the perceived authorities have the power of life or death[81].

Now, compare these conditions with what can happen when a patient is facing a challenging consultation, has been admitted to hospital or is facing a battery of complex tests. Food, clothing and contact with the outside world may be strictly controlled. The 'experts' use unfamiliar and distinctive terminology derived from an arcane science. Sometimes the patient is kept in the dark about the significance of medical or surgical procedures. The doctors and nurses may be perceived as mysterious and powerful figures with the authority to decide who lives or dies.

Questioning or criticism, especially of senior clinical personnel, is discouraged or ignored.

If we assume that these conditions have the potential significantly to increase the patient's susceptibility to suggestion, consider the potential impact of some of the phrases collected by (real) patients from their practitioners:

> *This is very serious surgery and there are risks attached to it. You will experience pain afterwards and it will be several weeks before you'll be able to move around comfortably.* (A surgeon to a pre-surgical patient)
>
> *You can't possibly be ready to deliver. You're not in enough pain yet.* (A midwife to a woman in labour)
>
> *People who take this medication often have dizziness or tingling in the hands and feet. Read the list of other side-effects inside the box and tell your doctor about any others you get.* (A pharmacist dispensing a prescription)

All the professionals above would argue that their intentions were impeccable and that they were obliged by law to deliver the information contained in their statements – and we would agree. However, in the light of everything discussed so far, we would strongly caution all health practitioners to *assume that the patient in front of you is in an altered and highly suggestible state and proceed accordingly.*

All the medico-legal requirements of informed consent, "safety netting" (instructions given to the patient for action to be taken should the condition worsen or persist) and discussion of side-effects can be met and simultaneously tempered by the judicious use of positive semantic priming and 'hypnotic' suggestion. Accomplishing this easily and elegantly requires planning and practice. We advise you to write out as many examples as possible; this makes it easier to tailor the language patterns to the individual patient and to deliver them confidently and effortlessly.

Spend some time on the following exercises before proceeding on to the next chapter. But, just before doing that, compare the statements above with the re-cast versions below:

> The surgeon: "*This is serious surgery and there are risks, but we have a highly trained and experienced team looking after you. Some people have*

some pain afterwards, but it may well be less than expected, and we'll do everything we can to have you up and about as soon as possible."

The midwife: "*Not everybody's as relaxed as you seem to be when they're ready to deliver, and you seem really comfortable. Let's check and see how close you are now so we can make sure it continues to go smoothly.*"

The pharmacist: "*I think you'll find this really helps. Some people who take this have dizziness or tingling in the hands and feet, but most people find it very easy to take. The drug companies list all possible side-effects, even when only one or two people might have had them. Read the list and tell your doctor about any you might have, but most people only have good results.*"

EXERCISES

Review and then write out as many patterns related to your specialisation as you can. We advise keeping a file of your efforts, adding to it as new ideas and situations occur.

Five patterns of positive influence

Positive priming

Notice in the revised versions of instructions delivered above how many words implying success are used compared with the original examples, where the emphasis is on negative experiences. Some words and phrases used include: smoothly, looking after you, comfortable, relaxed, really helps.

First, make a list of as many synonyms as you can for states of comfort, ease, peace, calm, relaxation and relief. Then, when you have at least 20, practise creating sentences that impart the required information but orientate the patient towards positive experiences and outcomes (for example, "when you're feeling comfortable again" as opposed to "when the pain goes away"). See how many of these words you can introduce into your consultations without interrupting the flow.

Presuppositions

Presuppositions are statements that assume something that is actually not verbalised. The subject must accept the presupposition in order to understand the statement, thereby 'bypassing' conscious resistance. An example is: "When you take the medication regularly, you will find your symptoms come under control." That the medication will be taken regularly is presupposed; the patient's attention is diverted on to the second part of the sentence.

Presuppositions most commonly start with words such as when, after, before, as, during etc.

Embedded commands

Embedded commands are self-standing 'orders' or 'instructions' hidden within a larger sentence. The example above also contains two embedded commands: "Take the medication regularly," and "Find your symptoms come under control."

Create your embedded command, and then create a secondary sentence within which it can be embedded while still making sense.

When they are delivered, embedded commands should be analogically marked – that is, spoken slightly more loudly or softly, with a gesture or a slightly more emphatic tone, etc – to mark them out to the patient's unconscious processes as significant.

Primacy and recency

Since people tend to remember and respond to the first and/or the last of a set of statements, ensure that the most important instruction is delivered or repeated last.

Turning words

Words such as "but" and "however" are what we call "turning words" and have the effect of negating or minimising the impact of the clause immediately preceding it - for example:

"You're an intelligent and thoughtful person, but you need to pay more attention." Our natural response is to ignore the 'compliment' and focus on whatever qualifying statement follows.

Another example: "Johnny seems fine, but if you have any worries during the night, you can always call." Doctors delivering instructions in this way often report an increase in unnecessary calls or visits by worried patients. A revised version might be: "You have our number and you can call if you have any worries – but I've examined Johnny and he seems fine."

In order to minimise overreaction to adverse but unlikely possibilities or experiences, place them first in the sentence, followed by a turning word, then a qualifier that presupposes a more positive outcome.

The formula is:

Possibility + Turning Word + Reassurance

5

Structure, Process and Change: the building blocks of experience

Exactly what constitutes the nature of 'reality' and the 'meaning' of life has preoccupied scientists, philosophers and spiritual thinkers for much of our time on the planet. And even though you are unlikely to be consciously aware of the questions that inform almost every moment of your life, they are there, directing your emotions, needs, moods, desires and behaviours: *What is happening to me? Why do I feel this way? What does it mean? What should I do?* At virtually every turn, and often unconsciously, we ask questions and make decisions about our world and our place in it as we navigate through the complexity of daily living, based on the assumption that we understand, or can understand, what's *really* 'going on'.

For much of the time, this way of managing the world serves our needs. We eat, sleep, have sex, look to people and things we hope will give us something we call "happiness". To many of us, the challenge seems to be to control the unruly, unpredictable, unreliable elements of life, thinking that somehow, some day, we'll make it all fit.

Sometimes it will seem to work; more often, it won't. Disappointment sets in, and we start all over again, trying to rearrange the pieces of an ever-changing puzzle. If it doesn't, then we turn to an 'expert' in the particular part of our dysfunctioning body-mind in the hopes that he can.

One of our problems as a species is that we use our superior ability to think, but seldom think about the *way* in which we think. Even less do we suspect that how we think directly affects our experience, happy or unhappy, functional or dysfunctional, sick or well. This should not be confused either with New Age "positive thinking" or the hunting down and challenging of Cognitive Behavioural Therapy's "negative thinking patterns". We are talking about the structure and process of thinking, believing and knowing – more epistemology and less psychology; more *how* and less *why*.

In order fully to understand what NLP means when it refers to "the structure of subjective experience", try the following exercise.

> Recall a pleasant experience from your past – perhaps a holiday, or a reunion with a loved one. Make sure it is a specific experience or event.
>
> Now, ask yourself how you were thinking about the memory, how you remember what you were doing and how you felt.

Most people answer vaguely at first, "I just remember it was good"; "We had a good time"; "I was feeling great".

Now, return to the memory and answer the following questions:

> How strongly can you re-create your good feelings by recalling the memory? Scale it from 1 (a little) to 10 (as if you were there right now).
>
> Do you remember the experience as a picture? If so:
>
> - Is it in colour or black and white?
> - Is it moving or still?
> - Is it near or far away?
> - Are you observing it as if on a screen, or through your own eyes?
>
> Are there any sounds to the memory? If so, are they:
>
> - Loud or soft?
>
> Are there:

- Words or music?
- Internal self-talk?

What feelings or sensations are involved, if any?

- Internal or external?
- Still or moving?
- Warmth or coolness?

What other qualities do you notice? Think of all your senses: visual, auditory, kinesthetic (feeling), smell and taste.

The experiment above demonstrates the following:

1. your memory was created out of sensory-rich information (that is, you needed to activate, albeit internally, your senses: sight, hearing, feeling and touch, and, perhaps taste and smell);
2. by acting 'as if' you were there, you re-experienced some degree of feeling or emotion that corresponded with the feelings or emotions you experienced during the original scenario. This is what we call "state" – the sum total of the psychophysiological changes that take place when you remember, imagine or experience a particular memory, behaviour or event;
3. your senses had certain qualities: colour, size, movement, degree of involvement, volume, temperature, etc; and,
4. you favoured one sense over the others.

Additionally, even though you might have experienced strong feelings or emotions when recalling this experience, you also somehow 'knew' that you were 'here', remembering, and not actually back 'there'. A simple remembered incident from your past turns out to have a host of qualities that permits you to sort information, code it and store it in a 'filing system' that allows you to distinguish one event from another, place it on an internal 'time line' and invest it with a unique emotional 'charge'.

Now, try something else.

Imagine someone raking their fingernails down a blackboard.

Or pretend you have a lemon in your hand. Feel the weight of it and the texture of the skin. See the colour of the

> peel and the flesh in your mind's eye. Hear the sound of the knife as you slice into it, and smell the pungent oil of the skin. Now bite into one half, and swill the juice around your mouth before swallowing it. Notice its sharpness, how it reacts on the enamel of your teeth.

If you did this vividly enough, you either winced at the sound of nails on the blackboard, or found your salivary glands going into overdrive. No 'real' blackboard, no lemon. Just the power of your imagination and a part of your brain that is unable to distinguish between what is real and what is imaginary, a cascade of neurochemicals, and a physical response.

The fact that people can activate physiological responses merely by imagining or remembering events will, as we will explain, serve an important function in the provision of health care (and contribute greatly to our own mental and physical health). By understanding more about how a patient 'sets up' and maintains his particular dysfunction, you will become more strategically positioned to develop practical interventions to empower him to move more systematically in the direction of self-regulation, health and well-being.

One of the fundamental messages of NLP is: *we act on our* ***representation*** *of the world, rather than on the world itself.* Information gathered from the external world is filtered through our preferred sensory modalities, and then through the constraints of our neurology and our social and cultural conditioning. This contributes to the creation of the internal model of 'reality' by which we function. The degree to which data are filtered dictates how expanded or constrained the model – and therefore our experience – is. 'Reality', then, is a construct of our neurology, in much the same way as 'vision' is an interpretation by the brain, rather than a literal reflection of the external world.

It follows, therefore, that (1) at best, the map can only *approximate* the world or 'territory' it represents, not least because the territory is too complex to render in exact detail, and (2) our maps, made up as they are from selective data uniquely filtered through personal sensory bias, *differ* from those of the people around us.

However, when we create an internal representation of the 'outside' world, we seldom question the accuracy or validity of that representation, or notice the differences between the maps of the people we meet. Alfred

Korzybski, the founder of General Semantics, said, "The map is not the territory", and attributed what he called "un-sanity" to the fact that we fail to distinguish between the two[82].

Acquiring access to the patient's map to ascertain how his representation limits his world is one of the first skills the effective practitioner should acquire. The patient is unlikely to have conscious access to his internal processing, but information nevertheless 'leaks' in a number of ways, both verbal and non-verbal. To gain insight into the patient's situation, we need to identify his sensory preferences, how he codes the 'meaning' of his experience, and how he creates and maintains negative feelings and repetitive behaviours. With that information in hand, it becomes relatively easy to interrupt and change his experience by changing the structure that supports it.

The information that follows is generalised, and it is important to remember that some people may display idiosyncratic patterns. Observe carefully before making assumptions.

Decoding the patient's inner experience

The speaker may reveal his or her sensory preference (or the pattern of the current experience) in one or other of the following ways:

1. eye moments ("eye accessing cues"), may be related to how information is stored in the brain and to innervation of the eye by four cranial nerves;
2. choice of words, also known as "sensory predicates";
3. position and movement of the body; and,
4. tone, rate and pitch of speech.

Eye movements

Classic NLP suggests that most right-handed people look to the left when remembering events, and to the right when creating new images (Figure 5.1).

Visual processing is suggested when the subject looks upwards, to the left, right or directly ahead, the vision slightly defocused.

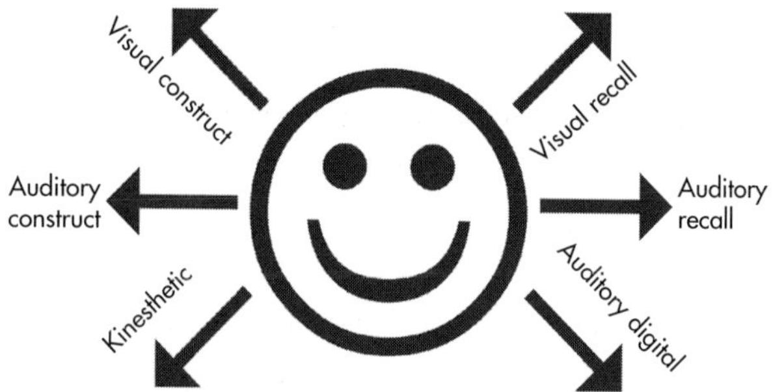

Fig 5.1 Eye accessing cues of a right-handed person. (©Dr Richard Bandler. Reproduced by written permission.)

Auditory access is indicated when the eyes are in the midline, more or less in line with the ears. The head is often tilted to one side, or it may be turned so that the listener's dominant ear is nearest the speaker.

Self-talk (also known as "Auditory Digital") is often indicated when the speaker looks down and to his or her left.

Internal kinesthetics (feelings/emotions) may be present when the subject looks down and to the right. It should be noted that olfactory and gustatory processing are usually included within the kinesthetic categorisation.

Sensory predicates

Many words and phrases indicate a preference for one or other sensory modalities – for example:

Visual: "It looks clear to me", "I get the picture", "We need to focus on this", "It's too much in my face."

Auditory: "I hear what you're saying", "That sounds good to me", "I can't hear myself think."

Kinesthetic: "I really feel for you", "You need to get a grip on yourself", "Everything feels as if it's getting on top of me."

Posture and movement

Visual: Sitting and standing erect, with the head up. Gestures are high, often as if 'sketching' in important details. Tight muscle tonus.

Auditory: Neither upward reaching nor slumped. Gestures are slower and more measured.

Kinesthetic: Often slumped, as if dragged down. Muscle tonus is slack. Gestures are slow and asymmetrical.

Speech

Visual: The pitch is often higher than average, and the rate of speech rapid-fire. There is considerable variation in tone.

Auditory: Speech is somewhat slower, pitched in the mid-range and with less variation.

Kinesthetic: Speech is slow and measured, often lacking colour or animation.

Some commentators have even suggested a correlation between physical build and sensory preference. The categories of the now largely discarded physical typology – ectomorph, mesomorph and endomorph – are said to correspond to visual, auditory and kinesthetic preferences*.

Annotation

In order to be able to analyse a subject's internal processes more easily, they may be annotated as follows:

V = Visual
A = Auditory
K = Kinesthetic

The following superscripts are then added:

^{i} = internal
^{e} = external
^{r} = recalled
^{c} = constructed
^{d} = digital (auditory digital is annotated as A^{d})

* Interestingly, many traditional health systems include physical-emotional categorisations similar to the visual-auditory-kinesthetic distinctions. The ancient Indian system of Ayurveda, for example, refers to *prakriti* (innate bio-psychological tendency), made up of different combinations of *pitta, vata* and *kapha*, corresponding to visual, auditory and kinesthetic.

The signs $^+$ and $^-$ may also be incorporated to represent subjectively pleasant or unpleasant feelings, and the sign > signifies a progression from one step to another.

Strategies: the sequencing of experience

Unpleasant feelings almost inevitably result from an inappropriate coding of a triggering event. Post-Traumatic Stress Disorder results from "flashbacks", usually experienced as if happening in the present tense (associated). Depression frequently involves melancholic or despairing self-talk (A^{d-}) or gloomy images (V^{i-}), which trigger negative feelings (K^{i-}).These, in turn, result in further pessimistic imagery or internal dialogue, leaving the sufferer physically and emotionally depleted. Anxiety is often a pattern-matching process, transferring a past experience into future possibility, thus setting up a "meta-state" (the fear that fear will come).

In order to assist patients struggling with disorders such as these, it is useful to understand the sequence, or "strategy", that their processing follows. We have internal strategies or "schemas" for all our behaviours, from making scrambled eggs and buying a shirt to feeling depressed or having an hallucination. In order to achieve the same result, the steps of the sequence will always be repeated in exactly the same order.

Eliciting strategies

The question, "How does it happen?" is useful in eliciting a strategy.

The answer might be, "Well, I wake up every morning and the first thing I feel is a weight on my chest (K^{i-}) and it's like: 'I can't go on this way!' (A^{d-}), and that's when the panic comes (K^{i-}), and I think: 'You're going to have a heart attack!' (A^{d-}) and the weight just presses down harder and harder, and it just never seems to stop…"

This can be annotated as follows:

$$K^{i-} > A^{d-} > K^{i-} > A^{d-} > \text{(loop back to } K^{i-}\text{)}$$

It will be clear from the above that this strategy is a self-maintaining "two-point loop" (that is, the subjective experience loops from K to A and then back again, repeating endlessly). The practitioner's role, as we will expand upon later, is to find an entry point in order to break the loop, provide an appropriate "exit point" and leverage change.

The sequence of eye accessing cues that patients use when re-accessing their experiences can give the practitioner further clues to the strategy being employed. The above sequence might be:

Eyes down and to the right > across and down to the left > across and down and to the right, etc. This repeating $K^i > A^d$ pattern is characteristic of people suffering from depressive and anxiety disorders.

Submodalities: shades of meaning

But how can we be sure that something we remember actually happened? By what mechanism do we distinguish differences in the time, quality, intensity and meaning of an experience?

Evolution has equipped us not only with senses by which we "sample" the external world and make internal representations of what we see, hear, feel, smell and taste, but each organ of perception also has specialised receptors that allow us to make distinctions that further drive the making of meaning.

The auditory input channel, for example, permits the reception of not only packets of data, but also qualities such as the direction from which a sound comes, the pitch and tonality of a voice, rhythm, direction and a myriad of other qualities.

Visually, we are equipped to detect colour, movement, patterns and relationships between items within our visual field, distance, etc.

Our kinesthetic senses permit physical touch, organ awareness and inner 'feelings', each of which in turn may be subdivided into an almost infinite array of subtleties. Likewise, smell and taste have qualities dependent on the receptors inside our mouths and nasal passages.

Our internal representations, therefore, are assembled not simply out of varying arrays of modalities, but each modality is 'tagged' by one or more characteristics that keeps it distinct from its associated modalities.

Given the almost limitless combinations that five modalities and their attendant submodalities possess, we have a powerful methodology for storing and accessing information in a relatively organised way.

Table 5.1 shows some of the more commonly encountered submodality distinctions, although this list is far from complete.

Table 5.1 Submodality distinctions

Visual	*Auditory*	*Kinesthetic*
Associated/dissociated	Tonality	Location
Colour/black and white	Loud/soft	Movement
Moving/still	Inside/outside head	Direction
Location	Location	Pressure/weight
Size	Pitch	Extent (start and end-points)
Near/mid/far	Tempo	Temperature
Vivid/pastel	Continuous/interrupted	Duration
Framed/panoramic	Distance	Intensity
Clear/vague	Clear/diffuse	Shape
2D/3D		
Single/multiple images		
Steady/jerky		
Flat on/tilted		
Smooth/jumpy transitions		

Changing the map

It follows that if submodality coding is part of how the perception-to-meaning transformation really works, changing the submodalities of an experience should, of necessity, change the meaning of that experience.

> Recall the pleasant memory from the exercise on page 52 and re-enter it as fully as possible. See in your mind's eye what you saw then, hear what you heard, notice the feelings you felt. Recall any smells and tastes that might have been present. Refer to how you scored the intensity of the remembered experience.
>
> Now slowly push the image away from you, or step back from it, so that you are seeing it as if from a distance. Continue increasing the distance between you and the image. If you recalled the original image through your own eyes, pull back until you see yourself in the scene as if on a screen or in

a photograph. Drain out any colour. Let the details diminish, as the image moves further from you.

Rescale the emotional intensity and compare it with the first time you calibrated it.

The majority of people who do this experiment find that feelings of pleasure are substantially diminished. Experiment by changing other submodalities. If you favour auditory or kinesthetic modalities over the visual, you might have to experiment with changing or turning down any sounds or sensations within the experience to notice an effect. You may also have observed that changing just one submodality triggered a domino effect on the others. This is what is known as the "driver" submodality – the single shift that alters the entire Gestalt. Remember to restore the original submodalities to your experience before moving on.

As a general rule, large, bright, close and colourful images usually intensify feelings, whereas smaller, distant, less distinct and colourless imagery reduces emotional impact.

Association (seeing through the subject's eyes) commonly amplifies responses, while dissociation (seeing the self as if in a picture or movie) decreases them.

Eliciting submodalities

Quite simply, ask. Ask, "How do you do that?"; "What happens when you think of that?"; "Where in your body is your (symptom)? If it had a colour (shape, size, weight, etc), what would it be?"

Take your time, and guard against being drawn back into 'content'. You are eliciting the structure of the experience, its component building blocks, not its 'story'.

Applying submodality change in practice

Simple issues can be resolved with submodality changes, literally within a few minutes. Since each person's unique coding system is the basis of his sense of reality, work systematically and ecologically, changing one submodality at a time, putting it back if no change takes place before moving on to the next. Ideally, you will find the one submodality that triggers a system-wide change.

> ***Case history:*** *The patient, a 66-year-old retired painter and decorator, had a six-month history of mounting anxiety. He was having difficulty sleeping and asked for sleeping tablets. He said he had found life difficult since retiring. He had to look after his wife, his house and his health, and worried about his ability to cope. A few weeks before the consultation, his roof had begun to leak, and he said his anxiety was stopping him doing anything to fix it – and this, in turn, was further exacerbating his anxiety.*

After carefully pacing the patient in order to lower his anxiety, the practitioner asked him to describe his 'anxiety' in terms of its location, size, colour, etc.

> *The patient said it was in his abdomen, "black", and spherical, "like a ball". He rated his level of comfort at 7, with 10 being the worst anxiety possible. The practitioner and patient then began changing the qualities of the ball, pushing it further back, changing the colour, size, etc. After a few minutes, he found to his great surprise that his rating had dropped to 3.*
>
> *The practitioner ended the consultation by asking him to practise this "relaxation technique" of changing the submodalities of his anxiety whenever necessary.*
>
> *The patient returned two weeks later saying he didn't understand exactly what had happened, but "for some reason" he felt much calmer and more relaxed, no longer wanted sleeping tablets and was planning to sort out his leaking roof.*

The initial consultation, the practitioner reports, took no more than 10 minutes, including history-taking and outcome-planning.

Notice in the above example that at no time did the practitioner offer advice or argumentation to challenge the patient's world-view. Rather than suggest he change his self-defeating self-talk, she moved to another level: that of the *structure* of patient's *model*, which she then helped him change.

Especially where more complex problems are concerned, bear in mind that how the patient describes his problem differs substantially from how the problem actually functions. This follows from the way in which we, both consciously and unconsciously, edit information in order to reduce it to more manageable proportions. George Miller calculated that we are only able consciously to process between five and seven 'bits' of information at a time[83]. More than that and details tend to be lost to both short- and long-term memory.

But what is left out or transformed in the process of creating our models of the world is as important as what is left in. As Richard Bandler emphasises, the transformation of direct, subjective experience (Deep Structure) into what is communicated (Surface Structure) is governed by three processes: deletion, distortion and generalisation:

- **Deletion** is the filtering of data to reduce it to levels we can handle. This, in part, explains why patients forget between 40% and 80% of medical information provided by health-care practitioners within minutes of leaving the consultation[84].
- **Distortion** is the inevitable consequence of deletion. Jumping to conclusions, 'catasrophising', 'remembering' something that wasn't actually said, are all examples of distortion.
- **Generalisation** is an inbuilt human skill that allows us to predict events from what has gone before. However, when only one or two elements of an experience become generalised to 'all' similar events, problems can ensue. Post-Traumatic Stress Disorder (PTSD) is a generalised response to traumatic events such as childhood abuse or car accidents.

NLP's Meta Model (see *The Structure of Magic*) defines several distinctions within each category and provides specific tools by which deletions, distortions and generalisations can be challenged. It is, however, useful, when gathering information, to favour questions starting with *how, where, when, with whom, how often*, etc, all of which provide grounded, fact-based data, rather than asking "why?", which often elicits speculation, justification and defensive behaviour (see Chapter 9).

EXERCISES

Building skill sets

Work with just one component at a time; take a day or two for each. This eliminates confusion. Practise consistently in the beginning to identify, rather than act on, what you observe.

1. Listen for sensory predicates, identifying the subject's preferred mode. (Be aware that many patients may present kinesthetically, simply because they are experiencing somatic distress; their preferred modality may, in fact, be different.)
2. Watch for eye accessing cues. Calibrate eye position with the emotional content of the subject's account.
3. Observe eye accessing sequences that repeat. These suggest a 'strategy' driving the behaviour.
4. Elicit submodality distinction of the problem states. Experiment with changing them and note the effect.

Note: To avoid "performance anxiety" with your subject and to inoculate against 'failure', use phrases such as: "Just before we begin, let's try a little experiment", or "I just need to find something out." When coaching submodality changes, it often helps to use examples and analogies to explain the process. Referring to the controls of a TV set or sound system is one way of doing this.

6

Taming the Runaway Brain: three thinking tools

Thinking is something we all do naturally, but not necessarily well. The process happens so quickly, naturally, and so far beneath our ordinary, day-to-day awareness that it seldom presents itself for scrutiny.

The human brain – the most extraordinary tool in the universe, the only one we know of that has the ability to rewire itself according to how we use it – is left largely to its own devices. 'Thinking about thinking' is something we are generally quite happy to hand over to other people to contemplate: the philosophers, neuroscientists and psychotics. Thinking 'just is', and for the most part we are quite content to leave it that way.

Astonishingly, given the number of bad decisions our species has chalked up, education has proved of little help. We have been taught *what* to think, but not *how* to think. Our ability to error-correct has not improved significantly as a result.

On the other hand, thinking skilfully – that is, with system and purpose, not to be confused with formal logic – allows us to consider information we might not even have noticed before; extract order and meaning out of apparent chaos; generate theories and hypotheses; and, create solutions we can then test.

The complex chronic conditions currently overwhelming the health services are deeply in need of a new reasoning approach. They are baffling, we agree. But they appear baffling not because of their intrinsic nature, but because of the way we have been looking at them.

The old folk story, attributed to Mullah Nasruddin, about five blind men, each trying to describe an elephant by feeling just one part of its body, is an apt analogy. The elephant is, variously, like a snake, a tree, a huge palm leaf. Any attempt to synthesise a whole from the parts is doomed to failure, no matter how eloquently each is able to sense and describe the part he is touching.

Most of us find the story amusing because it is so patently irrational. And yet research often follows the same thinking process – that, somehow, if the object is divided into sufficiently small parts, understanding of the 'whole' will follow.

Of course, this approach has served us well in certain areas in the past. We now know a lot about how a germ can cause a particular infection, and which gene can cause a specific deformity. Our knowledge about how people become sick is vast. But, as a result, our single-minded commitment to the twin beliefs of reductionism and causality tells us virtually nothing about how some people never get sick, and others get well.

This occurs largely because of the way in which we have chosen to think about a particular problem. The instant we decide to confine our attention to a specific set of events – the *text* of a story – we exclude information that may, in fact, explain the *context* in which that function or process occurs (see Chapter 8). To paraphrase Sir William Osler, we look at the disease the patient has, without looking at the patient who has the disease. *We are baffled at the condition we encounter because we are trying to apply a familiar and limited map to unfamiliar territory.*

On being comfortable with not-knowing

Of course, scientists are not alone in thinking this way. Ambiguity is, for most of us, an uncomfortable experience. The compulsion to avoid the discomfort of 'not-knowing' is so strong that often we will accept, without reflection, an explanation – either our own or one provided for us by some authority – that resolves our internal dissonance. And yet the ability to tolerate ambiguity, at least for a time, is an essential step towards widening our perspective. Just for the moment, we need to suspend our beliefs and biases in the knowledge that this way only will permit new information to flow in.

In order to break out of this particular box, we need to understand how easily our beliefs and perceptions are influenced by an ongoing interaction between the way in which our minds naturally work and the effect that unchallenged linguistic distortions (using language mindlessly) can have on our beliefs.

Consider the phrase "medically unexplained", one of the descriptors used almost synonymously with "functional", "somatoform", "psychosomatic" or "psychogenic" disorders. On the face of it, it means simply that *our current medical knowledge is not able to account for the condition under consideration.* It does *not* mean – as is so often assumed by default – that the condition is imaginary or intended to deceive or manipulate.

Although most practitioners will deny drawing these conclusions, it happens more frequently than we would like – especially when the health professional is under pressure. Here are three examples of phrases we have encountered in physicians' letters of referral for patients suffering from what is usually called "myofascial" or "fibromyalgic" pain syndromes:

> *"Physical basis for the pain has been conclusively ruled out by all tests … A psychiatric assessment has diagnosed somatoform pain disorder."*
>
> *"I suspect the patient has a hidden agenda, since I have determined that there is nothing physically wrong with him."*
>
> *"The patient's over-reaction during examination leads me to believe his problem is either hypochondriasis or malingering."*

Our argument here is not with whether the patient was or was not 'making it up', but with the cognitive mechanism employed by the attending physician in reaching his conclusion. The reasoning is as follows:

> All real pain has a physical cause.
> Therefore, if no physical cause is found,
> the pain cannot be real.

This reasoning process, known as syllogistic, is perfectly logical – but only within its own framework. If the propositions are correct, then the conclusion is correct. If the propositions are questionable, as in the example above, we – and the patient – are in trouble. The flaws in the reasoning include the facts that only pain with a physical cause is 'real' and that there is no physical cause, simply because one has not been identified.

The speed with which we often draw conclusions and make decisions tends to trick us into believing they are 'right'. If questioned, we insist (and feel) that we have selected our response from a range of possibilities, all duly subjected to full assessment.

But, as a number of researchers, including Benjamin Libet[85] and Daniel Wegner[86], have demonstrated, a series of complicated mental and physical processes takes place from a third to half a second before you 'choose' to act in a particular way. Conscious thought, therefore, *follows* a psychophysiological decision to act, rather than the other way around. This 'illusion' is so compelling that we tend to defend vigorously our intention to act, even where intentionality can be disproved.

One thing we can be sure of: the mind does not rigorously question the sense or logic of each chunk of information it receives. The sheer amount of data available to our senses would be overwhelming if we had to weigh up each incoming bit. We cope by streamlining. Information is chunked and processed according to general patterns; we respond to situations that resemble previous situations we have encountered, calling on the same feelings and responses as before. Inevitably, as we acquire more 'similar' experiences, these patterns coalesce into biases, mindsets and, if we fail to remain alert, stereotypes.

A number of other factors can dissuade us from freeing up our thinking and reasoning processes. Four of these are are as follows:

1. **Fear.** The fear of making the 'wrong' decision is a major concern within the health professions, and not only because of the risks to the patient's health and well-being. Litigation is increasing, forcing practitioners into an increasingly more defensive position. This results in an overdependence on referrals to specialists, multiple tests and opinions, invasive scans and surgery, and overmedication.

2. **Pressure.** As stress mounts, our tendency to revert to familiar coping patterns also increases. Complex and manifold problems encountered in unfavourable circumstances are likely to trigger limbic arousal. Constraints of time increase pressure. And so does a sense that we do not have the resources to help the person seeking our knowledge and expertise.
3. **Peer acceptance.** Doing something differently from our peers or our superiors is a risky business. Or at least it feels risky. If we depart from the 'norm', we tend to be concerned that someone will challenge us and, by doing so, 'prove' that our approach is inferior. Despite many organisations' claim that they encourage 'proaction' and 'individuality', disturbing the status quo is often penalised, implicitly if not directly.
4. **External demands.** An essentially market-driven model of health delivery as exists in the United States and is rapidly being imposed in the United Kingdom depends on external measures of 'effectiveness': audits, targets and guidelines, established, at least partly, on the basis of cost-effectiveness. Meeting targets, then, can easily become an easier option than meeting patient needs.

There are many highly effective means of developing rational thinking processes, but we believe the three tools we outline below are among the most easily understood and applied. The underlying intention of these is to make distinctions between fact and belief, to reduce errors that occur when we confuse one with the other, and to begin to explore some of the mechanisms that set up and maintain the patient's problem.

Thinking tool 1: The Fact-Evaluation Spectrum

'Facts' – especially if you're a quantum physicist or a politician – are pretty hard to come by. Much of what we regard as 'true' or 'objective' depends on evaluating the evidence on which we *choose* to place our attention. Psychologists, such as Edmund Bolles, now recognise that 'paying attention' requires us actively to choose information from a confused buzz of sensations and details to which we then ascribe 'meaning'[87]. This is what we call "evaluation".

But, the process of evaluation includes two other mental actions. In creating 'meaning' out of whatever we place our attention on, we also *exclude* certain information from what is available, and we *supplement* what is in front of us with what has gone before. Far from functioning as 'objective', 'scientific' beings, systematically uncovering meaning, we are architects and builders; we construct meaning according to blueprints, most of which exist and function well below our conscious awareness.

The labels we then select to apply to that which we have attended to are quick to develop a life of their own. As discussed above, the word becomes the 'thing', and we forget that we (or someone else) created that part of our cognitive map by a process of evaluation. It is now 'true'.

The Fact-Evaluation Spectrum is a tool designed to help our ability to distinguish between verifiable data (fact) and belief, speculation, judgement, opinion, evaluation, etc. In doing this, we reduce our tendency towards premature cognitive closure (making your mind up before all the evidence has been acquired), and acting 'as if' the individual in front of you is physically, psychologically, socially and spiritually identical to everyone else who matches some or all of the criteria of a particular class of 'condition'.

We (the authors) do not pretend to know what an incontrovertible fact is (we're not politicians); the guidelines in this section are intended more to caution against unknowingly applying beliefs, judgements, inferences, opinions, etc as 'true' simply because they are *believed* to be true.

Belief is a major trap in clear thinking. We need to understand that a belief differs from a fact, however dearly held. The distinction needs to be made. It is often debated whether a belief is 'true' or 'false', whereas it might be more productive simply to decide whether it is 'useful' or not*. Many of the descriptions we use in day-to-day practice may help us communicate to fellow professionals with some degree of consensuality; however, we need also to be cautious as to how they can (often unconsciously) inform and influence our beliefs and responses.

* Inevitably, the issue of religious belief is raised here. Our response is simply this: if your religious beliefs support the health and well-being of yourself and others, they are 'useful'. If not, they are not.

"Functional", the description of a very large class of complex chronic conditions without specific cause, is such a word. And the word itself often stands in the way of understanding and assisting the patient to restructure his experience. Definitions vary from source to source, but only slightly. Ideally, a functional disorder is one in which no evidence of organic damage or disturbance may be found, but, which nevertheless affects the patient's physical and emotional well-being. However, increasingly, the word is taken to suggest the presence of 'psychiatric' elements (see the *Oxford Concise Medical Dictionary*, as an example[88]).

Sadly, the belief (that if the cause of a condition cannot be established it can't be 'real') permeates everyday medical care. To the patient, there is a strong element of blaming and shaming, which, given our earlier investigation of the impact of stress on health, is hardly likely to help.

In a bid to minimise this kind of toxic labelling, our first 'thinking tool', therefore, is based on learning to recognise and distinguish between facts and evaluations (inferences, assumptions, judgements and opinions). Simply put, 'fact', as we use the word from now on, refers to sensory-based information – that is, whatever you (or the patient) can see, hear, touch, taste and smell. As far as possible, these data should be free of value-judgement or interpretation. They should not be evaluated. A group of independent bystanders would in the main agree with your observations.

Example of facts

- The man is sitting, slumped in his chair, head down, looking at the floor.
- The woman sits with her arms wrapped around her body.
- The child doesn't make eye contact when he says he didn't take the cookie.

Most observers would agree with these descriptions.

Examples of beliefs

- The man is depressed.
- The woman is defensive.
- The child is lying.

These are all evaluations that we may believe to be true, but have no way of verifying without further information.

Especially where patients' subjective (internal) experience is concerned, we seek to elicit sensory-specific, factual information. By this, we mean how the patient experiences his condition (what he sees, hears, feels, smells and tastes), rather than the inferences he makes from that experience. For example:

> Patient: *I feel very depressed. It's just awful. I feel really terrible.* (All the information here is inferential. The patient responds 'as if' this is the 'true' nature of his experience.)
> Practitioner: *How do you know? What specifically happens that lets you know this?*
> Patient: *I wake up every morning with a grey cloud over my head and it's just like … Oh, you're never going to get any better, and it's like a lead weight on my chest …*

As discussed in Chapter 5, this kind of information is separated out from inferences, judgements and beliefs. It describes the process of his experience using sensory-based information.

> Patient: …*I wake up every morning with a grey cloud* (visual) *over my head and it's just like … Oh, you're never going to get any better* (auditory), *and it's like a lead weight on my chest* (kinesthetic) …

As we report at various points in this book, sensory-based, factual information gives us something specific to work with. We can begin to change the experience by changing *how* the patient *structures* the experience.

Thinking tool 2: The Structural Differential

In the years following World War 1, Alfred Korzybski, a Polish nobleman and polymath, was puzzled how a species, already so advanced, could have plunged so deeply into chaos. With remarkable prescience, he formulated his ideas of the relationship of language with neurological function into a field he called General Semantics*.

Language, he said, emerged as a 'higher-order' abstraction from certain neurological 'events'. Put another way, 'something' happens in the subject's neurology, a perturbation, or Event, which exists formlessly and silently. This is also known as process. The subject then becomes aware of some 'difference' occurring. Korzybski called this the Object, since it had characteristics (submodalities), but, like the Event, no words have yet been attached to it. Both Event and Object are on a "silent", or pre-linguistic, level.

The subject's Description follows his experience. For the first time, words are involved and, of necessity, the words can only partially represent the experience itself. Then, based on the subject's description, comes Inference (I^1) – an *evaluation* about what this 'means'. And, following that, an Inference about the first Inference (I^2), followed by an Inference about that Inference (I^3), and so on, potentially to infinity (or, as Korzybski would put it, 'etc').

The language used to describe and infer from the silent level of subjective experience may be regarded as 'story' or 'content'. Since each level can feed back to the level(s) above it, Inference can affect the original Event, regulating it either upwards or downwards, changing the subject's experience of the Object. Thus 'story' is required to establish and maintain ongoing subjective experience, making it better or worse. Or, to put it another way, without story, structure cannot be maintained.

Korzybski represented this with a three-dimensional model of what he called the Structural Differential. Figure 6.1 is a two-dimensional representation of the process as applied to the medical or psychiatric investigation.

In practice, we can use the Structural Differential to map a patient's experience in the following way.

Some disturbance occurs within the patient's neurology that affects complex homeostasis, and compromises allostasis (for the sake of illustration, let's say he suffers confusion and anxiety when he tries to

* General Semantics should not be confused with semantics. The latter is concerned with the 'meaning' of words. Korzybski intended General Semantics to focus primarily on the process of 'abstraction' and its effect on thinking.

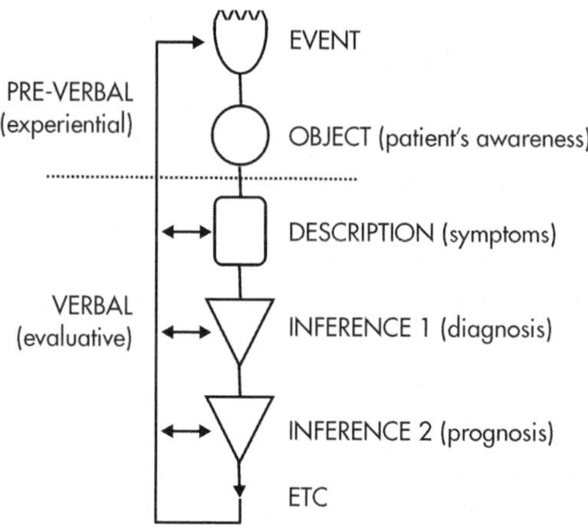

Fig 6.1 The Structural Differential as applied to the medical investigation. Note that everything that is verbalised is evaluative, not 'factual'. (Adapted with permission of the Institute of General Semantics.)

understand written information). We may never know everything about what causes the disturbance or how it occurs (Event level). Broadly speaking, this is the territory of neuroscience, and its companion fields of psychopharmacology and psychoneuroimmunology.

The patient becomes aware of a 'problem' (Object level), and then goes on to try to describe it (Descriptive level).

Based on the description, the 'expert' creates the first Inference ($Inference^1$), also known as "diagnosis"; the patient has 'dyslexia'. Further Inferences follow, both from the patient and from those around him ($Inference^2$, $Inference^3$, etc). These might include, "He has a learning disability"; "I am stupid because I have a disability"; "His feelings about having a disability are making him anxious"; "He needs treatment for his anxiety about his feelings about having a disability" … etc.

Any, or all, of these Inferences can loop back and intensify the experience of 'confusion' that first alerted the patient to an Event. Thus, he may become more anxious, more 'disabled' and even more confused.

Differences in treatments and schools of psychology develop when various theorists observe and develop models applying to different levels of Inference. One might try to curb the anxiety with medication, another might try to alter the subject's "negative self-talk", yet another might try to retrain the way he moves his eyes when he reads.

From this, it can easily be seen that all diagnoses are Inferences based on abstracted information, and all Inferences (including prognoses and treatment modalities) depend on the quality of the Inferences that precede it. Therefore, the diagnosis (Inference) is not the disease (Event), but only the currently accepted label for a collection of descriptions (symptoms). And these (the Inferences) will change. Indeed, they are changing all the time.

Let's look at some examples:

- World Health Organisation diagnostic criteria for diabetes were redefined in the late 1970s, revised in 1985 and changed again in 1996/97[89]. The diagnostic value of the fasting plasma glucose concentration was reduced from the former level of 7.8 mmol/l to 7.0 mmol/l and above[90]. In practice, this meant that many people had been told that they had normal blood glucose when in fact they were actually diabetic. Given the slow insidious progression of this disease one can only speculate as to how much untold organ damage had occurred to those individuals during the intervening years.
- A transient ischaemic attack is diagnosed if symptoms last less than 24 hours. If the symptoms last 24 hours and 1 minute it becomes a "stroke". The disease process is the same.
- The diagnostic descriptions of "acute coronary syndrome", "social phobia" and "restless legs" did not exist as separate entities with those labels until relatively recently.

Many diseases are notoriously difficult for clinicians to assign diagnostic labels to – yet this labelling process remains a cornerstone of current orthodox medical practice. The former world heavyweight boxer Mohammad Ali was originally diagnosed as having Parkinson's disease and treated accordingly. Years later, the label of Parkinson's was found to be erroneous, and has since been changed to spinal stenosis. Confusion apparently arose out of the presupposition that injuries received in the ring were responsible for his condition.

As suggested above, when prime cause cannot be established, the most proximate diagnosis is often selected, or a new condition may be created. But the further away from the Event and Object levels that the Inferences move, the greater the potential for confusion. Also, confusing levels of abstraction with each other (for example, treating an Inference as an explanation, or even a cause) can lead to the pathologising of body-mind events that may fall within the range of 'normal' experience and encourages excessive medical and surgical intervention, yet can leave both patient and practitioner still at a loss as to how to relieve the suffering.

Reference to the Structural Differential allows the practitioner to identify Inferences at various levels of abstraction (both his own and those of the patient), and to plan his response accordingly. It is an especially valuable tool to eliminate confusion caused by interpreting an Inference about the problem as a cause.

Thinking Tool 3: Function Analysis

In the corporate world, function analysis is designed to measure the cost and benefit of a new product or system against the cost and benefit of keeping the old. Whether or not we are consciously aware of it, we apply function analysis to almost every new decision we make, from buying a new sound system to which medication might be best for a particular patient. Problems arise when function analysis has been conducted 'intuitively' or derives from criteria we have inherited and accepted, without examination, from others.

In the Medical NLP model of whole-person health care, we aim to recognise and respond to the psychosocial components of complex chronic conditions and to accord them the same significance as biomechanical signs and symptoms. We want to understand context (the landscape in which the problem occurs) as much as text (the details of the problem itself). We seek answers to questions such as, "What is the value, need or purpose of the old condition/behaviour to the patient?"; "How can those values, needs or purposes be met by another behaviour or response that is more useful or appropriate?"; "What are the costs of making a change balanced against the costs of staying the way he is – and is he prepared to meet those costs?"

And, by "cost", of course, we mean the price paid or value expressed in emotional, social, spiritual and behavioural terms. Is it worth it to the patient to make the change? Function analysis helps us move to a higher order of investigation – looking for patterns that may explain the condition's resistance to treatment.

Supposing we are considering the possibility that a patient feels deficient in social support and connectedness (see Chapter 3). In applying function analysis to the presenting condition, we will be considering if and how the condition is related to that specific emotional shortfall. For example:

> ***Case history:*** *A single, middle-aged woman developed multiple chemical sensitivities after her neighbour sprayed his garden (and, inadvertently, hers) with an illegal toxic herbicide. She confronted him and reported that he was rude and unrepentant. The allergic response developed soon after the confrontation and spread rapidly to include a wide range of allergens, including house paint, cigarette smoke, perfume and aftershave and exhaust fumes. (**Note:** This is text.)*
>
> *In conversation, it emerged that the woman felt lonely and uncared for. She spoke several times about her father, whom she considered cold and uncaring; she became agitated and apparently angry when talking about him. (We noticed that her breathing became raspy and constricted and her eyes watered whenever the subject came up, typical of an allergic response.) The only time he showed any consideration for her was when she was confined to her bed with an "attack", even though she suspected he thought she was malingering. (This is context. It also reflects the process of abstraction and evaluation taking place inside her model of the world.)*
>
> *She also reported being immensely angry at her neighbour, and had abandoned conventional treatment, explaining that both her neighbour and doctors in general were "paternalistic" and disinterested in the welfare of others … "just like my father".*

At that point, the practitioner's focus shifted to: (1) the possible purpose or intention of her symptoms, (2) whether these needs were being met, and (3) whether it would be possible to find ways of meeting these needs in ways that would make 'being sick' no longer necessary.

From the information we elicited, the practitioner constructed several hypotheses for later testing. These included the possibility that she needed to expand her social connectedness (in this case, by reactivating supportive friendships she had allowed to lapse), to resolve or come to terms with her anger towards her father, that her neighbour's indifferent attitude was functioning as a subliminal reminder of her father's emotional unavailability, that she needed to be ill to get the love and attention she needed, etc. (Interestingly, when we sent her out, after ensuring there was no risk of anaphylactic shock, into a place where people were smoking, with the instruction to "make the symptom appear", nothing happened. That was the first step in her beginning to understand that she was not completely at the mercy of her condition.)

Our intention was not to impose these theories on the patient, but to seek out an 'entry point' in the behavioural loop, set up initially as a protective mechanism, with the intention of helping her to change. At best, we make cautious suggestions. More often, though, the patient notices patterns and connections himself. This is therapeutic gold. But, as with all other cases, change would not have been possible for this patient unless her unmet needs were addressed and the entire 'system' in which she functioned was effectively balanced.

Please note that *at no time did we suggest (or even consider) that her responses were 'not real'; they were.*

The purpose of function analysis, then, is to acquire "higher-order" information (about how something happens). With this and the other principles and tools already discussed, the Engagement phase of the consultation can begin.

EXERCISES

We recommend that you practise the three thinking tools so they can operate in the background of your experience. They are not intended to dominate your attention. As you become more familiar with the processes, you will find it progressively easier to apply them naturally and conversationally.

1. **The Fact-Evaluation Spectrum**
   Establish whether statements (including your own) are factual or evaluative. Make a mental note whenever a fact checks out as well grounded and sensory-specific. Likewise, notice how easily evaluation creeps in. Test for these by asking questions such as "How do you/I know?", "What is the (sensory) evidence?"
2. **The Structural Differential**
   Practise locating statements along the Structural Differential. How much, if any, of the patient's description is in fact evaluative? Are the Inferences you detect first-level evaluations, or are they evaluations of the evaluation(s) before it?
3. **Function Analysis**
   As you listen to the patient, keep in mind the higher-order questions, such as "What purpose could this symptom/behaviour serve?", "How does it work?", etc.

Part II: Realisation

Phase 1: Engagement

7

The Rules of Engagement: managing first impressions

The first 30 seconds can be critical to the success or failure of any consultation. Research and experience lead us to the incontrovertible conclusion that people make up their minds almost instantaneously. Reasoning comes later – and that may be too late. The instant your patient lays eyes on you, he has already begun to form an opinion, assembled unconsciously and at near-light speed, from the way you are dressed, your posture, facial expression, eye contact and body movements. Within the first few words you speak, the impression is all but fixed.

The phenomenon, extensively studied by psychologists as "thin slicing" and introduced to the general public by British writer Malcolm Gladwell in his highly readable book, *Blink*[91], is familiar to everyone in both social and professional settings. How many times have you taken an instant liking to someone you met at a party? Within minutes, you felt as if you'd known them "for ever". How times have you "just known" something was wrong with the person on the other end of a telephone conversation, even though nothing specific was said?

Aside from the spoken word, people leak information at every turn. This includes eye movements, facial expression, bearing, gestures, mannerisms, vocal qualities, breathing patterns, changes in skin colour and muscle tone. Most of this is absorbed below the threshold of consciousness, but it *is absorbed*. And, once absorbed, it acquires meaning through some of the processes we will discuss below.

The speed with which information is transmitted and received is staggering. Paul Ekman has identified micro-expressions of emotions such as anger, fear, disgust, happiness and sadness, lasting as little as 1/500th of a second and shared by cultures throughout the world[92]. Harvard University's Nalini Ambady and fellow experimental psychologist Robert Rosenthal have demonstrated that 30-second snatches of soundless videos of lectures are all observers needed accurately to predict the qualities of teaching as measured over an entire semester[93].

The key to concordance and adherence

Awareness that these processes are at work and understanding how to engage with patients at the most productive level have given rise to a set of skills that allows the practitioner to achieve maximum engagement with the patient. This, in turn, improves both concordance between patient and practitioner and adherence to treatment plans, while avoiding, as far as possible, accidental and damaging disconnects.

Lack of warmth and friendliness has been found to be one of the most significant variables aversely affecting patient satisfaction and concordance. Many busy practitioners underestimate how much their attention shifts from the patient to other concerns (computer screens, notes, calls, etc), and overestimate the time they give to listening, eliciting unexpressed concerns and giving information[94].

In order to get the feeling for this, imagine for a moment that you are a patient visiting a doctor you have never met before (in other words, move into **position 2**; see Table 3.1). As you enter the examination room, he is tapping at the keyboard on his desk, eyes fixed on the screen.

Without looking up from your electronic records, he says, "What's the problem?"

"Well, doctor, I have this headache and it's worrying me because –"

"When did it start?" The doctor pauses, fingers hovering above the keyboard, still not looking up.

"About three weeks ago, but –"

"Where about in your head is it?"

"Well, it's actually more a kind of pressure at the back. I'm worried about –"

"Is it sharp or dull?"

"Um – like I said, it's more a kind of … pressure, but I think it's –"

And, so it goes.

For you, as the patient, a number of things are happening, aside from your symptoms and any frustration, confusion or irritation you may be feeling at the repeated interruptions.

The first is a 'gut feeling' that something is not right. At this stage (and, had you been alert enough, you might unconsciously have noticed it the instant the physician failed to look at you when you entered his space), you will not have attached any words to the experience. In Korzybski's model, it occurs at the Object level – a kinesthetic internal experience that has qualities, such as heat, weight, movement and intensity. It is highly unlikely that it will feel good.

In NLP terminology, this is an 'internal kinesthetic'. Neuroscientist Antonio Damasio calls it a "somatic marker", and he believes that it is a learned response that serves as an automated alarm, a psychophysical signal communicating either "Danger!" or "Go for it!"[95]

Somatic markers are "paired" experiences, he adds. In other words, we learned to feel one way if Dad never praised us for our accomplishments, or another way if Mum gave us a particularly sunny smile every time she saw us. As we navigate through life, we link various experiences into groups or chains according to the characteristics they share. Each of these is experienced as a distinctive kinesthetic or somatic marker. And each of these markers, in turn, may be triggered at any later stage by a word, a look, a tone of voice – any stimulus, in fact, that is a broad pattern-match to the one that set up the original response.

The stimulus may occur unexpectedly, and at any time, long after the original experience has been forgotten. Only later (often much later, and sometimes in front of a lawyer) does cognition kick in and we try to explain the reasons for feeling the way we did. "He just didn't seem to care"; "He was too busy to listen"; "I tried to tell him my sister had died but he kept cutting me off." (Some lawyers are extremely skilled at helping clients 'translate' these somatic markers into the language of litigation – so be warned[96].)

This automated stimulus-response is known in NLP as an "anchor", and it is impossible to know how many have been set up over the years. It follows, then, that we need to do whatever we can in order to minimise adverse responses in the people we hope to help.

Entirely avoiding responses that bubble up from the patient's hidden past may be an impossible task. However, the *probability* of a mutually rewarding consultation is significantly increased if three propositions are borne in mind:

1. Patients expect "carers" to show that they actually care, by their warmth, interest and focused attention;
2. Helping patients "feel better" is an important factor in helping them to *get* better; and,
3. Patients tend to be reluctant to act punitively against practitioners they like, even when a professional mistake has occurred[95].

Our contention – and the balance of research that we present in this book – is that a major part of effective consultation is a mutually respectful relationship between patient and practitioner[97], and that, once set up, the relationship is maintained and measured through the medium of communication. What follows from this point on, then, is a collection of principles and techniques modelled from particularly effective communicators, reinforced by research projects, and verified by patients satisfied with the health care they have received.

We have also gleaned useful nuggets from less orthodox sources, including information technology, successful business consultants, presenters, observation, our own and that of our colleagues, experience and common (Korzybski would say "un-common") sense. Together, these form the basis of the Engagement phase of the three-part Medical NLP Consultation Process. Integrating them into your normal consultation style takes little or no extra time, and increases your sense of control in potentially problematical or challenging situations.

Your appearance

Appearance is a significant factor in creating good first impressions. Although the results of studies on physician attire are inconclusive regarding the white coat vs. no white coat debate, communication experts agree that patients expect health professionals to be well dressed and smartly groomed. The consensus is well-fitting suits, plain shirts and ties for men, neat suits or jacket and skirts for women. Both sexes should avoid overly strident patterns or colours, excessive jewellery and unpolished shoes. Many patients react particularly adversely to extravagant hair styles or overly trendy cuts.

Your voice

Most of us take the voices we were 'born with' for granted – until we hear ourselves for the first time in a recording. Even that is often not enough to prod us into taking charge of one of our most primary tools of communication.

Well, consider this: within less than a minute, your voice can reveal your height, weight, build, gender[98], age and occupation[99], and even your sexual orientation[100] – sight unseen. As sociologist Anne Karpf comments in her book, *The Human Voice*, we are doing something "terrifyingly intimate" every time we speak, even if all we do is to "read out regulations for the disposal of sewage"[101].

Such a powerful tool needs to be cared for and protected if it is to do its job effectively. If you are unsatisfied with the quality of your speech and are unable to correct it by applying some of the suggestions below, we urge you to consult a qualified professional to improve your presentation and to prevent damage to your vocal cords.

Vocal coach and therapist Janet Edwards identifies two factors particularly damaging to the voice: inadequate breathing and dehydration. "If you don't breathe into your abdomen, your voice has no support and lacks power," she says. "This is also a great drain on energy." She also suggests a minimum of a litre to a litre and a half of water ("not soft drinks, tea or coffee") sipped over a day to ensure adequate hydration.

Another recommendation often given to professionals who use their voices over sustained periods is to locate their unique "key". Broadly speaking, key refers to the most comfortable range of notes you can produce, while still retaining a wide range of 'highs' and 'lows'. By identifying the key of your speaking voice – which changes from day to day according to energy levels, the amount of talking you do, your physical and emotional state at the time – you can inject variation into your speech and sustain interest while avoiding strain.

Setting your key

We suggest one of the following ways to 'set' your key before starting any sustained period of speaking. The first is to sing (probably best when no-one else is around to witness your efforts) the lowest note you can produce. Then, sing five notes up the scale ('so' on the do-re-mi scale). This is the mid-point of your range, giving you flexibility to move up and down while still retaining a 'natural' sound.

If you prefer not to sing, or are not familiar with the notes of the musical scale, take a deep breath, imagine you are sitting down after a long and tiring period on your feet, and make that 'comfort sound' we all know so well – *hunh*! The *hunh* sound is the mid-point of your current vocal range.

Vocal qualities of excellent communicators

Communicating with purpose requires an understanding of how the 'shape' and rhythm of language can affect the listener as much as the words that are used.

As a general rule, only questions should inflect *upwards* (the voice going up at the end of the sentence), whereas neutral statements tend to be *uninflected*, and commands, orders or important information are all *downwardly inflected* (the voice going down at the end of the sentence). Some nationalities (Australian and Welsh in particular) have a tendency to inflect upwards whether or not a question is being asked. Women in the West sometimes follow the same pattern in the belief that it is a friendlier, more empathetic approach. However, this may sometimes be interpreted as a lack of certainty.

Credible or approachable

Effective communicators and presenters tend to share two qualities – credibility and approachability – both of which have distinctive vocal

Table 6.1 The vocal patterns of approachability and credibility

	Purpose	*Tone*	*Pitch*	*Eye contact*	*Physical movement*
Approachable	Rapport Concordance Information	Variable	Variable	Variable	Some
Credible	Instructions Advice Adherence	Monotone	Drop at end of sentence	Fixed	Restrained

patterns (See Table 6.1). It is important to distinguish between the two styles, and to know when to apply them.

Approachability (often associated with 'friendliness' and 'likeability') is an aid to gaining rapport, gathering information and encouraging disclosure. It is marked by variability in pitch, tone and rate of speech (what Edwards calls "colour"). The voice is animated, rising and falling naturally. Laughing and joking (if appropriate) and moving or gesturing while talking are also permissible in the approachable phase. Setting your 'key', as mentioned above, helps facilitate the vocal flexibility that characterises approachability.

Approachability alone, however, may be counter-productive when important information or instructions need to be given. Patients may like an approachable practitioner, but will not necessarily accept his advice as authoritative. This is where 'credibility' will improve concordance and adherence.

Credibility (being authoritative but not overbearing) serves analogically to 'mark out' the importance of a statement from the general 'noise' of conversational exchanges. This alerts the patient, consciously and unconsciously, to pay particular attention to what is being said, while also helping to increase memory and adherence.

Credibility and authority are dependent not on volume, but on vocal style. When striving to be credible, your voice should be less varied, and your movements and gestures more restrained. Information and instructions are delivered with a downward inflection at the end of a sentence. Eye contact should be steady throughout the statement, without being intimidating.

Accounting for gender differences

Both men and women may initially find it challenging to allow their voices to move up or down into registers they do not normally use. This is a common response, but one that usually disappears with practice.

It is also important to note that in British and American cultures, the 'meaning' of head-nodding can differ between the sexes. To generalise, men tend to nod when they agree with a statement, while women often nod to show they are listening. There is potential for confusion in both personal and professional settings ("But, the doctor said it was okay for me to keep drinking"; "But, you agreed when I said I wanted to play golf on Saturday instead of visiting your mother"). We suggest, therefore, that, as far as possible, both male and female practitioners inhibit nodding and affirmative phrases unless they intend to confirm or reinforce a statement or opinion.

Using the first 30 seconds

In a time-starved working world, you can carve out 30 vital seconds simply by getting up and going to fetch your patient (supposing that he or she is ambulatory, and that you are, too). During the walk back to your office, you can lock in two essential requirements for effective communication: rapport and concordance.

Much is made of 'rapport' in communication courses and NLP texts and trainings, and the usual means of accomplishing it is "mirroring" – reflecting the subject's physical postures and movements. This kind of phase-locked 'dance' can be seen anywhere two people are in close accord. Watch out in restaurants and public places for those couples who unconsciously reflect each other's moves: one picks up a drink, the other follows; one sits forward and folds his or her arms, the other follows.

We have some reservations about this single-technique approach to rapport-building. First, it takes considerable practice to lock in to another person, and the risk of detection is always present. Second, it takes time to achieve that level of mirroring, and, time, as we have agreed, is in short supply. Third, our suspicion is that "phase-locking" is often the *result*, rather than the cause, of two people gaining rapport.

The following method is easy and almost instantaneous, and has proved successful with hundreds of practitioners incorporating it into the "meet-and-greet" phase of the consultation. Four steps, performed almost simultaneously, are involved.

Achieving rapid rapport

1. Smile – a full-face, not a "social", smile. Get into the habit of smiling with your eyes as well as your mouth.
2. Look directly into the patient's eyes, mentally noting his eye colour. In contrast to the quick glance skating across the subject's face, this creates the effect of being fully "looked at" and "seen".
3. Silently project a 'message' of goodwill or well-wishing towards the patient. If you are good at mental imagery, you can create an internal representation of the patient looking healthy, happy and satisfied. The effect of this is subtly to alter your facial expression to suggest interest, involvement and positive concern.
4. If culturally and/or physically appropriate, shake hands. Frank Bernieri, chair of the psychology department at Oregon State University and an expert in non-verbal communication, believes a good handshake is "critically important" to first impressions. Strength is unimportant, he says, but "web-to-web" contact and alignment of the hands is. Handshakes should be avoided if:
    - you know or suspect cultural differences: when in doubt, don't;
    - the patient is very frail or in pain; the reasons for this are self-evident; or,
    - the patient is markedly distressed. The risk of linking a psychophysiological state to a touch (kinesthetic anchoring) is ever-present, and it is sensible to avoid the risk of associating your touch to another's distress, especially as you may have to conduct an examination later.

Other caveats include the following: do not present your hand with the back facing upwards (signalling dominance) or downwards (signalling submission); and, do not touch the patient's forearm, upper arm or shoulder with your free hand while shaking hands. This is sometimes interpreted as patronising or manipulative if occurring in the opening stage of a meeting.

Achieving concordance

The following four-part approach is derived from the field of social psychology and the work of Milton Erickson, whose expertise in gaining concordance with his patients was unparalleled. Erickson's language patterns, known in NLP as the Milton Model, were elegant, persuasive and respectful of his subject's needs. Since his medium was hypnosis, and 'hypnotisability' may be equated with a willingness to follow instructions, his methods were also designed systematically to predispose the subject towards a cooperative mindset.

Yes-sets and negative frames

Erickson knew from long experience that the more agreement he could extract from the patient, the more acquiescent the patient would become. Truisms – statements that cannot be denied – were his vehicle of preference. The process of asking questions that can only be answered affirmatively are known as yes-sets, and three seems to be the magic number.

Yes-sets are bundled as conversation or "small talk" – for example:

> "So you managed to get an appointment today?" (*Yes*)
> "Good. And, you found your way here okay?" (*Yes*)
> "It looks like it's still raining outside…" (*Yes*)

Note: Effective yes-sets should be incontrovertible. Avoid statements that can potentially be denied. "It's raining" cannot be denied (assuming there's a window nearby), whereas "It's a nice day, isn't it?" can be – especially if the patient is feeling depressed. Also, take care when using names as a yes-set ("You're Mrs Peterson, aren't you?") unless you're *absolutely* sure you have the correct details at hand.

At this point, some subjects may feel they have been too agreeable, so we depotentiate with another linguistic device called a "negative frame". This is a language pattern that prompts a negative response while still maintaining agreement. For example:

> "Well, let's go right through because we wouldn't want to keep you waiting any longer, would we?" (*No – meaning, "I agree".*)

The formula for the yes-sets and negative frames is as follows:

1. Truism + 2. Truism + 3. Truism + Negative Frame

A negative frame is, in turn, constructed as follows: begin with something that is desirable ("go right through"), add the word "because", and follow this with something that is not wanted (such as "we don't want to wait any longer"), then add the rhetorical tag: "do we?"

Desired action + "because" + undesired (negated) action + rhetorical tag

Reasoned response

The word "because" acts as a powerful releaser of decision or action – often regardless of what that decision or action might be.

Harvard social psychologist Ellen Langer once conspired with her university librarian to shut down all but one photocopying machine. As a long line formed, Langer sent in one group of confederates to go to the head of the queue and ask permission to use the machine, giving no explanation. Around 60% of students allowed the confederates to go ahead of them. A second group of confederates asked to use the machine, giving explanations such as, "I'm late for class." The percentage given permission jumped to 94.

Then Langer had a brilliant idea. She had another group go to the head of the queue and make bogus requests to use the machine, explaining, "...because I want to make some copies". Contrary to everyone's expectations, the requests went largely unchallenged. Almost nobody said, "Of course you do. We're all here to make copies, so wait your turn." The success rate dropped only one percentage point[102].

This, along with a number of subsequent studies, gives rise to the (slightly discomforting) realisation that many of us respond to linguistic patterns almost as readily as to the content or meaning of certain statements and requests ... so long as there's a reason. Any reason.

What this suggests is that our cognitive functions are often in "park" mode. We respond to the 'shape' of things rather more than what the things mean. In contrast to algorithmic thinking (the application of predetermined 'rules' to arrive at conclusions), this form of processing is "heuristic". For our purposes, heuristics may be thought of as mental 'tools' we use in order to conserve brain power, or as 'shortcuts' that aim to get more thinking done with minimum effort. Although the shortcoming of heuristic thinking is evident from the examples given above, heuristics themselves, as we will suggest later, can also be valuable tools *if consciously and contextually applied as a means to an end.*

Our hope, then, by presenting some of the evidence surrounding the issues of first impressions and decision-making, is to sensitise you to the fact that more – much more – is happening than simply inviting your patient to sit down.

The overall object of the Engagement phase of the Medical NLP Consultation Process is to increase a productive sense of 'connectedness' with the patient, and to reduce, as far as possible, the risk of avoidable mishaps and misunderstandings. The starting point of a safe, productive and mutually satisfying first contact is the congruence of the practitioner – that is, an alignment of attitude, intention, communication style and behaviour.

And, it's best to bear in mind that, while you are assessing the patient, the patient is assessing you. Diagnosis, for better or worse, is a two-way street.

EXERCISES

1. Yes-sets are key skills to master in this section. Review the four-part structure, and then create sets of your own. The challenge is to make them naturally conversational, but still based on truisms. Test these for effectiveness.
2. Read aloud any three paragraphs from the chapter above. At the end of each sentence, practise inflecting **downwards**. You may record this for learning purposes if you wish.
3. Rehearse giving lifestyle advice to a patient:
   - with an "approachable" delivery only;
   - with a "credible" delivery only;
   - with an appropriate combination of the two.
4. Practise the "rapid rapport" method with the next 20 people you meet.

Phase 2: Alignment

8

The Uninterrupted Story: beyond the 18th second

Listen to your patient, for he will give you the diagnosis.

Sir William Osler

The patient who arrives in the consultation room or hospital bed comes with more than just a collection of symptoms. He has a history, beliefs, fears, theories and frustrations. He has choices and resources, the means to help resolve his problems, even though these are as yet unrecognised and unapplied. He also functions – together with his problems – within a unique and complex set of relationships with the others in his group. In short, he has a 'story'.

This is seldom good news to the medical practitioner, pressured as he or she may be by targets, algorithms and guidelines. Patients' stories are relegated to the lowest point on the list of viable 'evidence', just below the practitioner's intuition, experience and insight.

And when the patient complains of being treated "like a number", he has inadvertently put his finger on the problem. The growing reliance on statistical analysis, specialist referrals and technology-based diagnosis, in its bid to demystify the mystery of illness and standardise treatment, can also serve to degrade and depersonalise the complexity of human experience.

Regrettably, this is the way medicine is still largely taught in both the United Kingdom and the United States. Standardised diagnostic criteria, on which both medicine and psychiatry increasingly depend, are created to assist the practitioner in reaching sound conclusions, upon which effective treatment can be based.

These linear details (what Robert Ornstein originally called "text"[103]) are seldom enough to describe or understand the experience of chronic 'functional' disorder. As French philosopher Henri Bergson observed: no matter how many hundreds of buckets of water we analyse, we will probably never understand the tides. In an undifferentiated patient population, text is not enough. People do not live, think, become sick or die according to a set of logical propositions. They are much more creative than that. Their experience, physical and emotional, is made up of complex relationships, both internal and external, that give their present condition meaning – Ornstein's "context"[102].

And the place to start with 'decoding' the intricacies and interrelationships within chronic 'functional' disorders is with the uninterrupted story. Text needs to be understood in context. (Note that we are not encouraging the patient to become 'stuck' in his story. The practitioner's intention is to understand the themes, patterns and emotional forces driving the patient's condition.)

Concerns persist that the garrulous patient will consume what little time is available to him and the other patients on the busy practitioner's list. But this is not as big a risk as it might first appear. Most doctors and medical students know of the 1984 Beckman-Frankel study reporting that the average practitioner interrupted the patient just 18 seconds after he had begun to talk[104]. Later studies show very little improvement. "If I didn't do that," doctors tell us, "I'd never finish one consultation, let alone my whole caseload for the day."

In reality, research also showed that patients given the freedom to talk beyond the point where the practitioner believed he had identified 'the problem' averaged just five minutes to tell their stories. Longer stories were later agreed to have been entirely clinically significant. Just for a moment, imagine that you are sitting watching a movie with a friend. After just 18 seconds, he whispers, "What's happening now?" Quite apart from the irritation you are likely to feel, how much of the plot-line could you be expected to know after less than half a minute?

Time, like physical energy, needs to be spent in order to create more. But it needs to be spent wisely, with purpose and design in order to have the investment yield returns. And, in all time-management systems that work, time well spent is, in the longer run, time saved. If the patient's needs are not met in this consultation, he will be back.

The purpose of stories

Stories are essentially the way in which we attempt to organise our experience and extract meaning out of a collection of apparently random events. By allowing the patient to talk, you gain insight into the forces that drive his unique narrative (the same kind of situations, characters, challenges, conflicts and tensions that you were looking forward to unfolding before you when you were so rudely interrupted by your movie-going companion).

Story helps you understand how your patient's map of the world no longer serves to help him navigate through the bewildering territory in which he finds himself. The greater our ability to detect themes, patterns and relationships within items of information that we might otherwise have disregarded as "irrelevant", the easier it becomes to help the patient update his model of 'reality' and move forward.

At this point, accept this reassurance now. We are not asking you to abandon the logical, left-brain reasoning that is the cornerstone of accurate differential diagnosis. Rather, we are offering an adjunctive approach – a way of gaining, managing and applying knowledge that supplements, and can dramatically enhance, your understanding of the patient's experience.

So the first recommendation is that you relax. Relax while reading this, and relax with the patient in front of you. Remind yourself of the advice given to anxious students by Sir William Osler more than 100 years ago, "Listen to your patient, for he will give you the diagnosis." Just for the moment, put aside the need to 'know' what is happening. Your formal training and experience will automatically deal with text. You are listening for context, for meaning and effect, and, it is the patient, not the practitioner, who is the expert on this.

"Listening", in this model, is much more than the non-directive "active listening" of the Rogerian client-centred approach, or the sympathetic head-tilt of the psychodynamic counsellor ("… and, how does that make you feel?"). You are accumulating raw data from a number of sources, verbal and non-verbal, in order to form hypotheses that will later be tested. You are deliberately activating all your sensory receptors, with as little internal judgement and commentary as possible. Out of this, structure, process and meaning emerge.

Gathering quality information

Auditory

We naturally extract meaning out of the words used. But the Medical NLP practitioner is also paying attention to:

1. the language used (direct communication);
2. comments and observation about the communication used (metalinguistic);
3. the pauses and tics and verbal mannerisms that punctuate the language used (paralinguistic); and,
4. metaphoric, symbolic and analogical communication (the speaker's way of representing experience in terms of codes and symbols).

Noting the class or quality of communication permits the practitioner later to enter the patient's model of his world at the same level at which he organises his experience, as well as to match language patterns during the Reorientation phase. Examples of the linguistic cues available in any communication might be:

- **Direct** communication: "I feel tired."
- **Metalinguistic**: "I'm such a complainer. I can't stop moaning about being tired."
- **Paralinguistic**: "I'm … uh … (*sighs deeply*) … you know - I'm, like – bleugh!"
- **Metaphoric**, symbolic and analogous communication: "I've completely run out of steam. It feels like I'm wading through treacle." Listen especially for submodality distinctions, such as "It's like I'm carrying the world on my shoulders"; "If only I could get a bit of distance from my problems"; "It's always in my face".

At this stage of the consultation process, you are simply making mental notes (or physical ones, if you can do so without interrupting the patient's flow). At the same time, you are also *watching* for non-verbal forms of communication, including 'body language', such as changes in posture, distinctive gestures, repetitive movements and 'spatial marking', as well as minimal cues (such as pupil dilation, flushing, paling and other colour changes, engorging of the lower lip, etc).

Visual

Along with spiders, frogs and meerkats, we're designed to focus on what's important to us. Or, in our case at least, on what we *think* is important to us.

Evolutionary psychologists suggest that our ability to focus closely on series of events and extract patterns from what we observe was vital to our survival as a species. If we did not immediately fix on what caused that rustling in the undergrowth, we were very likely abruptly to be selected out.

Culturally, too, the use of foveal vision, associated as it is with 'logical' reasoning, is highly valued. In the few years from birth to being deposited in a playgroup or preschool, we're encouraged to focus on and label whatever our caregivers and teachers believe is significant to us: shapes, colours, sounds, animals, people, events.

The ability to notice sequential information, create meaning from it, store it and access it whenever required is how 'intelligence' is popularly perceived. Foveal vision has evolved to receive fine detail and patterns (Table 8.1). The processing of the information we take in through deliberate focus is entirely conscious, sequential and cortical. Compared with the responses of the defensive limbic system, it is slow. Focus seeks to relate what we are seeing with something we believe we already know – a "pattern-matching" mechanism.

Peripheral vision, activated when we get that 'far-away' look in our eyes is, on the other hand, usually associated with 'losing focus' or 'zoning out'. When the activity shifts away from the densely packed cones in the centre of our retina, and towards a more primal 'instinctual' part of our brains, the quality of both vision and consciousness changes. Despite the sheer size and number of the peripheral rods (125 million compared

Table 8.1 Foveal and peripheral vision

Foveal vision	*Peripheral vision*
Details	Broad shapes
Derived patterns	Relationships
Colours	Light/dark
Sequential data (scanning by saccades)	Movement and change
Similarities	Differences
Associated neurological processing	
Slow	Fast

with only 6 million cones), peripheral vision is either considered inferior to 'close focus', or is virtually ignored. Peripheral vision can detect large objects and differences between light and dark, but is regarded as 'deficient' for its lack of colour perception and detail.

But it wasn't always so. In the 15th Century, legendary Japanese swordsman Miyamoto Musashi wrote in his arcane 'training manual', *The Book of Five Rings*, about a kind of perception that permitted the warrior to perceive the movement of an opponent "before movement itself arises"[105]. He called this style of 'seeing' *kan*. In contrast, *ken* was the more familiar form of close focusing – the style presumably adopted by his opponents since Musashi died, revered and undefeated after many scores of battles.

Try this as an experiment:

> Find a point on the opposite wall and rest your gaze easily on it. Now, relax and become progressively more conscious of how much you begin to become aware of on either side, up and down. You will not be able to make out much detail, but you will become aware of a flatter, wider field, in which all the details have more or less equal value. Notice, too, how everything in your environment seems to 'fit together' as a whole.
>
> Now, slowly extend your arms to either side and move them slowly backwards until they're barely in your field of vision. Wiggle the fingers on one hand, very slightly, then the fingers on the other. Make the movements as small as you can.

Without any effort at all, you will find that your peripheral vision picks up the tiniest activity – for a very good and, as it turns out, useful reason. Peripheral vision picks up movement and change. Its 'attention' is caught by whatever is different and new, and it functions unconsciously. It is peripheral, not foveal, vision that picks up the flight path of the insect headed for your eyeball and snaps your eyelid shut. It has other important qualities, too.

It would seem from the above that both ways of seeing contributed to our survival. Moving cautiously through the savannah, sequential scanning with its 'dead zone' between saccades would have made us vulnerable to a predator we had not yet located. Equally, since peripheral vision is more useful when light conditions are low (we can detect a match flame 20 km away in the dark with our peripheral, but not our foveal, vision), it would have supplemented our defences during nocturnal hunts. However, as civilisation advanced, rational, sequential, linear reasoning became increasingly more valued, whereas our talents for a more 'instinctual', simultaneous, other-than-conscious way of 'knowing' were shunted out of awareness.

Now, here's a problem. Our instinct for creating patterns out of a collection of discrete packets of information overrides almost everything, *including the fact that sometimes there's no pattern to be made.* If we cannot immediately find a pattern, we experience an internal dissonance – a vague, but disturbing, feeling of disquiet.

There's more. Where we *believe* we have identified a pattern, or *want* to see a pattern, we will often edit out additional information to fit the model we have created. If the pattern has been handed to us by a higher authority - current treatment guidelines, or an 'expert' interpretation of symptoms, such as the Diagnostic and Statistical Manual (DSM), for example - the effect is even stronger, and we will often ignore information that could throw us back into uncertainty and internal dissonance.

The phenomenon is called "representative heuristics", and it occurs more frequently in medicine than we might expect. A simple example would be a smoker who develops a medical problem that is seen to be a product of his smoking, even though his condition may, in fact, be unrelated[106].

The danger of this kind of misdiagnosis was dramatically illustrated in the early 1970s, when David Rosenhan set out to test psychiatrists' ability accurately to distinguish between the 'sane' and the 'insane'. He and several associates gave up shaving and bathing for several days, then turned up at various psychiatric hospitals reporting only that they heard a voice inside their heads saying "Thud!"

All the confederates were diagnosed with paranoid schizophrenia and other serious psychiatric disorders, and were duly institutionalised and medicated. After a while, Rosenhan reports, he tried to leave, but the authorities dismissed his story as a symptom of his 'illness'. Finally, after considerable effort, he and his colleagues were released, and the experiment was revealed.

Fury erupted throughout the psychiatric community. One senior psychiatrist at a leading institution publicly challenged Rosenhan to try to deceive his staff at some time over the next few months, promising that all pseudopatients would easily be detected. Rosenhan accepted the challenge, but craftily sent no confederates to the institution – and the psychiatric chief confidently announced that his staff had identified no fewer than 41 phoney patients[107].

Understanding how representative heuristics, pattern-making and vision can work either for or against decision-making is necessary to help cut through the Gordian knot of chronic 'functional' problems. Using wide vision is another tool that may be used adjunctively with your more everyday close focusing to expand your sensory acuity and help you detect minute physical changes. Once mastered, it is effortless and automatic to apply.

Together with the auditory data mentioned above, this comprises what Medical NLP knows as "syntactic perception" – the ability to detect the hidden 'rules' (the syntax) of communication, as well as its textual content. This can open up information of a depth and quality that can have a profound impact on how you regard illness, healing and health. The method is as follows. To build your confidence we suggest you practise while talking with friends and family before introducing it into formal consultations.

Wide vision

Take a few deep breaths through your nose to help you relax.

Ensure you're sitting a little back from your partner (but not so far back that you seem distant and disengaged). As you look at his face, allow your gaze to relax and widen. Become consciously aware of the walls on either side, the ceiling and floor, without shifting your gaze to look directly at them.

Notice that you can see your subject from head to foot. Even as you talk, changes in his or her posture, facial expressions, gestures – no matter how slight – will seem to 'pop' into your awareness. Remember, we are observing in a neutral, non-judgemental way. If something appears significant (for example, you may notice that your partner 'marks' the 'location' of a problem in the same place in the space around him every time he talks about it), simply make a mental note for possible later use. We'll discuss the application of new data you acquire in later chapters.

Should you find yourself talking to yourself about what is happening, or what you should be doing (auditory digital), you have moved out of wide vision. Gently widen your gaze again.

Two changes take place automatically in your state when you enter wide vision: you physically and mentally relax, and your internal dialogue, the chatter of the 'meaning-making' part of our mind that equates 'thinking' with internal commentary and evaluation, begins to quieten down.

You will find that you shift in and out of wide vision. This is perfectly natural, especially when you are new to the technique. Using your peripheral vision feels unnatural in the beginning, but you can easily acquire proficiency by practising regularly in different locations: social occasions, meetings, walking down the street, watching television, etc. Using wide vision in group settings is particularly interesting as you become increasingly aware of the interactive 'dance' that takes place. You will often notice subtle elements you have filtered out before – such as the way one person's body stiffens every time another talks.

Note: When using wide vision with a partner or patient, start first by looking into only one of their eyes, then soften your gaze. This avoids a 'spacey', slightly disconcerting look.

We seldom look at other people with the deliberate intention of gaining unedited information. Yet vast amounts of data are available to enrich information-gathering, and often to apply later to a positive end. Also, since light travels at 186,000 miles a second, your brain registers visual information far more rapidly than your cognitive circuits can process. An almost imperceptible headshake as the patient assures you he has been taking his medication regularly, for example, may provide clues that would otherwise go unnoticed.

But remember this: we avoid 'mind-reading' other people on the basis of the changes we notice. They may not mean what you assume they do. The rule is (as it is throughout any Medical NLP-based consultation): calibrate to the individual's idiosyncratic mannerisms and responses, and test each hypothesis thoroughly. We do not presume to know the 'truth' about all people in all situations. We can entertain the probability or even just the *possibility* of understanding what's going on – but be suspicious of certainty.

And, by learning to include the 'syntax', the hidden rules and structure, of communication, we can dramatically increase the probability of helping others by recognising, respecting and responding appropriately to the uniqueness of each.

Emerging patterns

Patterns that are allowed to emerge provide more reliable evidence than those imposed from without. Paying attention to the network of family and social relationships will often reveal important information – including 'causes' of problems, triggers and the purpose they serve. This may allow the astute practitioner to work holistically and systemically, rather than to limit himself and his patient to the symptoms at hand.

Extensive family histories, including relationships, are seldom included in patient notes, and even less frequently are they looked at as relevant to a presenting 'functional' disorder. And yet clues to many – if not most – psychosocial dysfunctions may be teased out of the relational web.

Questions such as, "How is this a problem for you and for those around you?"; "Who else in your family has had to deal with something like this?"; "What do you think this means to others in your life?"; "Who will benefit most when you recover?"; and, "Who will be adversely affected by your recovery?" may seem unusual, but could provide important insight into the dynamics of the presenting problem within the context of the patient's life. (Visit the reader support site, www.magicinpractice.com, for further suggestions in exploring family histories.)

EXERCISES

1. Begin by practising wide vision. Try walking for several blocks using your peripheral vision, and then ask yourself a series of questions, such as: "How many men have I passed?"; "How many women?"; "How many blue (or red) cars?" etc. Keep a record of your results to track your improvement.
2. As you listen to patients, friends or members of your family, mentally note what parts of their stories are text (factual linear details of the speaker's experience) and what parts are context (the landscape in which these events occur).

9

The Clinical Questioning Matrix: eliciting quality data

Acquiring quality information in any interview or consultation depends largely on the quality of the questions we ask. As we observed in the previous chapter, the process of 'paying attention' simultaneously involves acquiring and excluding data. Quite simply, we tend to look for, and find, mainly the information we expect.

To facilitate an exchange of quality (that is, useful) information, we strongly recommend that the practitioner hold three organising principles in mind.

1. Reduce the patient's anxiety. This is a priority. All patients in distress suffer allostatic load to some degree or other; unless some neurological coherence is restored, they are unlikely to be able to organise their thoughts, communicate the real issues that concern them, and even accurately hear and remember what you say. Therefore:
   - Pace the patient, by matching either his rate of speech or his breathing (supposing he does not suffer from a breathing disorder); then gradually slow down.
   - Acknowledge the patient's discomfort, but avoid telling him to "calm down". Lead by example. As Richard Bandler says, if you want people to enter a particular state, *go there first*.

- Pacing also involves matching the patient's representation of a problem. The following extract is from a video recording of a doctor's consultation with an elderly patient. Note the mismatches in the doctor's responses.

Patient: *I've had this … uncomfortable … this feeling for some time now (gestures towards abdomen).*
Doctor: *What kind of pain is it? Sharp or dull?*
Patient: *No, not exactly … not a pain. More a kind of sensation…*
Doctor: *When did it start to hurt?*
Patient: *Well, not really hurting. Sort of … About three and a half years ago. (The patient had earlier mentioned being suddenly widowed three and a half years before, a fact not picked up on by the doctor.)*
Doctor: *Do you have pain all the time?*
Patient: *It's more – pressure, I'd say. It's like I'm … holding too much inside. (looks down and right, left, and back again, indication of an internal kinesthetic accompanied by self-talk, or auditory digital)*
Doctor: *Pain can be caused by a number of things. What I'm going to do is to send you for some tests. (The doctor's attention shifts to organising referral of the patient.) We'll see what's causing it then …*

2. Listen and watch for structure and process.
    - People organise their behaviours and responses into sequences called strategies (see Chapter 5). These sequences have to be repeated in order to result in the same outcome. Strategies may have to be elicited since they function out of conscious awareness. Note especially any two-point loops (that is, any strategy that does not end when it has served its purpose). This is how the patient becomes 'stuck'.
    - Notice repeating patterns of behaviour, gestures or phrases. Patients will often 'mark out' their problem with a particular gesture. This is useful information; rather than recapping the problem, the practitioner can often simply mirror the gesture (in the patient's subjective space, not his own) to recall the entire process. Adopt a curious attitude. Patients will often leave 'clues' as to the real problem for the practitioner to pick up.

3. Explore the context in which the patient and his problem function. Maintaining or resolving a problem may adversely affect the system in which the patient exists, and this needs to be resolved if treatment is to continue successfully. For example:

Case history: *The patient, said to be "mildly learning disabled", had suffered a serious fall and was unable to walk without constant support. The practitioner noted that her father, who had become her primary caregiver, supervised her every move, including ensuring she was seated "safely" on the chair before leaving the room.*

The approach, which involved building the girl's confidence and using some of the techniques outlined elsewhere in this book, was hugely successful. She was able to jump in and out of her chair, and stand on one leg, and was clearly excited at her renewed abilities.

Since the father had given up his job to look after his daughter, the practitioner was still concerned about how such a change might affect the father's function and self-image as primary caretaker. He said to the girl, "Your Dad has been looking after you and keeping you safe for a long time because he loves you so much. Now that you're doing so well, how are we going to make sure he doesn't feel you don't need him any more?"

The girl recognised the potential problem immediately, and, after some discussion, decided she would make an effort to involve him fully in all her decisions, including her plans to return to college.

When her father returned to pick her up, the girl excitedly jumped out of her chair, stood on one leg and waved her arms around. Apparently without noticing the change, the father said, "Don't do that, you'll hurt yourself," and gently pushed her back in the chair. The daughter shot a conspiratorial smile in the direction of the practitioner, and said gently, "You're right. We'll need to practise together."

The importance of attention

Too often today, the practitioner's attention is divided between the patient and the computer screen. Far from streamlining the consultation process, electronic note-taking has opened a new level of risk in health care. Aside from the unspoken message communicated to the patient ("I'm busy; get on with it. Just give me the facts"), new research indicates that multi-tasking reduces, rather than improves, the quality of information gathered, instructions imparted and conclusions reached.

Contrary to popular belief, the human brain is designed to deal with only one conscious task at a time. In some cases, it is possible to learn to speed up processing, but we remain vulnerable to what psychologists call "attentional blink" (a momentary drop-out in the ability to take action) and "response selection bottleneck" (quite literally, a competition between conflicting actions that leads to delay and even temporary cognitive paralysis). These phenomena can occur so fleetingly that we are not consciously aware of them, but important data can be obscured. We are simply not as good at multi-tasking as we like to think[108].

To minimise this risk, we suggest separating out computer-based tasks from interaction with the patient. In order to avoid loss of rapport, ensure you give the patient "orientating statements", such as: "I'm afraid I need to get this information down. But, as soon as I have, we can settle down and have a chat about things … ."

Hemispheric lateralisation

In many ways, 'whole-person' consultation is also a 'whole-brain' activity. We need to allow input of data we are inclined (for reasons discussed in Chapter 8) to disregard, and – rather more challenging – we also need to understand and outwit what cognitive neuroscientist Michael Gazzaniga has dubbed "the spin doctor" in our heads[109].

Almost everyone who witnessed the business boom of the 1980s got to hear about "right brain" thinking. Split-brain experiments had long suggested that the two hemispheres of the brain were specialised: left brain logical, right brain creative. It was a seductive idea, but not a particularly accurate one. We know now that we use both sides of our brains for much of the time. Few, if any, functions are located in only one hemisphere. However, we also know that each side is uniquely specialised to carry out certain tasks. With the caveat in mind that what follows is generalised, four important distinctions are outlined below:

1. **The brain and body are cross-lateralised.** The left hemisphere controls the right side of the body, and the right hemisphere controls the left side of the body. Medical NLP regards this as important for a number of reasons. These include the role of homolateralisation (one-sided dominance) in certain so-called 'learning disabilities', such as dyslexia, childhood behavioural problems, depression, strokes and even immune function[110]. Incorporating re-lateralisation exercises and activities has shown encouraging results with our patients and those of other Medical NLP practitioners who are developing approaches along these lines (See Appendix B).
2. **The hemispheres process differently.** The left hemisphere processes data sequentially. Sounds, symbols and sequential behaviour are all predominantly under the control of the left hemisphere. This is what we mean when we speak of text. The right hemisphere processes data simultaneously. It sees and extracts meaning out of many different elements. It notices relationships. This is what we mean by context. As Daniel Pink comments in his book, *A Whole New Mind*, "the right hemisphere is the picture; the left hemisphere is the thousand words"[111].
3. **The hemispheres 'make sense' of experience differently.** The right hemisphere wordlessly 'experiences'. The left hemisphere evaluates, explains, justifies and defends. Gazzaniga also calls the left hemisphere "the interpreter", and writes amusingly in *The Mind's Past* about its tendency to work overtime to 'spin' explanations out of experiences – sometimes with bizarre results. (This is characteristic of what in hypnosis is called "trance logic"; the subject's 'explanation' for carrying out a post-hypnotic command may make perfect sense to him, but is a patent concoction to bystanders who have not been hypnotised.) Note, too, that as we move down Korzybski's Structural Differential (see Chapter 8), we call increasingly on left-brain processing, to the exclusion of the right's.
4. **The hemispheres separate and combine information.** When working together optimally, the hemispheres synthesise data to provide holistic 'meaning'. While the left hemisphere registers the

individual features of an approaching friend, the right 'recognises' his face. One hemisphere hears notes, the other combines them into melody; one side can read words, the other recognises the emotional tone of the words etc.

It follows from the above that the quality of the meaning we extract from our neuronal processes should increase when both hemispheres are engaged, each contributing its own particular skills. Physical damage can adversely affect this – as, regrettably, can eduction.

For various reasons, Western teaching – especially in the sciences – favours the logical, linear, sequential mode of left-brain processing, and mistrusts the rather more exuberant, untrammelled, creative activities of the right. The kind of syllogistic reasoning we mentioned earlier is exclusively the province of the left hemisphere. Its objective (that is, measurable, reproducible) 'evidence' is valued over the subjective, emotional 'experience' of the right. We are encouraged to believe that only by refining data enough can we eventually arrive at 'truth'.

The differential diagnosis

The differential diagnosis – essentially an evaluative exercise that aims to arrive at a diagnosis by a process of elimination – is a cornerstone of Western medicine and a primarily left-brain activity. Valuable as it proves in many areas, it does not always rise to the challenge of certain complex, chronic conditions. Information derived from this kind of thinking alone may be valued, but is not necessarily always accurate. Research has shown that overdependence can lead to a "high control style" on the part of the practitioner, increased patient dissatisfaction, an overly narrow approach to hypothesis-generation, a premature focus on medical explanations, and inaccuracies in diagnosis[112].

Where deductive reasoning does not provide us with the results we are looking for, we need to engage another of our highly developed, but largely overlooked, human capabilities, one which does not reside in the left side of our skulls. We need to cross the *corpus callosum* that bridges left and right, and listen to the melody of the patient's experience, rather than just studying the notes.

The 'open' practitioner

Adopt what Zen writers call "beginner's mind". Raw data unfiltered by preconception are valuable data. The practitioner should become comfortable with periods of 'not knowing' what the problem is or how to approach it. As the consultation progresses, information will accumulate, patterns and distinctions emerge, and responses begin to suggest themselves.

It is important to manage one's own sense of pressure when listening to the patient's response to open questions. The patient may need time to find his way through the tangle of his own feelings and symptoms. And while time may be at a premium, quality information will lead to more effective approaches and conclusive results.

The 'open' practitioner not only engages the patient, but also gently encourages further disclosures, with questions such as, "What else is it like?"; "How would you describe …?"; "Exactly how does this happen?"; and, if the patient seems stuck for words, "Just so I understand – if I were having this problem that you've been having, what would I be thinking, feeling, doing … how would I be talking to myself?" etc. In order to elicit a strategy, you may find it useful to ask, "What happens just before that … and before that …?" until you can identify the first step in the sequence (See Chapter 5).

Open and closed questions

Most medical and communication training programmes refer to the differences between "open" (contextual) and "closed" (textual) questions. Open questions usually elicit stories, anecdotes and subjective analogical responses. Closed questions tend to lead to yes/no, digital replies.

The method usually taught is to begin with open questions, and move gradually down to closed questions. Known as "coning" or "funnelling", this approach, moving from the general to the specific, is widely believed to provide all the data needed to translate the patient's story into the data needed to make an accurate diagnosis.

However, busy practitioners often revert to predominantly closed questions, unaware of the different functions and rich potential of each when skilfully applied. And, when patients are confronted with closed questions, communication and the relationship can suffer[113]. Furthermore, information relevant to making an accurate diagnosis may not surface if the patient is prevented by excessive closed questioning from responding more fully[114].

Our broad distinction between the two different classes of question is simply this: open questions seek information (including meaning, beliefs, emerging patterns and systemic impact), whereas closed questions are intended to gain agreement or confirmation. To put it another way, open and closed questions engage the right- and left-brain functions respectively of both patient and practitioner, resulting in a richer and more productive sharing of information. Applying one or the other exclusively, or confusing the purpose of each, will result in data that are difficult to manage, risking overwhelming the practitioner and causing frustration for the patient.

The structure and value of open and closed questions

Open questions

While open and closed questions may be interspersed, we prefer to begin with open questions. These invite information rather than demand it. The history is *received* rather than taken. Although the practitioner is the expert on the mechanisms of illness, the patient is respected and acknowledged as the expert in how *his* condition manifests itself in his body and life. Open questions encourage the patient to adopt an active, rather than submissive, role, and invite him into a mutual, adult relationship.

Open questions usually begin with words such as: Who? What? Where? When? How? and, sometimes, Why? We tend to be cautious of "why" questions for two reasons: they elicit speculation, and can seem authoritarian ("Why haven't you been taking your medication?"). The information gathered from open questions often involves 'story' and metaphorical and analogical language ("It's like a hot knife in my back"). The answers to open questions often provide an enriching insight into the context within which the patient and his problem function.

Closed questions

Closed questions help sharpen focus on specific details, as well as elicit agreement or confirmation (the yes-set in Chapter 7 being an example of the effective use of closed questions). If overemployed, however , they can dramatically reduce rapport and patient satisfaction. This class of question usually begins with phrases such as, "Is it…?"; "Has it…?"; "Can you…?"; Have you…?"; "Are you ...?"; etc. The "any" question is also closed ("Any pain?"; "Any problem sleeping?"). Closed questions tend to elicit digital (yes/no) responses.

The practitioner should not only aim to become proficient at discriminating between open and closed questions, but also at converting one form to the other 'on the fly' (see the exercises at the end of this chapter).

Starting to question

The first question sets the tone for the remainder of the consultation. "What's the problem?" is common, but may be regarded as too abrupt. "How can I help you?" is better, but may place the practitioner 'one-up' on the patient. Our questions of preference are "What brings you here today?" and "What would you like to talk about today?"

To help the patient express himself more fully, especially where the problem that concerns him has not yet been voiced, we suggest you respond to his initial statement with gentle probing. "Is there anything else you'd like to talk about?" and "If we can sort this out today, will that help with everything that's been worrying you?" are typical questions that both accept the possibility that the patient has several concerns, and ensure that the practitioner will not be blind-sided by a succession of new concerns just as he is about to close the consultation.

Establishing boundary conditions

The problem, however pervasive it seems, is limited, either physically (being localised in the body) or in time. It has an 'edge' or a boundary to it. It also had a beginning, a middle (now) and, we trust, an end. We will address the issue of physically perceived location of the symptom in later chapters, but where and when the problem began needs to be established early, as do any events or situations surrounding it (the context).

Consider questions such as, "What was happening in your life around the time, or just before, this began?"; "How is this problem for you now?"; "Who else is affected by this and how?"; and, "What will happen when the problem you've been having is resolved?" Any of these will help establish where the problem begins and ends.

The patient's opinion

Inviting the patient's opinion about his problem requires delicacy and discretion so as not to surrender your role as a trained professional. However, patients often have insights of which they are unaware until asked. We suggest a gentle inquiry along the lines of: "We sometimes find that patients have ideas about their own situation. In case I've missed something important, do you have any inkling or hunch about what's been happening?"

The importance of emotional cues

Do not allow signs of heightened emotion to go unacknowledged. These might include agitation, reddening eyes, a downcast or darting gaze, changes in breathing rate or skin colouration, or a breaking voice. Equally, do not presume to 'know' what these minimal cues mean. Physical distress alone accounts for only a quarter of the reasons patients seek help from health professionals, even when the presenting complaint is somatic[115]. Use a gentle remark such as, "I notice you seem to have some emotion right now. Would you like to talk about it?" Accept the patient's decision, whether or not he decides to open up.

If the patient loses direction

If it is clear that the patient is departing radically from his concerns (and this happens less frequently than many practitioners fear), you can gently bring him back on track with a remark such as, "I think that's probably important and we'll remember that so we can come back to it. But can I just clarify …" (and return to the main thread of the consultation).

If the patient has a 'shopping list'

Patients sometimes bring a number of concerns to the same consultation. We disapprove of the notices appearing on the doors of some centres saying something like: "Appointments: 10 minutes each. Only one problem per appointment."

Two options exist: the first (which we will expand on in Chapter 18) is to look for a shared theme – for example, excessive stress. The other is simply to say to the patient, "There are a number of things here. I'd like us to deal with the one that's most important to you. Which would you like that to be?"

A key question for follow-up visit(s)

In follow-up visits, "What have you noticed that's different or better?" will orientate the patient towards solution and resolution. Failure to do that will direct the patient to access what has not yet improved, or what is 'not there' (for example, absence of pain).

Our intention is to guide the patient towards noticing change, however small, and building on that. Around 60% of patients presented with a solution-oriented question that presupposes change have been shown to report a positive result, whereas, if the question inquires about their problem state, 67% report little or no change[116]. Sometimes, patients will respond, *"Oh, I've been up and down …"* Inquire first about the "downs", then elicit the "ups" in full, sensory detail … and anchor their response (see page 129).

The Clinical Questioning Matrix in Table 9.1 outlines the different functions of each method of questioning.

Table 9.1 The Medical NLP Clinical Questioning Matrix

Open questions	***Closed questions***
Lead to:	*Lead to:*
Analogue information	Digital responses (yes/no)
Process	Content
Internal locus of control (proactive)	External locus of control (reactive)
Consideration	Decision/agreement
Subjective meaning	Objective response
'Being listened to'	'Revolving door syndrome'
Association	Dissociation
Metaphorical and symbolic representation	Literality
Emotional content	Physical content
Deep Structure	**Surface Structure**
(What is really meant)	(What is actually said)
Open questions	***Closed questions***
are preceded by …	
Who?	Does it…?
What?	Is it…?
Where?	Can you…?
When?	Have you…?
Why? (Use with caution)	Are you…?
	Any … (for example, 'Any problems with your bowels?'
Prompting questions (aimed at extracting further information)	
Such as …?	
What else…?	
What's it like …?	
Do you have any idea (who/what/where/when/why) …?	
And…?	

EXERCISES

1. Identify whether the following questions are open or closed:

Question	***Open***	***Closed***
1. *Is it a sharp/dull/aching, etc. pain?*		
2. *Can you move your arm easily?*		
3. *What have you tried so far?*		

	Open	Closed
4. *How would you describe your relationships at work?*		
5. *Are you feeling stressed?*		
6. *What else can you tell me about it?*		
7. *What is the (symptom) like?*		
8. *Where do you feel it?*		
9. *Any problems at home?*		
10. *What do you mean by (patient's description)?*		

2. *Convert the following open or closed questions into their opposite form:*
   1. *Do you understand these instructions?*
   2. *Have you had this a long time?*
   3. *What brings you here today?*
   4. *How well do you sleep?*
   5. *Is the pain worse when you move?*
   6. *Is the depression very bad?*
   7. *How is your appetite?*
   8. *Which side is the pain on?*
   9. *Any worries about your family?*
   10. *Do the anxiety attacks come often?*

3. Question three patients (or willing friends) about a problem or concern, and annotate their strategy as described in Chapter 5. Pay particular attention to any two-point loops in their strategies.
   Strategy 1:
   Annotation:
   Two-point loop? Y/N
   Strategy 2:
   Annotation:
   Two-point loop? Y/N
   Strategy 3:
   Annotation:
   Two-point loop? Y/N

Phase 3: Reorientation

10

Accessing Patient Resources: the potential for change

One of the presuppositions of NLP, and a guiding principle of the work of Milton Erickson, is that all patients have the resources needed to produce change. To some, this may seem overly optimistic, especially where both patient and practitioner feel baffled and helpless when confronted with a particularly complex and chronic condition. To those patients and physicians who genuinely feel they have 'tried everything', the statement may even seem platitudinous or blaming. In Medical NLP, we modify the statement slightly. We suggest that both patient and practitioner have resources that have not yet been investigated or applied, and *of which they may not yet be aware.*

Problem-based medicine tends to regard illness as the result of a deficit. A patient regarded as deficient in some way or other requires 'fixing'. The role of practitioner and patient then becomes one of the active and informed acting on the passive and uninformed.

The patient's resources

Among the resources that patients bring into treatment, may be included:

- the desire to achieve a healed state (or else he would not have sought help);

- the evolutionary drive of all living entities to strive for allostasis at every point in their lives until the moment of death;
- successful changes and healings they have accomplished in the past; and,
- the ability, under guidance, to envisage an existence in which allostasis is restored.

Several factors may, however, initially stand in the way of identifying resources.

It may be (and often is) that the patient has not yet fully engaged with one or all of the resources mentioned above. "Secondary gain" (psychology's assertion that people sometimes stay sick to achieve some hidden benefit) may often be used to explain a patient's "resistance" to treatment, thereby aborting further investigation. Many patients (and, we would say, many practitioners) have not even considered the presenting condition as a symptom of the body-mind system's attempt (albeit unsuccessfully) to regulate itself. Also, the patient's problem-state of mind may preclude recollecting 'successful' or 'happy' times in the past, or to imagine improvements in the future, simply because, at this stage, it seems too risky.

Some "patient-centred" approaches suggest that only a "non-directive" approach is ethically acceptable, and that interventions that take place outside the patient's conscious knowledge are unacceptable. We disagree. We have no problem in regarding the patient's request for help as a mandate to proceed *in his interests*. The fact that he might be better served when some parts of the intervention take place covertly is, in our opinion, unavoidable. The *outcome* (and this part of the treatment *must* be negotiated with the patient's full consent) informs everything else we do.

Identifying, accessing and stabilising resources

Resourcing, then, is accomplished by three processes: "behavioural shaping" (or "response shaping"); "informative feedback"; and the NLP core skill of anchoring.

Successful resourcing requires a creative balance between an overt uncovering of patient strengths and more oblique methods bringing together as yet unacknowledged positive experiences, abilities and behaviours. It is important to pace the patient's experience appropriately. Focusing too soon or too directly on what is *not* wrong will damage rapport and engagement and be perceived simply as a things-are-not-as-bad-as-you-think attitude.

Since effective anchoring is a technique critical to all successful NLP interventions, and one that is particularly important to resourcing, we recommend that some time is spent in mastering it.

The power of anchoring

Anchors are often explained in terms of classical conditioning as a stimulus that elicits a particular response. Russian psychologist Ivan Pavlov's experiments at the turn of the last century demonstrated how the sound of a bell, rung when a group of dogs were given food, could eventually trigger salivation, even when food was not present.

The experiment, together with a series conducted later by B. F. Skinner, much of it with pigeons, excited some psychologists. They envisaged being able to correct human behavioural 'errors' with little effort, and even less concern for how the "black box" of the human brain functioned. It was a belief that led to many spurious and inhumane 'treatments' and child-rearing models.

The fact that we are deeply patterned – and patternable – organisms is undeniable. We respond automatically to many stimuli (think of hearing a song that automatically recalls emotions belonging to the distant past). But we are also much more than that. Unlike a dog or a pigeon, we have the capacity to reflect on our behaviour, act (when we know how) on our patterning, and even use it for our own self-regulation and personal evolution.

Anchors, then, are a means to an end. As stimuli that predictably evoke specific psychophysiological states, they may be incorporated as tools to facilitate the integration and effective functioning of a wide range of other psychophysiological capabilities.

An anchor may be set up accidentally or deliberately. It may result from several repetitions or a single, traumatising incident (as with some phobias). Heightened emotion, such fear or grief, makes us more susceptible. Anchors can occur singly or in sequences. Triggers may occur in any of the senses: sight, sound, touch, smell or taste. The more senses involved in creating both stimulus and response, the more intense the 'internal' experience is likely to be.

Anchors, not pathology

Until we are aware of how they are established and how they function, most anchors are set up and triggered outside our conscious awareness. Many responses, otherwise thought of as pathological, may, in fact, be seen as caused by negative anchoring. Take, for example, the following:

> ***Case history:*** *The patient complained of developing a "social phobia" when meeting new people. The practitioner noted that the condition had surfaced some weeks after the sudden and tragic death of the patient's mother, and had progressively worsened since then. Interestingly, he described the symptoms of his "phobia", not as "anxiety", as might be expected, but as "sadness" and "despair".*
>
> *During the consultation, the practitioner anchored the "sad" feeling and asked him to "follow the feeling back" to when he had first experienced it. The patient recalled with considerable emotion the funeral of his mother at which he was battling to contain his grief, while meeting and shaking hands with scores of mourners.*
>
> *When the patient had recovered his composure, the practitioner asked permission to "test something". He reach out, shook hands with the patient, and the patient instantly collapsed back into the sad and despairing state he had felt at the funeral. Immediately, he recognised that his "phobic" response was not caused by meeting new people, but was triggered by the physical act of shaking hands: an anchor that had been set up at a time of heightened emotion.*

Anchors, as we will demonstrate later, not only explain aspects of many chronic conditions, but can be effectively 'installed' to therapeutic effect. Anchors may be intrapersonal (self-anchoring) as well as interpersonal (operating between people). The triggers may be real and external (a handshake, the sound of fingernails raking down a blackboard), or entirely imaginal – that is, the response may be triggered simply by thinking of a particular event. Anxiety disorders often involve a physical response to the memory, or future imagining, of a sensitising event that is long past.

Setting anchors

The most commonly applied therapeutic anchor is kinesthetic. But although it is significantly easier to link a physical touch with an emotional or physical response, it may not always be appropriate to touch a patient. However, when touch is permissible, such as in taking a pulse or palpation, we suggest that you *tense* the muscles of your hand and fingers as you touch the patient, *then relax them*. This subliminally cues the patient himself to relax (see behavioural shaping below), as well as anchoring relaxation to your touch.

Auditory anchors might include a specific word or phrase, a sound or a tone. We advise practitioners to set up a specific phrase (such as the Ericksonian favourite, "That's right…") as early as possible in the consultation each time he notices a positive response from the patient.

Visual anchors could be set by nodding, smiling or making a specific gesture.

Olfactory and gustatory anchors are less likely to be deliberately used in consultation. However, we need to be aware that the smells associated with hospitals and clinics may set up negative anchors in some patients. We have found that we can help some patients minimise nausea while undergoing chemotherapy by addressing the issue of smell and sensation as anchoring.

Conditions of anchoring

In order for anchors to be effective, the following conditions must be met. Anchors link a specific trigger to a specific response. Therefore:

1. Remember, or create, a desired state. Heighten the state by making the sensory detail as rich as possible. Make it big, bright and appealing. If anchoring overtly, agree on a name to avoid confusing it with any other states.

2. The anchor needs to be precisely timed, set just as the state begins to 'peak'. Make sure that it is released a moment before the state begins to subside. The intention is to stabilise the most intense stage of the experience, not to capture its dissipation.
3. The trigger must be unique. An anchor that can be accidentally 'fired', by a casual touch or ambient sound, will rapidly lose effectiveness. Use more than one sense to create the trigger, if possible (for example – a tense-to-relaxed touch, together with the words, "That's right …".)
4. The process must be tested for effectiveness. Don't trust to chance.
5. The process must be repeatable. If it is to be used therapeutically at a later date, an anchor needs to be durable enough to be re-fired when needed.

Later, we will discuss the setting and application of anchors more specifically, but, at this point, we would like to explain why we have spent so much time on the engagement phase of the consultation.

The practitioner as 'meta-anchor'

Clinical outcomes may be demonstrably enhanced by positive expectation and belief (including that of the practitioner)[117,118,119]. Some studies even claim that strong belief and positive attitude can measurably affect the patient's cellular function[120]. While this research is regarded with scepticism in more orthodox circles, there is no doubt in many patients' mind that certain practitioners have the ability, somehow, to make them "just feel better".

Whether or not the connection between practitioner attitude and patient response is ever widely accepted, we believe a practitioner who exhibits strong congruence, optimism and engagement may function, at least in part, as a 'meta-anchor'. His state, if strong and coherent enough, may, in fact, collapse the patient's state in whole or in part – that is, he becomes the doctor-drug to which Michael Balint refers[121].

Pitfalls to avoid

Given our susceptibility to anchoring, the practitioner should avoid accidentally setting up negative anchors or reinforcing unwanted behaviour.

Practitioners are often encouraged to practise "active listening" by regularly acknowledging the patient's disclosures by nodding, sounds such as "uh-huh", and encouraging statements like, "I see." These should be carefully timed. Nodding, smiling and other gestures of acknowledgement made at the precise point where the patient is expressing his pain or distress may well anchor in the response we are striving to modify.

Difficult as it might be in the beginning, remain fully engaged, but neutral, at these times, reserving comments and other acknowledgements to be used in ways we will discuss later in this chapter.

Case history: *One of the authors was commissioned by a large London hospital to help chaplains of all denominations who were reported to be suffering from burnout. When interviewed, they all agreed they felt exhausted and debilitated by their perceived inability to help the many patients they encountered who were suffering from chronic and painful illnesses. As is our usual procedure, the job began with a period of observation – and the following was noted.*

Patients often appeared to be fairly relaxed and in good spirits, chatting, reading or watching television. When the chaplain appeared, he would sit down with a concerned and serious expression on his face, lean in towards the patient and inquire along the lines of, "So, how are you feeling today?"

The sonorous words and body language of the chaplain clearly signalled that he expected the patient to report negatively – which is exactly what happened. The patient visibly slumped, his expression becoming inwardly turned and reflective, then he would reply in some variation of, "Not so good today…". Patient and chaplain each appeared to be 'performing' the way the other expected of them. To the observer, it seemed clear that the chaplains had become anchored to the perceived suffering of the patients, and patients, in turn, to the chaplains' overserious and concerned demeanour.

The chaplains were taken aside, and the principle of anchoring explained to them and rehearsed (somewhat reluctantly at first) in adopting a more upbeat and positively expectant manner.

After a couple of days, the tone of the meetings changed noticeably. The chaplains became more 'human', teasing and joking with their charges, and the patients responded with visible pleasure at the chaplains' visits. Later, the chaplains reported feeling more relaxed, energised and optimistic about their work.

Anchors and strategies

When you experimented with the third part of the exercise at the end of Chapter 9 (and, if you haven't, we suggest you return and do so now), you might have noticed that each part of a subject's strategy depended on the part that immediately preceded it. Without that part (or any other), the strategy cannot run as a sequence. In terms of the conditioning process, a specific stimulus leads to a predictable response (S > R). The important thing to note here is that the response, in turn, functions as a stimulus to the next S-R unit, and so on, until the strategy has run its course. This is known as a "chain". Anchoring, as we will now see, becomes the building block of the principles and techniques designed to identify, access and stabilise the patient's resources.

Behavioural shaping

All conditions have limits or boundary conditions. There are times, or places in the body, where they are not experienced. The patient has a repertoire (as yet unrecognised) of behaviours that divert him from his suffering. No experience – however much the subject may protest to the contrary – can be maintained at the same level all the time. The human nervous system is not structured in a way that permits this to occur.

However, since the patient may feel overwhelmed by a problem and be incapable of finding his way past it, the purpose of shaping is gently and respectfully to guide him towards a greater awareness and activation of his capabilities, and to help him develop a more proactive and self-efficacious attitude.

To this end, we are interested in: exceptions to the problem state (times when the problem does not occur); the ability to shift and maintain attention to experiences outside the problem state; past successes and achievements; reducing the problem's size and impact by attending to its components, rather than the whole (splitting); and, accessing and developing solutions and solution-states (also referred to as desired states).

The patient will already have some, if not all, of these resources. But it is almost certain that he will not be aware of them. As long as he is associated into the problem, his (unsuccessful) struggle will be to dissociate – and 'dissociation', in his terms, will be to engage in the frustrating attempt to not-have the symptom. By trying not to have the problem, he has inadvertently placed himself in the paradoxical bind we call a "bonded disconnection".

Shaping is not in itself a therapeutic technique. As with elements of the earlier stages of the consultation (including engagement, lowering systemic overload, priming, respecting and listening to the patient's story, and applying the Clinical Questioning Matrix), the purpose is to orientate the patient in the direction of improvement, healing and health. By incorporating elements presupposing the capacity to change, you are assisting him to expand his incomplete or deficient map. In doing this, you also help him to change the qualitative feel of his experience[122].

It is important to gauge your patient's response, and to move at a pace that is comfortable for him. To move from his problem-state to a desired state may be perceived, consciously or unconsciously, as an unbridgeable gap. The processes outlined in this chapter are intended to prepare him to 'receive' the elements of change*.

Thus, the practitioner's role here is twofold: to help the patient successfully dissociate so he can more easily perceive his situation within a *wider* context (the rest of his life), without collapsing back into it, and, simultaneously, to begin to notice some of the resources mentioned above.

Stacking anchors

Initially, the practitioner's role will be to collect and build on the elements he elicits indirectly and conversationally. The process of "stacking" anchors is his instrument of choice.

Stacking is accomplished by setting multiple anchors in the same location, using the same trigger. The intention is to build a 'mega-state'

* In training, we sometimes use the metaphor of those old-fashioned computer floppy disks that needed to be formatted before they could store data. Alas, not everyone is old enough to get this one.

by adding together the qualities of each component (see Chapter 15 for further details). For example, a stacked anchor may be built out of qualities such as optimism, curiosity, humour and adventurousness.

Once you have created a stacked anchor, test for a response. First, change conversational direction momentarily ("By the way, how did you get here today?"). This is known as "breaking state". Pause, then re-fire the anchor using exactly the same trigger, watching to ensure that the patient re-enters the target state. If he does, the consultation continues. If not, return to the elicitation and anchoring stage of the process. *Do not assume that an anchor has been set simply because you have gone through the steps.* Always test it before proceeding.

Feedback

The British astrophysicist, Sir Fred Hoyle, once calculated that a blind man trying to solve the Rubik's cube by trial and error at a rate of one random move a second would take 1.35 trillion years, or, around 300 times the supposed age of the earth[123]. However, if he received feedback in the form of yes/no guidance from an experienced cubist, it would take him less than 90 seconds.

In today's politically correct atmosphere, students are often warned against 'telling' people what to do. This uncompromising approach is regrettable, especially as the patient arrives in your office or greets you in his hospital bed with the presupposition that you have knowledge by which he can benefit. We agree the autocratic 'orders' delivered by some egocentric practitioners have a detrimental effect (and may get you sued). However, with rapport and deep engagement, and simple good manners, giving effective feedback to the patient enables an efficient transfer of your knowledge to his resource-bank.

In giving informative feedback, you have three verbal options:

- right-wrong (R-W);
- no response-wrong (N-W); and,
- no response-right (N-R).

Without doubt, telling people what they are doing wrong has a negative effect. As any good schoolteacher knows, the learner can easily become demoralised and passive when progress is measured by failure. Research indicates that reinforcing 'correct' responses is considerably better – but by far the best results are obtained by consistent and appropriate guidance as to right *and* wrong manoeuvres[124]. The following technique achieves this conversationally without patronising overtones.

The "And … But" pattern

The practitioner can deliver feedback while continuing to shape the patient's responses and behaviours, weaving them in with the And … But pattern.

"But" is an example of a "turning word" that reduces or negates the impact of the statement immediately before it. "And" is a conjunction that connects thoughts, clauses and sentences sequentially into a single whole. For example:

Patient: *It's just so difficult to lose weight…*
Practitioner: *I know it's been a challenge (pace), **but** (directs away: **W**) you have to admit you have lost some weight, **and** (connects: **R**) that deserves some credit, doesn't it?*
Patient: *That's true (practitioner may choose to anchor here) … but I'm always hungry.*
Practitioner: ***But** (directs away: **W**) that only means you're not yet eating the right kind of foods, **and** (connects: **R**) some good foods are better and fill you up more, wouldn't you say?*
Patient: *Well, I could do better, I suppose. I'm not very good at this.*
Practitioner: ***But** (directs away: **W**), you've already lost quite a lot of weight. You're already doing pretty well (pace). **And** (connects: **R**), if you do a little planning ahead, it will be much easier. **But** (directs away: **W**), of course, that means thinking ahead a bit.*
Patient: *I guess I could do a bigger shop on Saturdays …*
Practitioner: *Good thinking (pace). **And** (connects: **R**) then you can enjoy the rest of the week without having to run out to the supermarket …*

Conducted elegantly, the process may be seen as a gentle, good-natured game. However, the practitioner is urged to avoid at all costs what is known as a symmetrical argument, which arises when he responds to the patient's "Yes, but…" with a counter-argument. If the patient's argument is met by a counter-argument, be sure he will follow that with a counter-counter-argument, and so on, until the practitioner surrenders. This is known colloquially as "being yes-butted", and it's a frustrating and fruitless experience.

Your options are to use the patient's responses to reshape meaning and direction before that happens … and to avoid the 'bait' when it's dangled in front of you.

EXERCISES

1. Anchoring is the core skill of effective NLP. We urge practitioners to become as proficient as possible in the technique, not just to link positive states to external triggers, but because, as we will illustrate in subsequent chapters, anchoring is a fundamental principle involved in virtually all Medical NLP techniques – including ones you develop yourself.
   - Begin by practising self-anchoring. The process involves accessing and amplifying a strong desired state, and then linking it to a specific physical trigger (e.g., touching finger to thumb, or pressing on a knuckle). Break state, test and repeat, until you can re-enter the state at will. Give some consideration to the quality of the state. Identify the submodalities involved, and then intensify them to a desired pitch.
   - Extend your skills to creating kinesthetic anchors with others. Guide and amplify your partner's state, then anchor it. Break state, test and repeat, until your partner can re-enter the state at will. Pay special attention to your subject's minimal cues (changes in colour, breathing rate, posture, etc) so you can also begin to learn to 'read' state changes in your patients.
   - Extend your anchoring to the auditory and visual channels. We have made some suggestions for non-

kinesthetic anchoring above. Another aid is to visualise a transparent screen between you and your subject and place your gestural anchors precisely in place each time you set and fire them. Should you shift the position of your body in relation to the screen, you must ensure that you stretch or bend your arm precisely to position the anchor in the same place.

2. Feedback and the And … But Pattern are best practised in stages. Simple feedback might initially involve a simple "That's right" accompanied by an affirmative nod of the head where you are reinforcing a desired behaviour or response, and a slight head-shake when you wish to divert the subject away from a position he has taken. Ensure that you immediately follow the 'negative' response with a more resourceful alternative. Adding "and" or "but" to the process should follow naturally as you become more comfortable with delivering feedback in a way that remains respectful of the patient's world-view.

11

The Symptom as Solution: when the body speaks

You may already have experienced this. You're in a café in a country where nobody speaks your language. You have an overwhelming desire for a coffee and the waiter is standing by to take your order. If you're lucky, you can get by with the universal language of gestures (miming sipping from a cup, pointing at the Lavazza machine).

But supposing your needs were a bit more complex. You want half-caffeinated, half-decaf. Skimmed milk, topped up with hot water, but extra foam. And, since you're watching your weight, you want to know if he'll bring you some artificial sweetener.

Suddenly, it's not so easy. On an unequal battle-ground, neither side can win. You may even 'kiss your teeth' and throw your head back in exasperation, but if this happens to be in a country where that gesture means "yes", he rushes off to bring you something you don't want. Or, if your waiter is African or West Indian, where 'teeth-kissing' is a supreme insult, you may get a lot more than a sugar substitute for your pains.

This is the position the patient suffering from a complex, chronic 'functional' disorder finds himself in. At some level, he knows a lot about his dis-ease, but words just seem to widen the gap of understanding.

Now, put yourself in the waiter's shoes. He's confronted by a gesticulating, increasingly angry or frustrated customer, whose mimed gestures are becoming increasingly bizarre ("What on earth does a little square shape drawn in the air followed by several pats on the midriff have to do with coffee? Oh, good – he's said, "Yes". At last …"). This is the position the practitioner finds himself in when he tries to sort through the avalanche of signs, symptoms and complaints the patient is sending in his direction.

In a world where logical, linear, sequential, digital data are considered superior to feelings, imagery, relationships and subjective experience, it's no wonder that the practitioner and the patient in our analogy will attempt to generate even more words in the hopes that some consensual 'explanation' will emerge. And it's no surprise that the person who holds most power in the relationship will jump at a piece of information (the head-toss and teeth-kissing) that seems to make sense, *in terms of his own map*, and run with it.

But, as this happens, both parties slide further down the greased pole of the Structural Differential, away from the patient's experience and into the abyss of ever-increasing abstraction.

There is another way, and this is what this book is about.

But, first, a case history:

Case history: *A woman in her mid-30s had returned to the doctor's practice after the latest, unsuccessful, investigation into a painful allergy that had been making her life miserable for the previous three years. Because it usually occurred at night, marked by large, inflamed wheals, suspicion fell on possible allergens, such as dust mites, laundry detergents and synthetic fibres. However, extensive tests had failed to identify the cause, and the patient despaired that her problem would ever be resolved.*

Depressed, anxious and suffering from sleep deprivation, she described how her condition was destroying her relationship; she felt "cut off" from her partner, who was becoming increasingly frustrated with her reluctance to have sex. "It's as though we're living in different worlds and we're separated by a wall we just can't get through," she remarked bitterly.

As always, we suggest practitioners go back to basics when a problem seems overwhelmingly complex. This is similar to what therapist Sheldon Kopp calls going "back to one"[125] *– temporarily abandoning* *theories and assumptions, and returning to the baseline of the Medical NLP consultation: gathering sensory-based information. Pursuing a conventional investigative approach had, so far, proved fruitless, so the practitioner decided to re-enter her "beginner's mind" state.*

*Hoping, at least, to be able to restore a more optimistic direction in which they could both work, she asked the patient, "When the problem is finally resolved, what will you be able to do that you haven't been able to do so far? What will be different and better about your life?"**

To the practitioner's surprise (and, she admits, to her dismay), the patient began to weep. Sensing that the woman needed to dissipate her grief and despair, she resisted the urge to comfort her, remained engaged and present, and did what many health professionals find particularly difficult to do in their busy and pressured world … absolutely nothing.

After a while, the woman raised her head, dabbed at her still streaming eyes and said indistinctly, "I want a baby. My life is empty without a child."

"And, have you talked about this with your partner? What does he think?"

The woman drew a long, shuddering breath, and then let it out. "He wants one too – very much … but, I don't think it's possible."

On reflection, the practitioner admitted that she responded according to what she believed the woman was saying, rather than to what was actually meant. She said, "You might have to approach it differently, especially if making love is painful, but I don't see any reason why you shouldn't be able to have a baby."

The patient paused, then leaned forward and spoke softly, but emphatically. "You don't understand. It's not that. It's that I know he's not the right one. I want a baby, and he's willing to have one, too, but I don't want it with him. I've never admitted that to anyone, not even myself. The idea of having a baby with someone I don't love makes my skin crawl."

* These are standard, presuppositional, solution-oriented questions characteristic of Medical NLP. They are usually applied early in the first consultation, but, the practitioner should feel free to check back at any point to see if the patient's outcomes have clarified or changed.

It took a moment or two, the doctor later admitted, "but, then it was as if all the lights went on". Some gentle questioning fleshed out the picture. The 'allergic response' occurred only at night, and only when she was with her partner. She hadn't noticed it before (and, nor had any of the specialists she had consulted), but on the few occasions she'd been away from home on a work assignment and sleeping on her own, the symptoms hadn't appeared.

"What do you think that means?" the practitioner asked.

The woman smiled faintly. "That it's all in my head? That's what the other doctors think. I can see that from the way they talk to me."

"Of course it's in your head," the practitioner said. "But, it's also very much in your body. It can't be in one and not the other."

The remark seemed to resonate with the patient, so the practitioner continued. She explained that the function of the immune system was essentially protective. Its role was to distinguish between 'me' and 'not me', and to defend against anything it perceived as threatening the boundary between the two. "It's just a guess," she added, "but it may be that your immune system knew something you hadn't really thought out clearly for yourself. What do you think?"

The patient's words tumbled out. She had known "at some level" that the relationship had to end. She realised she was being unfair to her partner by not telling him that she didn't love him. She thought she had to be open with him. She was nervous, she said, but added, without a touch of irony, that she needed to "grow a thicker skin".

The premise that unresolved emotional issues can be expressed as physical symptoms is almost as old as the practice of medicine itself. But, the search for the 'deeper meaning' of "psychosomatic" disorders has traditionally been long, arduous and often unrewarding. This is further complicated by the abundance of theory-driven schools and models of therapy, each of which competes for supremacy over the others.

Our proposal, then, is that the process of helping the patient to restore both physical and emotional balance can be substantially quicker and easier when we learn to defer less to dogma and more to the expertise and communication style of the undisputed expert in the problem at hand: the patient who is presenting it.

When permitted to speak freely, the patient usually presents a narrative rich in detail and meaning. But, unlike the logical, linear signs and symptoms that traditionally govern clinical investigation, meaning emerges in a form of description that is usually overlooked. This is densely packed with words, phrases, imagery, actions and behaviours that re-present (present again) the problem state in a more dynamic form. More than mere linguistic and behavioural artifices, these 'stand for' a much more complex inner landscape. This is what linguists refer to as metaphor.

The significance of metaphor

Traditionally, a metaphor is a figure of speech which, normally used of one class of object, action, etc, is extended to another.

In everyday conversation, and, especially in consultations, metaphors are everywhere – so much so, that we rarely notice them. If we return to our analogy at the start of the chapter, we can point to a number of examples: the health professional as "waiter", the patient as "customer"; their communication problems as a "battle" fought on an "uneven battle-ground" where there could be no "winners". Then there are the non-verbal metaphors: the little square packet of sweetener 'drawn' in the air, the patting of an expanding waistline, representing "I'm watching my weight", the 'kissing' of the teeth and the tossing of the head.

Similarly, imagery used by the patient whose case history is presented above includes various forms of walls and barriers that, nonetheless, create "emptiness". She craves something to fill the emptiness, but 'part' of her is repulsed by the idea of that happening with someone she does not love. Failing to speak out about and resolve this inner conflict, her immune system takes over the job. In evolutionary terms, we might even propose that it is preventing her from reproducing with an unsuitable mate. Her skin, literally, "crawls" to prevent that happening.

Metaphor in whole-person healing

The metaphoric content of communication cannot be ignored if we truly mean to practise "whole-person" health care. In either screening metaphors out or dismissing them as verbal flourishes that have nothing to do with 'fact', we lose information that could considerably increase our understanding. We choose text over context, facts over story, left brain over right. We drain off the lifeblood of subjective experience, and then blame the corpse for its lack of cooperation.

The truth is: *we cannot communicate without metaphor.* It is not merely the way in which we add colour, depth and poetry to bald facts, but it is how we organise and make sense out of our experience, express the inexpressible, and seek resolution when our complex homeostasis becomes dangerously upset. Above all, *the symptom itself can function as a metaphor* – and, as such, can help practitioner and patient uncover the structure, origin and meaning of the presenting problem, and therefore arrive significantly more quickly and easily at resolution.

The origins of metaphor

In Chapter 5, we looked at the component parts – the 'building blocks' – of subjective experience. The sensory modalities and their distinctive qualities, the submodalities, are to our sense of 'reality' what bricks and mortar are to a building. But what gives meaning and purpose to the building is metaphor. If the building is a house, is it also a "home", or perhaps, a "sanctuary" for you and your family, or perhaps a "showpiece" that places you in a particular position in your society? Size and shape may expand the possibilities for its use, but the *concept* driving its design and construction dictates how we will relate to it.

Linguist George Lakoff and philosopher Mark Johnson believe that our language and thinking are both metaphoric in nature[126]. Additionally, they suggest that both our verbal and non-verbal actions are metaphorically structured. We cannot accurately describe our inner world in linear sequential terms, simply because our experience of that unique landscape *precedes* its arrangement into the grammar of communication. And we cannot *act* without in some way expressing the greater complexity of that inner world.

Some cognitive linguists believe that our primary metaphors are unconsciously acquired in our early years, largely by associating experiential domains (say, the closeness of your mother's embrace with enjoying "close" friendships in later life)[127].

Metaphoric constructs, each with its own neural network, both trigger and shape our physical and emotional responses in hundreds of different two-way interactions. The fact that they usually function below the level of conscious awareness is significant. The neural circuits that allow us to operate on both literal and figurative levels leave their traces indirectly – through certain words, phrases, actions (such as distinctive gestures), and, as we have already said, the appearance and development of symptoms themselves.

Metaphor in NLP and Medical NLP

Traditionally, NLP uses practitioner-generated metaphors adjunctively with other techniques. These are usually isomorphic – that is, stories or anecdotes that follow the structure of the problem but with a suggested solution appended. Derived from the work of Milton Erickson, who had a vast repertoire of therapeutic stories, they are intended to bypass conscious awareness to be embedded in and acted upon by the patient's unconscious mind.

Practitioners trained in Medical NLP use metaphors in this manner wherever relevant; telling a story about "someone else" who solved a similar problem can be immensely encouraging to a patient. However, our focus in this chapter is on another class of metaphor – that spontaneously generated by the patient.

Patient-generated metaphors

The metaphors that emerge spontaneously in the patient's story and during information-gathering fall into two distinct categories: linguistic metaphors, and the symptom itself.

The felt sense

Although from our earlier discussion about submodalities, it is easy to understand that metaphors derive from the way we use our sensory modalities, all problem-based metaphors have at their core a kinesthetic, or "felt sense". This is almost a truism; all patients seek help because, in one way or another, they 'feel bad'. In Korzybski's model, there is an awareness of some neurological disturbance at the Object level. It is this felt sense which disturbs them and from which they seek respite.

However, unlike conventional medicine that may seek reduction or elimination of the felt sense, Medical NLP regards it as an entry-point to the silent, flowing level of the Event. Integrating transformational approaches into the regular consultation process requires that the practitioner works at 'tuning' his senses to listen for and observe the patient's metaphoric communication.

Linguistic metaphors

Some years ago, Western medicine recognised and paid attention to what was then called "organ language". Phrases such as "pain in the neck" and "heart-broken" were given equal weight along with objective signs and symptoms in arriving at diagnoses. Today, we (the authors) prefer the term "somatic language", which should not be confused with what physicians often refer to as "somatisation". Somatic language comprises figures of speech, used unconsciously, but semantically related to the physical and/or psychological problem presented by the patient.

When practitioners begin to pay attention to this phenomenon, they are often astonished by the layers of meaning present in the patient's speech. Here are just a few examples of somatic language phrases encountered in our own consultations:

> *My boss makes me so hot under the collar. I'm scared one day I'm just going to blow up at him* (from a man with high blood pressure)
>
> *I've had enough. I've had a gut-full of things* (a patient diagnosed with irritable bowel syndrome)
>
> *I'm always there for other people, but they don't give me the support I need* (a woman whose rheumatoid arthritis reduced her to walking – when she could walk – with sticks)
>
> *I know I should leave my husband, but each time I think about it I get cold feet* (a woman diagnosed with Raynaud's disease, a condi-

tion "of unknown cause" marked by highly reactive arteries of the fingers or toes, painful spasms and unduly cold hands and feet)

People always expect me to mother them, but nobody ever asks about what I want (a woman faced with a diagnosis of breast cancer and the prospect of a mastectomy)

I feel as though I'm going to drive off a cliff (a car salesman with agitated depression)

My father always told me to keep my head down and not draw attention to myself (a golf pro who developed the "yips"* each time he came near to winning a championship)

It should be emphasised that patients never consciously use true somatic language. The words and phrases occur without any discernible awareness or irony. We caution against drawing them to the patient's attention lest we abort the unconsciously driven communication process, or embarrass him with his "Freudian slip". Equally, guard against jumping to conclusions. Without supporting evidence, it would be presumptuous and potentially damaging to attribute a specific meaning where meaning may not exist.

Using patient-generated somatic language

Patients will often report feeling "really listened to" when the practitioner simply matches the somatic language used. But, utilising it therapeutically requires exploring and expanding the imagery to include the potential for solutions. Sometimes a simple reframing of the patient's metaphor is sufficient. Here is the practitioner's response to the golfer who had lost his form:

> "*Well, 'keeping your head down' when you swing is a good thing, isn't it? So, your Dad gave you some good advice there.* (This is said lightly, and the patient gets the joke.) *But, we know he wanted the best for you, so what else could he have intended by telling you not to draw attention to yourself?*" (Here the father's positive intention is presup-

* "Yips" is a term used by golfers to describe a nervous response that causes them to lose form.

posed; contrary to some psychoanalytical beliefs, we believe very few parents deliberately set out to make their children miserable.)

"*...Maybe not to take risks in case I failed? Perhaps, in his way he was trying to keep me from getting hurt ...*"

"*Maybe. And, you mentioned earlier that he'd never had the experience of really achieving anything important in his own life. Did I understand that correctly?*" (The patient agrees.) *So, I wonder how that will change for him when he experiences real success through his son's achievements.*"

This reframing simultaneously suggests that the patient will return to form and that his achievements will serve both him and his father. The conversation continues in this direction with some further tips about managing stress, etc, as a win-win solution for everyone, and is negotiated without recourse to, or even any suggestion of, antidepressants or beta-blockers to deal with the golfer's nerves.)

The symptom as metaphor

Taken as a whole, the patient's story, including his language patterns, provides the practitioner with tools further to explore the condition. All of the above presupposes a kind of 'enfoldment' of all the characteristics of the problem – including its history and biology – into the symptom. Attempts to 'unfold' the complex nature of this complex state have, thus far in Western medicine, been essentially linear, left-brained, logical and, clearly, incomplete. By alternating this essentially left-brain approach with the creative, right-brain, relationship-detecting talents of your cognitive processing abilities, a 'bigger picture' will begin to appear.

The questions to bear in mind when reviewing the totality of the condition as presented are:

1. How does it work?
2. What are its origins?
3. What need is it trying to meet?
4. What other (healthier, more resourceful) behaviour or response would satisfy that need?

How it works

How the condition 'works' has already been discussed at some length in Chapter 5. The way the patient structures his experience – his preferred sensory modalities, submodalities and the sequences involved (strategies) – may be elicited directly by questioning, or indirectly by noting eye accessing cues and sensory predicates. Be sure to calibrate and test to ensure that your observations match the patient's internal experience.

Origin, purpose and intention

Medical NLP is less concerned with 'causes' than with solutions. Nevertheless, understanding how the problem was established (or is perceived to have been established) and its purpose or intention can provide a useful starting point for restructuring the experience. Our intention in establishing a symptom's origin is *not* to dwell unnecessarily on a stressful experience, but to understand how the patient set up his *response* to the experience.

Here are some useful guiding presuppositions:

1. At some time in the past, the patient's ability to respond and adjust effectively (restore allostasis) was compromised, either by a single sensitising experience, or by a series of unrelieved stresses;
2. The autonomic arousal presently experienced by the patient results from both the "imprint" of the original stressor(s) and his ongoing failure to resolve the problem. He has failed to fight or flee. Now he is 'frozen';
3. At the time, the patient, consciously or unconsciously, may have drawn certain generalised conclusions about his situation: e.g., "If I'm sick, my parents will look after me rather than fight with each other"; "All men (or women) are untrustworthy"; "If I get fat then my stepfather won't want to touch me again" etc.

   The symptom, therefore, functions protectively. It is striving to prevent the patient re-experiencing the original sensitising experience by diverting him to some response or behaviour that is (unconsciously) perceived as preferable. (In this way, rather than being regarded as an exogenous and inexplicable force creating disease, the symptom is reframed as a disturbing, but nonetheless, positively intentioned, aspect of our own internal system of checks and balances).

Detecting origins

The origins – real or perceived – of the problem may be simply detected by a process known as "Affect Bridging". The technique is explained in detail in Chapter 18.

Once the origins of a problem have been identified, we may need to explore its purpose or intention and the sequence of actions involved in its execution. One process for achieving is the NLP principle of "chunking" (Figure 11.1).

Establishing purpose or intention

Chunking is a term borrowed from computer programming. It refers to how we group and organise "bits" of information. The technique linguistically shifts a subject's consciousness, either deeper into the details and sequences of a particular experience (chunking down), or towards a more generalised, experiential 'core' state (chunking up). Chunking down may also be seen as the molecular approach, chunking up the molar.

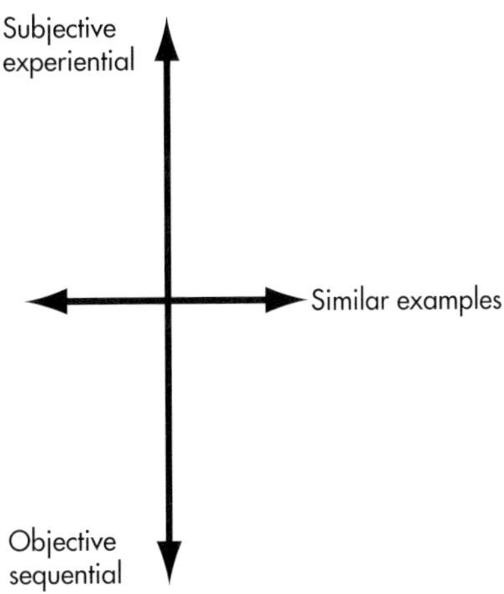

Fig 11.1 Chunking

Chunking across reveals similar examples of the same experience. Metaphors, similes and analogies are examples of chunking across. We will discuss the therapeutic application of chunking in greater detail in later chapters. For now, though, we can apply chunking to access the purpose or intention of a symptom, and to explore alternative means of satisfying that need.

To do this, simply ask the patient, "If (the symptom) had a positive intention, what would it want to accomplish for you?" Whatever the patient answers, respond with, "So, if you had (the reply), what would *that* want for you that's even more positive?" Repeat the question until the patient is unable to access any more levels. The word or phrase he uses will usually be a nominalistion, with somewhat abstract or even 'spiritual' connotations. Examples given during a consultation about excessive drinking are:

It relaxes me.
I'm better able to cope.
I feel less of a failure. (*Reframed by the practitioner to, "I feel more successful"*)
More fulfilled.
More at peace.
More connected.

Meeting the need

Solutions are often self-evident, once the origins and purpose have been disclosed. For example, the woman with the mysterious allergy decided to review her relationship with her partner; following through with her decision to leave him was enough to resolve her emotional distress. The 'allergy' was still absent a year later.

The practitioner can also assist the patient by chunking across to explore alternative responses. All questions in this class are variations of *in what healthier and more resourceful way can the purpose or intention of the symptom be met?*

Here are some 'solutions' to a few of the cases mentioned earlier:

- The woman diagnosed with Raynaud's decided her "cold feet" actually prevented her from rushing headlong into potentially problematic situations. Now, she regards the symptom (when it occurs) as a warning signal for her to look more carefully at whatever she might be intending to do.

- The patient with rheumatoid arthritis realised that her family and friends might not have realised she needed support, but she felt she lacked the confidence to approach the subject. She asked for help on how to ask for help, then laughed when we pointed out what she'd just said. She added, "I guess I just have to do it!"
- The woman with breast cancer decided to focus her attention on those people who saw her as an equal partner in their friendship, rather than striving to satisfy those who continually made demands on her.

At the time of writing, all these patients are alive and well.

EXERCISES

1. Start by keeping a metaphor log. Pay attention not only to your patients, but to newscasts, television programmes and conversations with your family and friends. Listen for words and phrases that suggest something is 'like' something else*. Notice when someone doesn't feel "grounded", or is "off-centre", or whether they see life or their work as a "battle", a "journey" or a "bowl of cherries". How much of a match can you detect between the metaphors they present and the way they lead their lives?
2. Write a mini-saga (no more than 50 words) about patients' symptoms. Start with the words, "I am X's symptom. I want ..."
3. Without necessarily applying an intervention, gently probe for the unspoken, unmet need of a patient's symptom. Use the questions suggested in this chapter, or ask yourself, "What could this be doing for X? How is it protecting him? From what?"

* To our more pedantic readers: yes, we do know the difference between "metaphor" and "simile". However, we use the word metaphor as a ... well, metaphor, for all other analogous forms.

12

A Different Kind of Reason: entering the patient's world

First the patient, second the patient, third the patient, fourth the patient, fifth the patient, and then maybe comes science. We first do everything for the patient; science can wait, research can wait.

Bela Schick[128]

The astute practitioner, confronted with a condition that is not readily identifiable, recognises that he needs to do something both challenging and rewarding. He needs to enter the patient's world.

This is a reversal of the conventional relationship in which the patient is expected to submit to the superior knowledge and expertise of the practitioner. That dynamic has been shown by studies to be counter-productive. Where the patient feels intimidated by the 'authority' of the medical encounter, he will often not disclose the information necessary to arrive at accurate diagnosis and appropriate treatment. In fact, he may even prefer to reveal sensitive information to a computer, or by filling in a questionnaire – even in the knowledge that his confidentiality may be compromised[129].

Within the patient's world, the problem-behaviour will have a logic that extends beyond the symptoms and their cause. The landscape in which he has lost his way needs to be explored and understood before the problem-behaviour can be changed.

This approach is, to borrow George Engel's terminology, "biopsychosocial". As the word suggests, it recognises that the patient's biology is intimately related to, or may even be affected adversely by, his relationships and emotions[130].

We derive the metaphor of "entering" the patient's world from the martial arts. Many styles historically evolved out of social and religious conditions that forbade meeting violence with violence. Instead, the nature and direction of the attacker's own energy was captured and redirected in a direction other than its original target. Later, more 'spiritual' forms, such as Aikido, re-cast the attacker as a "partner", and developed elegant, almost balletic, strategies to avoid injury, either to the attacker or to the defender.

In the Medical NLP model, the practitioner is required to 'enter' the patient's map of the world, without necessarily colluding with its distortions, with the intention of reorientating him in a more useful and appropriate direction. Just as the skilful martial artist needs knowledge, flexibility and practice to resolve conflict in a spirit unfamiliar to the rest of society, so the Medical NLP practitioner benefits from three skill-sets not normally encountered in a medical context.

Normalisation

The first of these is "normalisation". In essence, normalisation means we accept whatever the patient presents to us as 'making sense' *within a certain context.* Ultimately, the practitioner's job is to understand what that context is.

Normalising the patient's experience can be deeply transformational, not least by removing feelings of shame, blame or being 'beyond help'. Only then can the patient relax his efforts enough to entertain the possibility of change. As an example, we cite the many patients we see whose tension visibly begins to dissolve when we explain their 'anxiety disorder', or, 'Post-Traumatic Stress Disorder', as simply a name given to a natural, evolutionary response that "needs to be updated".

Dissociation

Thus far, the patient has been striving unsuccessfully to dissociate from the symptom in the belief that this will solve the problem itself. In doing this, he inadvertently establishes a bonded disconnection.

Medicating his feelings, or suggesting that he will get better if only he challenges and reforms his "negative thinking patterns", collude with this belief by failing to recognise and validate the purpose and reality of his pain. By providing only symptomatic relief, both these approaches leave the structure of the core problem intact, and may even risk weakening the patient by removing the 'challenge' to his system, without facilitating his biological and psychological capacity to adapt and grow.

Change, however, cannot take place from within the problem-state, so the patient needs temporarily to be able to step back from his current response or behaviour to view it from a more detached perspective. This can be done overtly, by suggesting he see the response or behaviour literally on a screen (with himself in the picture) or, indirectly, using language patterns presupposing temporary detachment – "If we could look at this a different way, a bit like a fly on the wall …" etc.

This serves to reduce the patient's anxiety when reviewing the problem, as well as opening opportunities for you both to generate new meanings and responses.

Utilisation

Utilisation recognises everything the patient brings to a consultation as raw materials of change.

The most obvious of these is, of course, the symptom itself. Many interventions evolving out of the principles of NLP are created by symptom-solution linkage – that is, by connecting the 'trigger' of the problem-state to a new and more appropriate response. This is highly effective in many conditions otherwise considered intractable – and even more so, when the new response more effectively meets an underlying need. Chapters 17 and 18 expand on this theme. For immediate application, though, we offer here several 'indirect' interventions based on utilisation.

Paradoxical binds

How often does it happen that you *absolutely know* that if only someone did what you suggested, he would get the result he wants? In real life, of course, people often don't, or won't, follow what you might regard is excellent advice. This is not necessarily because they are being obstructive, but because the change somehow doesn't seem to 'fit'.

"Paradoxical binds" are linguistic devices that recursively link action X to the outcome Y by making *not* doing Y the motivation to do X. Confused? *Well, the more confused you become, the more determined you'll be to understand.*

Try this with a friend:

> Have him clasp his hands tightly, palm to palm, and extend both forefingers so they are parallel to each other. Deliver the following instruction exactly and with conviction:
>
> "Now, notice how your forefingers will automatically come together until they touch. I want you to try your best to resist, but the more you resist, the more you exhaust your ability to resist, until those fingers move together and touch..."
>
> ... and simply sit back and watch. After a while, you will notice signs of effort. Your friend will pull the fingers apart, but each time the tendency to move together becomes stronger until he surrenders.
>
> Whatever explanation he chooses to give, the result is the same. By binding the response directly to the amount of effort he expends resisting it, the outcome becomes inevitable.

Here are some examples:

> *The more you allow the fever and runny nose to run their course, the more quickly your body will destroy the germs causing your cold.*
>
> *You say it's difficult to relax, so, instead of trying to relax, become as tense as you can be before you allow yourself to relax.*
>
> *You don't have to stop worrying. In fact, you may be the kind of person who needs to worry – so, I'd like you to set aside exactly 30 minutes at the same time every day so you can concentrate only on worrying as much as you can until you don't need to worry any more.*

(This latter approach – setting a special time during which the symptom must be indulged – has proved useful as an adjunctive treatment to Obsessive Compulsive Disorder.)

Framing and reframing

"Framing", "preframing" and "reframing" – setting up or changing the context in which a particular situation or problem is experienced – is a core skill of Medical NLP.

There is no doubt that our attitudes to certain events alter according to the context in which we experience them. There is also considerable evidence to suggest that the meaning and degree of emotion we attach to our experiences directly affects the performance of our immune system through the mediation of the complex orchestration of our hormone, peptide and cytokine flow. The sound of a creaking stair during the day may not even be noticed; in the middle of the night, it can trigger feelings of fear and anxiety. Sustained anxiety may eventually result in a deterioration of both performance and the function of cells and organs.

Adrenalin-fuelled experiences create different qualitative experiences according to the context in which they occur – "exciting", where the subject is involved in activity he enjoys, "stressful" when it is activity he fears or dislikes. Since the biochemical impact of 'excitement' differs from that of 'anxiety', reframing proves a useful tool*.

Three of the most useful applications of framing follow.

1. Preframing

Since the "expectations" of patient and physician have been identified as a significant component of successful treatment outcomes[131,132], preframing is designed to set up both patient and practitioner for improvement and change. In general, preframes involve suggestions and assumptions

* A Medical NLP-trained physician colleague approaches stress-related angina pain by reframing his patients to have the same, symptom-free response to day-to-day tensions as they do to the football matches and other social events they enjoy. In doing this, he changes the 'meaning' of sympathetic arousal and thereby alters the negative physiological response. His patients demonstrate increasing resilience to everyday stressors.

rather than direct statements. Preframes are therefore also classed as presuppositions.

Avoiding the negative preframe. Clinicians often deliver negative preframes while seeking informed consent. This can increase the patient's anxiety and elicit a "nocebo" response. For example, an overemphasis on side-effects of medications is known by most practitioners to increase patients' experience of some of those effects. Negative preframes often prompt the patient actively to search for these events; they may even *cause* the adverse response by the same mechanisms that underlie the placebo response.

Examples of commonly used negative preframes in everyday clinical practice include:

> *After the surgery, you may experience some swelling, pain or tenderness and notice some bruising over the scar site. It will be uncomfortable for some weeks afterwards.*
>
> *The glyceryl trinitrate spray you use under the tongue when you get angina will probably give you a headache.*
>
> *The pain may actually get worse following the injection in your knee.*
>
> *We need to do an exercise ECG, chest X-ray and blood tests to check whether you have heart disease, or whether you might get a heart-attack.*

It is relatively simple to deliver relevant information while at the same time actively seeking to reassure the patient, encourage him to tolerate unavoidable discomfort and orientate him towards improvement and recovery:

> *After the surgery, some people experience tenderness and bruising over the operation site. This is quite natural, and, if it does happen, as you begin to recover the swelling goes down and the bruising and pain usually clear up over the next few days.*
>
> *The glyceryl trinitrate spray used under the tongue can give* ***some*** *people* (presupposing "not you") *a headache as the angina pain clears and your breathing gets better.*
>
> *You may notice the pain gets worse after the joint injection before it begins to get better and your knee becomes more comfortable.*

We need to do an exercise ECG, chest X-ray and blood tests to make sure your heart is okay. If anything shows up on the tests we'll be able to give you the best possible treatment to make sure your condition improves.

2. *Content reframing*

The content reframe specifically seeks to change the *meaning* the patient has attributed to his experience without directly challenging it. A content reframe is specifically called for when the subject has used one or other of the Meta Model* violations known as "complex equivalence" (X is the same as, or means, Y) or "cause-and-effect" (X *causes* Y).

Meaning and appropriate action are further constricted where nominalisations (processes represented as events) are used. For example:

Statement: "*My anxiety* (nominalisation) *gets really bad as soon as I get behind the wheel.*"
Content reframe: "*Being anxious* (process returned to the nominalisation) *whenever you get behind the wheel could also remind you to stay alert and drive carefully* (the 'meaning' of anxiety is changed)."

Reframes should be never be delivered without adequate pacing and rapport to avoid seeming dismissive. To give another example:

"*Being over-anxious* ***can*** *be worrying* (pace). ***But*** (turning word) *being anxious to just the right degree* (presupposes 'degree' of anxiety can be adjusted) *can remind you to stay alert and drive carefully … so let's take a look at how we can be sure that the level is just right* (preframe)."

The following are examples of practitioner-generated statements patients brought into our consultations, followed by the reframes that reassured them during subsequent, probably unnecessary, appointments:

* The Meta Model as presented in *The Structure of Magic* is a revolutionary tool for extracting Deep Structure (the actual meaning of a statement) from the Surface Structure (what is said). We urge practitioners to become fully conversant with all the patterns to clarify their own thinking and reasoning and to increase their effectiveness when working with patients.

Statement: "*Your lifestyle and lack of exercise are causing these symptoms and increasing your risk of getting heart disease. You have to change all this.*"
Reframe: "*Your symptoms are your body telling you that now is a good time to start eating more healthily and getting some regular exercise.*"

Statement: "*Colds are caused by a virus. We don't give antibiotics for that.*"
Reframe: "*The mild fever and the stuffy nose are signs that your immune system is fighting off the virus really well. We wouldn't want to do anything that might interfere with your body's natural responses.*"

Statement: "*The growth was cancerous and if left it could have spread and become terminal.*"
Reframe: "*The growth was cancerous, but luckily we've found it early enough to remove it and do everything we can to make sure you remain well in the future.*"

3. Context reframing

As its name suggests, "context reframing" seeks to normalise or validate responses or behaviours by transferring them to a wider or different context.

One of the earliest presuppositions out of which NLP developed was that all behaviour has value, although sometimes that behaviour is better suited to a different situation. For example, 'anxiety' may be perceived as a 'problem'. 'Being anxious', though, is a natural and protective response to a real or potential threat, and can serve to help us avoid the perceived danger or create contingency plans to deal with it when it comes.

In order to create a context reframe, ask, "*Where else might this response or behaviour be useful?*" Context reframes are appropriate when the speaker reasons or explains an experience using a Meta Model violation that involves judgement while deleting information that could justify the judgement. Listen especially for the word "too", although this might be implicit in the statement. Examples are "I'm too busy"; "I'm too anxious"; "He's demanding"; "I'm stressed".

Asking where else this behaviour or response might be useful or relevant, we replace the problem frame with one that suggests relevance and change. "Being busy", for example, may be reframed as useful "when there are specific tasks to be done" (implying, or stating overtly, that there is also a benefit to relaxing, where appropriate). Obsessive behaviour may often be brought under control where treatment includes providing a context frame in which the behaviour would be appropriate (we know of a woman who had a cleaning obsession that she re-directed into setting up a popular and highly profitable celebrity housekeeping service).

Patients may even be comforted by context reframes applied to certain organic disorders – the sickle cell anaemia trait, for example, may be regarded as 'useful' in an area with a high incidence of malaria, since it confers added resistance to the malarial parasite.

Reframes of all kinds will not 'take' if they are not matched to the situation at hand. Richard Bandler suggests using all sensory modalities to replicate the subject's complaint, and then asking the questions, "What else could this response/behaviour mean?" and, "In what other situation could this be useful?"[133]

Utilisation in practice

The following is a transcript of part of a consultation with a young professional woman referred after being diagnosed as having 'psychotic episodes'.

> **Case history:** *The patient reported problems with a former boyfriend who was making her life a misery. According to her version of events, it was a classic case of "stalking": wherever she went, there he was; silent calls and hang-ups several times a night; suddenly appearing when she least expected it. She would often look out of her bedroom window in the middle of the night and see him standing in the shadows of the trees on the other side of the road. Sometimes he would ride past her, motorcycle helmet covering his face, "just to let me know he knows where I am at any time and can reach me whenever he wants".*
>
> *There was just one problem: the ex-lover was in Canada, and she lived on the other side of the world. Moreover, she* ***knew*** *he now lived*

abroad. But her explanation was "simple": he had profound psychic powers that allowed him to appear wherever, and in whatever form, he desired.

Many practitioners we speak to report similar cases: spell-casting, psychic control, 'spirit' manifestation. Some of these are examples of different cultural beliefs and interpretations, others of 'psychiatric' disorder. Problems occur when the subject fails effectively to resolve conflicts caused by a collision between internal and external 'realities'.

Whether we regard these experiences as 'real' or not is irrelevant – and frankly we don't presume to know. However, responsibility for helping sufferers of such conditions, broadly diagnosed in the Western paradigm as 'psychiatric', increasingly falls on primary care physicians.

This pressure, coupled with the belief that 'mental illness' is the result of a chemical imbalance in the brain, is confusing, and we sympathise with those who resort to psychotropic medications in the hope that the symptoms will come under control. Not only are these problems perceived as complex and deep-seated, but, to the unskilled practitioner, complaints as apparently bizarre as 'remote stalking' can be unnerving. Our assertion is: they need not be. By focusing on structure and process, we can supplement our existing helping skills without colluding with the patient or directly attacking his beliefs.

This is especially important when consulting with people from cultures in which such beliefs are not exceptional. Many cases of 'disordered thinking', when viewed in the context of the culture in which they occur, turn out to have reasonable explanations. Only relatively recently, for example, has it been recognised that many patients of Caribbean backgrounds diagnosed by British psychiatrists as 'schizophrenic' were in fact suffering from a particularly acute form of stress triggered by racism[134].

Our approach, then, seeks not to challenge and replace the patient's 'reality' with our own, but to help the patient discover new choices and coping strategies. To accomplish this, we need to look at the symptomatic behaviour and ask ourselves two questions: how can this be acting to protect the patient, and how, in his model, could it be explicable or 'true'?

With the patient referred to above, the practitioner's reasoning went in the following way. When people experience the loss of a loved one, they often refuse to accept that the relationship has ended[135]. Even though the loved one has died or left, they seem to see or hear them unexpectedly. Thoughts about the loved one occur frequently and unbidden, and attempts to exclude these thoughts seem to increase their frequency and intensity. They try to cope with their feelings of loss and grief by attempting to separate from them – but, at the same time, they might feel guilty about 'forgetting' the loved one in those moments in which they succeed in thinking about something else. All these responses are commonly experienced and generally regarded as 'normal'.

Now, supposing the subject succeeds to some degree in separating out from the unwanted experiences (that is, she successfully denies responsibility for generating the thoughts and feelings), but the experiences themselves persist. *Her left-brain "spin doctor" then has to come up with a 'rational' explanation for why it is happening.* Creating explanations for irrational events is a characteristic of altered states, and often appears bizarre to the observer.

The only explanation this patient had was "psychic control". In all other areas of her life, she was, by any assessment, entirely reasonable, rational and sane. On any other subject, in any other situation, she had a grounded, realistic and reliable perspective. She was, quite literally, being 'driven crazy' by her inability to cope with her loss.

The following is part of a transcription of the intervention that followed. Comments and responses are in the left-hand column, and details of the intervention in the right. The practitioner's speech is italicised.

He was always trying to change me – make me into something else.	The patient demonstrates resistance to being changed by an outside element or person. The practitioner notes this; change needs to be within the patient's control.
In what way?	
To make me a better person. More assertive, he said. To stand up for myself.	The practitioner notes the phrases "a better person" and "to stand up for myself".

Is that something you'd want for yourself?	The practitioner tests whether the patient really does want to be in control
Well, yes, but not when someone's putting so much pressure on you all the time.	… but, it needs to be self-directed.
So, if you could find a way that you could do that yourself?	The practitioner tests for concordance.
Yes. Of course.	The practitioner anchors the agreement by nodding and smiling, then seeks gently to prompt her into rejecting her own earlier presupposition (that the ex-boyfriend was too powerful to resist).
That's right. So, when you have this experience of his "powers" … does that mean his powers are stronger than anyone else's? (said in a slightly disbelieving and contemptuous tone). *That nobody in the world could stop him?*	
(Grimaces) He thinks he's great, but I think he's actually very weak. That's why he has to use psychic stuff to get at people.	The practitioner anchors her response, and then begins to employ primes directed at protecting herself by "reflecting" and "deflecting", rather than by counter-attack. This is an ecological consideration. We seek to provide peaceful resolutions to both internal and external conflicts wherever possible.
That's right. So, he's not the strongest wizard in the world? That may be what he thinks, what he sees reflected in the mirror? So thinking he's great is a kind of shield, a protective barrier, would you say?	

Oh, yes.

And, if you find you have real powers of your own – they don't even have to be psychic – to deflect his powers, would you use them?

The practitioner analogue-marks the embedded command, "you have real powers of your own … to deflect his powers … use them".

(Uncertainly) Uh … well, I wouldn't want to hurt him, even now. That's not the kind of person I am … .

Oh, I'm not suggesting that for a moment. But, if there were a way for you to set things up so that if he or anyone else did anything that wasn't in your best interests, you wouldn't be responsible for what happened to them, would you? I mean, if I throw a ball too hard against the wall and it bounces back and hits me in the ribs, is that the wall's fault?

The practitioner paces the patient's concern, and then reframes it to return the responsibility for any actions to the 'originator'. This is reinforced by the ball metaphor. Note, too, the faintly confusing 'hypnotic' language.

(Laughs). That's an idea. Like a shield. It'd need to be really tough … .

The patient begins to assemble and solidify information suggested subliminally (at no point do we say, "Do this" or "Do that", to avoid symmetrical argument and the "yes but" response). By processing unconsciously and then formulating a solution, the patient is 'taking ownership' of her own response.

It would.	
Like a really strong mirror … .	
Made out of?	
Steel maybe, only light enough not to bother me as I move about … .	A practical solution: armour that is strong but portable.
Steel, light. That's right. So, if you could set that up and kind of forget about it, knowing it would continue protecting you, would that be something worth having? And then you can forget the whole thing?	The practitioner anchors the qualities and also presupposes that, by taking the proposed actions, the patient can then safely forget (note the embedded command) about consciously responding to a perceived threat.
For sure!	Strong concordance.
And then the problem you've been having isn't your problem any more. So, when that happened, how would you be feeling and acting differently and better now?	Note the temporal shifts in the practitioner's language. The problem is expressed in the past tense and the solution (acting differently and better) is presupposed to already exist in the present ("now"). The question also prompts the patient into a transderivational search to provide subjective meaning to the "artfully vague" words "feel", "differently" and "better". This is intended to increase the patient's adherence.
Great. I could just – live my life and enjoy it.	

And what's interesting to me is that you would be a more assertive person. You're standing up for yourself. In a strange kind of way, he might just have helped you to get something you wanted – except he was going about it the wrong way, and now you've done it for yourself … .	Embedded commands, reframing, and 'handing over' responsibility for change to the patient.
(Laughs, nods)	
So, let's just go through it and make sure it fits. Close your eyes and think about what your shield, your protective mirror, would be like … .	Begins to coach the patient into adopting her new strategy.

Thus, in Medical NLP, we move, invited, through the patient's territory, with respect for (but not necessarily collusion with) his world-view. The changes we help him make accord with and expand his map of reality. Then, when the patient takes ownership of the change, we withdraw. There is no room for "therapist's ego". *The patient always comes first.*

EXERCISES

1. Select three symptoms a patient might bring to a consultation (e.g., "My mind races so much at night I can't get to sleep") and write out ways you can:
   - normalise the experience within the context of the patient's life;
   - find a utilisation for it; and,
   - reframe it – first by content, then by context.
2. Become alert to narratives and symptoms that suggest 'disordered' thinking. Each time you encounter an example, pretend you are the patient and seek out the possible (not necessarily the actual) logic that would need to make the details "hold water". Write down your explanations.
3. Regard everything the patient says as 'true', then ask yourself the questions:
   - How could this appear true?
   - What could this be true of?

13

Getting to Where You Want to Go: directions, outcomes and goals

Imagine turning up at the airport booking desk and asking the clerk for a ticket.

"Where would you like to go?" he asks.

"On holiday," you reply.

"Yes, I understand … but, where?"

You shrug. "Just … you know … somewhere that's not here."

A look of exasperation flashes across his face, but he quickly regains his composure. "Well, yes, of course. But, where exactly is not here?"

You glance at your watch; your holiday time is ticking away. You lean across the desk and speak in measured tones. "You're a travel agent, aren't you? Well, I want to travel. Give me a ticket, and give it to me *now*!"

Logic and common sense tell us that if we don't know where we're going, we're likely to get nowhere fast. Few people would even consider embarking on a long-awaited vacation without spending some considerable time and effort deciding on a destination. And, when we get to where we want to go … what then?

A consultation without established outcomes is analogous to trying to buy a ticket from a travel agent without knowing where you want to go. Despite the United Kingdom's description of the doctor as a "health navigator", remarkably little outcome-orientation occurs, either in medical training or in official proclamations regarding health "delivery". The word "outcome" is starting to appear on forms and discharge summaries from various clinics, but this is usually a summary of the end-point of the consultation. And, patients and health professionals alike assume that the end-point should be either an absence or a continued 'management' of the condition.

This is not altogether surprising. Two factors influence this thinking style: Western society's overall problem-orientation (relationships, work and health are all considered to progress as a result of removing or solving problems), and our lack of practice in identifying what we *do* want, in place of the problem we presently have. Test this for yourself.

> Think of an ongoing problem or shortfall in your life. Ask yourself what your preferred state would be.

Chances are, you answered either in terms of an *absence* of the problem ("less stress at work"), with a nominalised (reified) goal, or a lack of specificity ("more recognition for my efforts"). Both classes of response reflect a problem- or deficit-oriented thinking style. For several reasons, attempts to rectify the situation without having alternatives to move forwards will almost inevitably lead to further problems.

The most significant of these is that 'success' can only be measured in terms of the problem itself. This shifts our attention back on to the problem or deficit, and runs the risk of reactivating the very psychophysical patterns we are trying to resolve*. Equally, if problems (especially behaviour patterns) are removed without replacing them with more resourceful alternatives, new patterns may emerge to fill the 'neuronal gap'. This is especially evident with purely behavioural approaches to Obsessive Compulsive Disorder, in which new obsessions and compulsions often replace the old.

Why plan?

A solution-oriented approach that truly combines the resources and expertise of both practitioner and patient requires thought, planning and application.

* We are reminded here of a patient diagnosed as schizophrenic who complained that the more he tried to ignore or challenge his "voices", as suggested by a cognitive therapist, the more strident and disruptive they became. We suggested that he try to ignore the "quiet times" between the voices, which he later reported, was "incredibly difficult". Anyway, he added, he wasn't going to bother because the voices had "gone away".

Although health care in the West is said to be "patient-centred", many patients still expect health professionals to take most of the responsibility for managing their treatment. Patient-centredness, as developed out of the University of Western Ontario "Disease-Illness Model", sought to redress the overwhelmingly "doctor-centred" approach that preceded it. Echoing the "customer is always right" retail model, it encouraged patients to be proactive and involved in important decisions regarding their health care[136].

In practice, though, this "transformed clinical method" overlooks the fact that patients are often reluctant to make suggestions and may be unaware of what is required of them. The health professional, nevertheless, remains legally liable in the event of misadventure. Our contention is that this 'patient passivity' occurs mainly because no clear outcomes have been negotiated.

The Medical NLP model contrasts with most existing models currently presented in education and practice. Few make reference to "outcome", except in terms of adherence to treatment programmes, in seeking to understand the reason for the patient's attendance or to answer questions, such as, "What further help can I receive?"

What is singularly lacking in these models are tools for formulating, as a partnership, well-formed, practical, measurable, *continuing* outcomes. In other words: *How does the patient get, and stay, better*?

Medical NLP seeks to develop directions, outcomes and goals that answer questions central to the patient's well-being, such as: *Can I get better? Will I get better? How can I get better?* and *How will I know I'm getting better?* In sum, we need to answer the question posed earlier in this book: *What does this person need to live a fuller, happier and healthier life?* And then we work in partnership to meet those needs.

The requirements of effective outcomes

In order to negotiate effective outcomes, a number of requirements need to be met. The most important is to distinguish between "direction", "outcome" and "goals".

Direction may be thought of as essentially solution-oriented. As discussed in Chapter 10, we regard the patient as bringing with him previously untapped resources, including the innate biological drive towards allostasis, previous successes, and a desire to be well.

The practitioner needs to keep this in mind to avoid encouraging passivity in the patient. It is important, too, to recognise that, once the general direction towards healing and health has been established, the patient may elect to follow an equally productive path that the practitioner had not foreseen. This should be recognised and respected, even though it might not fit accepted wisdom or belief.

Example of direction: *Following a specifically defined healthy lifestyle.*

Outcome broadly corresponds with clinical effectiveness. Quite simply, has the treatment been a success *from the patient's point of view?* Outcome should not be confused with the kind of measurement imposed by medical economists, politicians or insurance assessors. Patient satisfaction as measured by reduced waiting times is not to be equated with patient satisfaction with the outcome of treatment.

Example of outcome: *Enjoying the (specified) benefits of a healthier lifestyle.*

Goals, often confused with outcomes and solutions, are measurable markers of progress. This is a business model that is useful to measure incremental change, but, in the absence of overall direction and/or outcome, however, an overemphasis on goals at the expense of direction and outcome can limit the ongoing process of healing and health.

Example of goal: *Reducing weight by 1.5 kg a week, exercising three times a week, etc.*

For simplicity's sake, we will, from now on, refer to "outcome" to mean the synthesis of direction, outcome and goal, unless we specify otherwise.

In the Medical NLP model, the practitioner acts as a guide, teacher and mentor to the patient, as well as a companion on the healing journey. Our criteria for well-formed outcomes are not intended to be dogmatically applied, but merely to provide a kind of checklist so the practitioner can help the patient keep his outcomes within the bounds of possibility or reason.

Obstacles to effective outcome-planning

Effective outcomes require careful thought. The patient (and, it must be admitted, the practitioner) can often inadvertently limit the possibilities for change by committing to ill-defined outcomes:

- **The problem is too narrowly defined** ("Your serotonin levels are low. That's why you're depressed.")
- **The problem is too broadly defined** ("If in the past month you have felt down, depressed or hopeless, and have been bothered by having little interest or pleasure in doing things, then you are suffering from depression."*)
- **The solution is too narrowly defined** ("You need to take medication to correct the serotonin deficiency.")
- **The solution is too broadly defined** ("You need to get out more. Don't sit around worrying so much.")
- **The outcome is premature.** Although it is important that the patient is introduced to solution-orientation as early as possible in the consultation process, an outcome that is fixed too early will limit options that may emerge during the rest of the consultation process.
- **Favouring a familiar or 'established' approach to the problem, or intuitively acting on subjective bias.** If an outcome occurs very early on in the consultation, it needs to be closely examined.
- **Talking without purpose.** While "talking it through" may be helpful to some people, especially those who have little social support, it should not be confused with developing solutions.

* This "two-question test", recommended by Britain's National Institute for Health and Clinical Excellence (NICE), is under attack at the time of writing as resulting in a considerable overdiagnosis of "depression". Note that the two questions focus on text at the expense of context (for example, the loss of a love one, redundancy, etc).

Finding yourselves "going round in circles" is often the result of an overemphasis on 'story' or content.

- **Getting caught up in content at the cost of process.** Remember to be cautious of answers to the question "Why?"; the risk of triggering a torrent of speculation is high. Instead, favour answers in response to questions asking, How? Where? When? With whom? How often? etc.

Now, go back to the problem you were thinking about a few moments ago, and ask yourself what you'd like instead.

Unless you are familiar with solution-oriented thinking, you might have experienced a kind of mental hiccough. We seldom think in terms of alternatives to 'not having' the problem state. And yet that question alone is sometimes all that is needed to open the patient up to proactively seeking resolution. (Asked this question on the phone, patients frequently arrive for their appointment with a solution already in mind.).

Return to your problem and begin redefining it positively – that is, in terms of a desired (or solution) state rather than as an absence of the unwanted state. Restore process to any nominalisations by turning abstract nouns into verbs. Identify which part of the problem is within your control, and focus your attention on exploring that.

Thus, "less stress at work" might become, "I would like to be able to relax and think clearly even when I have a lot to do", and, "more recognition for my efforts" might be reframed as, "I would like to measure my own achievements so that I know when I have done a specific job well".

The NLP change process is often presented as moving from a present or problem state to a desired state (the solution) through the application of appropriate resources. But even before we introduce those resources (*how* he will change), we need to ensure that the patient knows *where* he is going. He will also need to be able to see for himself *that* change is occurring. Not only does he need an expanded map, but he also benefits from new coordinates.

Measuring for change

Details of the problem-state will, of course, have emerged during the information-gathering stage of the consultation. Since part of our intention is to have the patient share responsibility for his healing and health, it is important that a system of measurement is in place, and that *the measurement is relevant to the patient*, rather than to the therapist or 'expert'.

Quantifying the patient's level of comfort

The simplest of these scaling devices is what in Medical NLP is known as the Subjective Measurement of Comfort Scale (SMCS). Unlike existing scales designed to measure the severity of a condition (often regarded as an 'objective' guideline to arrive at a diagnosis), the SMCS was designed to provide the patient with a means of focusing on progress, rather than pain.

Before any intervention begins (as early as the closing stages of the questioning phase of the consultation) ask the patient the following:

> *If your problem could be measured on a scale from one to 10, with one being most comfortable and 10 the least comfortable it's ever been, where would you put it right now?*

The wording is important. Notice especially that "pain" and "discomfort" are excluded. We are measuring *comfort.* Be sure the patient understands this, or self-measurement will be slewed.

Second, we do not give the patient the option of a zero point. This is to avoid a return to the pursuit of a state of no-symptom; we presuppose in the wording that there is enough comfort to make 1 a desirable goal, even though some of the problem is still present. This is intended to encourage coping behaviour.

Third, prompting the patient to reframe his condition in this slightly disorientating way (locating the degree of comfort rather than discomfort) begins the process of dissociation, a prerequisite of effective transformation. He starts to 'look at', rather than 'be in', his experience.

Make a note of the patient's SMCS level, and suggest the following,

So, when the level moves down from (whatever number is selected) to anything less, you'll know you're making progress, isn't that so?

The process of eliciting outcomes can begin as soon as the SMCS measurement has been completed.

Eliciting outcomes

Although the patient's outcome is important, the practitioner may need to help him edit it for well-formedness. Start by asking the following questions, or variations thereof:

After you've been able to find a way past the problem you've been having, what will be different or better? What will you be doing differently? How will you be thinking about yourself? What will other people notice about you?" etc.

Structure your questions to elicit responses expressed in all sensory modalities. In order to experience ourselves and our world differently, we need to see, hear, feel (and sometimes smell and taste) things differently. Prompt, if necessary, to fill in any gaps.

Note: At this stage, the patient might say simply, "I don't know…" Since he has probably never before been asked what he wants instead of what he *does not* want, he may simply not understand the question. In which case, clarify it (we find explaining that "the brain needs a direction to go in order to make changes" often helps). Another possibility is that the patient is worried about saying 'the wrong thing", or is suffering from simple performance anxiety.

In any event, do not back off. Simply utilise the patient's response and proceed as follows:

Of course you won't know exactly *what will be different and better yet. At this stage, we're just imagining how it could be better. Just make it up … ."*

Or jump-start the process by using a variation of the "Magic Wand Question" popularised by brief therapist Steve De Shazer[137]:

> *If tonight, while you're sleeping, someone waved a magic wand and you woke in the morning to find your problem had been resolved, how would things be better?*

Once the patient has expressed an outcome in all sensory modalities, check that the following criteria are met.

Positive, specific and active. As already mentioned, an outcome should be formulated in terms of what is wanted, not what is not wanted or, in the case of behaviours, a desired direction in which to move. The outcome should be detailed, without becoming overwhelming. Ensure that it is stated in the present tense.

The practitioner can assist in this process by exploring the patient's own model of health, as opposed to his model of disease. Patients with chronic or 'functional' conditions (as well as the professionals they consult) often focus on the latter, thereby depriving both parties of viable, salutogenic alternatives.

Realistic and achievable. This can be challenging to some health professionals, especially where conditions have been declared 'incurable' or 'terminal'. Our contention is that to install or reinforce the belief that a patient's condition is 'hopeless' could, in itself, be injurious. We simply do not know *with absolute certainty* that a given outcome will be the same for every patient, every time. However, we might need to adjust the outcome where instantaneous results are not achievable, or the patient has clearly unrealistic expectations.

Process-orientated. What does the patient need to do as a first step towards change? What specific actions and behaviours does he need to follow in order to maintain progress? It is especially useful here to restore all nominalisations to their verb (action) forms – even if you need to 'invent' new words to fill the need. Adding the suffix "-ing" is one way to accomplish this. "Cancer*ing*" suggests a greater possibility for change than does the noun "cancer". Restoring process suggests the condition is something that the patient (or the patient's body) is 'doing', rather than something he 'has', or that has him. It presupposes the possibility of change.

Within the patient's control. As far as possible, especially where behavioural changes are required, the locus of control should rest predominantly with the patient. It is especially important that any outcome dependent on someone else's behaviour or response ("I'll feel better when my wife stops nagging me") is re-negotiated. We often find it necessary to point out to the patient that, although we have no power to change other people, we *are* able to control our responses to them.

Positive intentions preserved. The purpose or intention of a condition should be thoroughly explored (see Chapter 11), and these should be preserved or met by the new response or behaviour. Occasionally, the need may be fairly straightforward. For example, one benefit of a state of elevated anxiety, low mood and poor motivation may simply be to allow the person to get some rest from the stress of overwork.

Deleted information restored. Missing information should be followed up or explored, as discussed in Chapter 5. Common responses include deletions such as, "They've tried everything and nothing helps". Consider who "they" are, what specifically they have tried, whether absolutely nothing has helped, or whether something might have helped, even if just a little.

Presuppositions explored. Consider the statement, "I've tried absolutely everything and it's just getting worse." The presupposition in "tried everything" is that there is indeed nothing at all left to try. The patient's complaining tone may indeed conceal the fear that his condition could end in disability or even death. Exploring presuppositions helps reveal undeclared reasons for seeking consultation.

Ecological. Outcomes should be tested for ecology to ensure they will have no negative impact on areas other than the specific context in which change is required. This includes the effect on immediate family members, associates and work, as well as in areas such as entitlement to state benefits, housing, access to carers, etc. For example, a patient with a past history of epilepsy who has been fit-free for 10 years may wish to stop all anticonvulsant medication. However, he also needs to consider the risk, however small, of losing his driving licence, which may, in turn, affect his employment.

Time-related. Certain interventions benefit from a specified time frame – for example, periodic targets for each stage of weight loss, number of minutes spent exercising, etc. Defining times and specifying "chunks" keeps outcomes well grounded and measurable.

Trouble-shooting outcome-planning

The importance of having well-formed outcomes cannot be overestimated. The following suggestions are offered to overcome any problems you might encounter.

- **Performance anxiety.** The phrase, "Just before we begin …" is a useful linguistic device to depotentiate your patient's fear about doing things 'right'. Others that can take the pressure off include, "I just need a little information, first …" and "Let's try a little experiment …"
- **Speculation vs. certainty.** Patients may be disinclined to commit themselves to an opinion with any certainty. You can circumvent this by inviting speculation. Ask questions such as, "If you did know (X), what would that be like?" or, "If you were to take a guess, what would that be …?"
- **Identifying obstructions to progress.** "If you could think of one thing that stops you from (Y), what would that be?" Any answer to this question can offer additional information useful in developing strategies and intervention. For example, "I'm afraid of falling" (as opposed to "I can't walk properly") can direct treatment to resolving fear, rather than focusing entirely on any physiological problems related to walking.

Acclimatising to the new outcome

Once a well-formed outcome has been successfully negotiated, the patient will need to acclimatise to the changes involved. The purpose is to create a new neural network to facilitate transition from the problem state. (In certain circumstances, clarifying outcomes alone may precipitate change, even though the process is not intended to be transformational in itself.)

Apply the following process to your own redefined outcome:

1. Run through an entire day in your imagination from a dissociated perspective, watching yourself from the moment of waking to going to sleep at night, with the new outcome in place. Do this vividly, engaging all sensory modalities except the kinesthetic. 'Edit' the scenario, if necessary, to correct any problems or deficiencies.
2. When the scenario has been optimised, associate into the scene, ensuring that you see, hear *and* now feel all aspects

of the new behaviour or response 'as if' it were actually happening.
3. Repeat this several times until you find the process running comfortably and easily.

This method, important in effective change work, is further explored in Chapter 18.

EXERCISES

1. Write out an outcome of your own, and then refer to the conditions of well-formedness referred to on pages 177–180. Rewrite any sections that need editing.
2. Review any lifestyle plans you may offer to patients to ensure they meet all the conditions of well-formedness.
3. Listen carefully to plans expressed by patients, friends or family and (mentally) test for well-formedness. If there are any violations, suggest how these might be corrected.

14

Thinking in Time: temporal language, permanent change

Presumably, you eat. So, think about the last meal you had. Did you enjoy it? Did you linger over each mouthful in full appreciation? Or perhaps it was a sandwich, grabbed at your desk?

Now, think of the meal you ate before the last one. And, the one before that … . And, here's the question:

> *How do you tell the difference between your last meal and the ones before?*

Take a minute to think about this. Compare the two memories. Notice the distinctions between the two. Check the submodalities, first of one, then of the other – then together. Here's a guess. The two representations are in different positions in your internal field. One is probably smaller and less distinct than the other. One may even be still, like a slide or photograph, the other moving, like a movie or video.

Now, to challenge yourself, think ahead to your next meal. Decide what you'd like to be eating, where you'll be, who your dining companions will be. More differences.

And, whatever they are, there *are* differences. If there were none, you would have no way of making the kinds of distinction that allow you to separate your life into the categories we call past, present and future. Without those distinctions, your internal and external life would descend into chaos. Quite literally, you would not know whether you were coming or going.

On a day-to-day basis, most of us have a kind of consensual agreement about 'time'. We agree that everything before today happened in the 'past'. Where we are now (roughly) is the 'present'. Later today, tomorrow and everything after that is in the 'future'.

We also agree, more or less, when we are 'on time', or not. But after that, things start to become somewhat less clear. Some of us have 'time on our side'; others are always 'running out of time'. We try to get our kids to calm down during exams, reassuring them that they have 'plenty of time' in which to answer the questions. On the other hand, we tell each other how there 'just don't seem to be enough hours in the day', or how that patient who wanted to talk about his family concerns was 'wasting' too much of our precious time. And of course, as we get older, time starts to 'go by' more quickly each year.

Time seems to be something that 'happens to' us – and it happens very differently, according to the situation we are in at the time. Remember, for example, how slowly times passes when you are standing at a bus stop on a rainy day without an umbrella, or how quickly it whizzes by when you are having fun.

Equally important is the distinctive way in which each of us codes time and its passage. This determines not only whether we seem to have enough or too little, but whether the past or the future directs our subjective experience more than the present moment.

Most of us run into trouble over the issue of time because we fail to notice that it is a nominalised word, suggesting a commodity, rather than a process. Time, we are saying, is not a 'thing'. We have subjective ways of measuring movement from one place or event to another; we have clocks and watches and an awareness of the cycles of day and night and the seasons. But the 'passage' of time – as Albert Einstein upset the scientific world by demonstrating – does not exist in the way we think it does.

The framework of time

Happily, when things are going smoothly, we can continue along our daily lives without too much concern about the 'reality' of time. But when they are not, we can benefit ourselves and our patients by recognising that, as physicist Sir James Jeans puts it, the "framework" of time in which we place our experience is personal to individuals or small groups"[138].

The 'personal framework' of time, as experienced by the patient, is the focus of this chapter. Should you repeat the experiment at the start of the chapter with a friend or colleague, you will almost certainly find that the way in which he distinguishes between his last meal and the one before that differs in some degree from your own.

Patients experience and respond to their chronic condition in a number of different ways: in terms of the anxiety it produces; the extent of the effect it has on their lives; the meaning attributed to the condition; the implications for the quality of their future existence, etc. And one of the most prevailing influences concerns time – how long the condition has existed, the duration of an 'attack', when they can anticipate some respite or, in the case of conditions said to be 'terminal', how long they have 'got'.

In fact, enormous semantic confusion surrounds our sense of time. Einstein and the New Physics showed us that all knowledge about 'reality' begins and ends with experience. Experience, in turn, is dependent on our senses. Certainty begins to dissolve before our eyes (and our ears and feelings) when we start to recognise that how, where and when we apply our attention can affect that quality of our experience. Quite literally, then, we are 'making time'.

The 'meaning' of time

Our attitude to the passage of time is a quality of our relationship with both our internal processes and the world outside. As mentioned above, the experience of waiting for a bus in the rain is likely to be not only 'dragged out', but also unpleasant. "Type A" people are characterised by an exaggerated sense of urgency. Both their internal 'sense' of the passage of time and their behaviour appear restless and 'driven'[139]. Conversely, athletes, artists, musicians, meditators and martial artists are among a group of people who regularly experience something widely known as "flow" – a highly pleasurable, timeless state in which activity seems to happen without effort or intention[140].

The subjective experience of time is a black hole in medical science. Aside from the number of days a patient will occupy a hospital bed, or how long the patient himself will have to endure his pain, time simply does not enter the clinical picture. This is a major omission. How we perceive time can kill or cure.

The birth of time as we know it

Not that far back in our collective history, our attitude to time was different. We lived according to natural cycles – the rising and setting of the sun, the changing of the seasons. Fine measurement was a crude affair. We have used dripping water, trickling sand, knots on a string and marks on a burning taper. But these units of measurement were arbitrary. An hour or a minute or a second simply did not exist as such. Most of us got up as soon as the sun rose and went to bed when it set, until two inventions changed all that. And, in changing the way we marked the unfolding of events, we changed our lives.

Dutch scientist Christiaan Huygens's pendulum clock brought sequential, rather than cyclical, time to our immediate attention[141]. This was followed by the invention of the electric light, and, suddenly, we were no longer bound by the rhythms of nature – so work, usually for the poorer classes, could extend deep into the night. And while the material benefits were far-reaching (for those who 'controlled' time and the means of buying it from others), for most of us, the separation from nature was profound.

Problems with linear time

As a chronocentric (centred on time) society, we have lost our sensitivity to the cycles in nature and to those of our own bodies. We eat, drink, make love, have children, sleep, wake, work and retire according to the linear measurement of time, instead of when we are hungry, thirsty, horny, paternal, tired, feel rested, or, are ready to slow down. Most of us live and die in the thrall of linear time without ever realising that it does not really exist. Everything we do (in our Western culture) is based on multiples of something arbitrarily called a 'second' – in fact, nothing more than 9,192,631,770 cycles of the frequency associated with the shift between two energy levels of the isotope caesium 133[142]. This is the nearest we can get to a 'thing' called Time.

Here's a little experiment about how the myth of linear time runs your life:

> Using a watch or clock with a second hand, close your eyes as it points to the 12 o'clock mark. Now, mentally review what you have to do today – then open your eyes when you 'feel' one minute has past.

Supposing you didn't cheat by counting off the seconds, how accurate was your estimation? Was your guess less or more than one minute? If it was markedly less than a minute, you are likely to feel tense, 'rushed', as if 'there is never enough time'. If it was markedly more, you are likely to be feeling calm, relaxed, laid back – or bored – with the experiment.

> Now ... what was your emotional response when you interpreted your particular estimate?

Interestingly, most people are vaguely unsettled by either response: the first because of their underlying sense of hurry, the second because, somehow, they are 'wasting' time.

The toxicity of time

So profoundly influential is the experience of linear time on the health and well-being of both patient and practitioner that we have felt compelled to create a word – "Chronopathic" – to describe the disorders in which the perception and experience of time plays a significant part. To that we have added "hyperchronic" (the sense of time passing too quickly) and "hypochronic" (time dragging) to describe the experiences and responses of those suffering from chronopathic disorders.

At the top of all the surveys of *doctor* dissatisfaction we have reviewed from both the United Kingdom and the United States is lack of time. At the top of all the surveys of *patient* dissatisfaction we have reviewed from both countries is … lack of time. It is saddening that the very interaction intended as a healing encounter should be marked by one of the disorders it should be seeking to resolve. In earlier chapters, we discussed stress and allostatic load as underlying factors in all chronic conditions. Here, we contend that the subjective perception of time can be one of the most important contributors to allostatic load.

The 'toxic' effects of time-perception are not entirely restricted to feeling its lack. The 'passage' of time is experienced in different ways, each with its own impact on the individual. But the most prevalent, and arguably the greatest, risk factor is the feeling of having too much to do with too little time in which to do it. Hyperchronicity is virtually unrecognised as pathological in Western medicine, except perhaps as an element in the catch-all diagnosis of "stress". Medicine's response to this is limited: take time off, reduce your commitments, or, take the pills.

Time-poor patients, once described as suffering from "hurry sickness", are vulnerable to a wide range of illnesses[143]. These include abnormal heart rate and blood pressure, elevation of blood hormones, including adrenalin, insulin, norepinephrine and hydrocortisone, increased gastric acid and insulin production, breathing disorders, sweating and musculoskeletal pain. Patients suffering from hyperchronicity are particularly susceptible to cardiovascular disease, type II diabetes and metabolic syndrome.

As may be expected, hyperchronicity affects high achievers driven by goals, deadlines and targets – all characteristics of what economists call "turbo-capitalism". A short time ago, this was considered to be essentially a male response, but an increasing number of women are reported to be presenting with similar life and work patterns – and the consequences thereof.

To our knowledge, only one country in the world has officially recognised the consequences of time poverty and turbo-capitalism on the individual. Japanese researchers have made a positive connection between a model known as "lean production", purported to improve economic productivity, and sudden death from cardiovascular and cerebrovascular disease. These types of death, known as *karoshi*, are said to be caused by increased workload, shift work and abnormal demands on the worker's time[144].

But 'too little time' is also a health factor for patients lower on the socioeconomic scale, especially unemployed single mothers. Hurry sickness is not simply the price you pay for being rich.

Time and chronic disorders

The patient's *felt sense* of time will usually differ from his experience of its *duration*. The felt sense is often one of constriction. As we have said elsewhere, feelings of discomfort are usually constricted, localised and intense. Duration – in chronic disorders – is expanded; the problem seems to stretch endlessly across 'space'.

Time distortion is a characteristic of altered states, and illness is, by definition, a state that differs from the patient's default 'normal' state. Depending on the condition, the degree of discomfort is related to the degree of attention being paid to both felt sense and duration, and to how and where on the continuum of his personal model of time the patient places the 'cause' of the problem.

The former (focusing on the problem) is a well-known amplifier of the experience of pain. Conversely, when our attention is diverted (for example, while playing a sport we enjoy), we may not even notice an injury when it occurs. The second form of coding – in which the patient places the cause of his problem in his 'past' or 'future' – is always a factor in conditions such as depressive or anxiety disorders. 'Panic attacks' recur wherever the patient, consciously or unconsciously, runs an internal representation of a past event happening some time in the future. Reactive depression is always a response to an event (real or imaginary) in the past.

Likewise, Post-Traumatic Stress Disorder and phobias are present-time responses to earlier, sensitising events. However, as Viktor Frankl pointed out, since two people experiencing the same 'objective' experience may have entirely different reactions and interpretations, it is evident that it is less what happened in the past that causes present-time problems, but the way in which we are responding to it. The past (or the future) is experienced 'as if' it is happening now – and our physiology responds 'as if' it is real.

A number of other conditions can affect our experience of the passage of time, including age (a sense of time ranges from undifferentiated at birth, through various phases until around the age of 16, when the 'existence' of linear time is established[145]); socioeconomic status (an extended sense of time is more prevalent among middle-class children[145]); and, even body temperature[145]. Certain drugs, both prescription and recreational, ranging from thyroxine and caffeine, through cocaine to cannabis and amphetamines, directly affect the experience of time[145].

Time, healing and health

Paradoxically, the experience of time changes when we learn to pay attention to specific symptoms or sensations 'as they are', in the present moment, without judgement or expectation (awareness at the more fluid, wordless Object level). The 'felt sense' of time expands, while duration contracts.

It is our belief that many systems, such as some forms of meditation; yoga; T'ai chi; hypnosis; certain breathing techniques; reorganising the patient's model of time (see below); and, some of the Medical NLP techniques we will discuss further in Chapters 17 and 18 and Appendix A, affect therapeutic change by reversing the constricted sense of time, and activating the mechanism that counter-balances the fight-or-flight response. This "Relaxation Response", as it has been named by Herbert Benson[146], seems to transcend linear time.

NLP and the time line

One of NLP's many major contributions to applied psychology is the observation that, just as people have individual sensory preferences, they also have unique ways of coding their experience of time.

As the example at the start of the chapter showed, we make and store distinctions between experiences that occurred in the past, are occurring in the present and may occur in the future. We also organise these experiences sequentially, characteristic of our culture's tendency to represent events spatially. That is, when we think of the meal we ate two days ago, it will tend to be placed in our internal landscape 'as if' it occupies an actual position different from where we placed the meal we had yesterday. This became known as a "time line" – a personal construct or 'map' of experiences in time-space.

Most NLP books and courses have a fairly lengthy method of 'connecting' similar experiences in order to reveal each person's construct. We consider the following method easier for most people to understand and to use in some of the ways we will discuss later. Here is the kind of suggestion we offer to patients:

> *Imagine your life, from birth until now, represented by a road, a pathway or a stream, with the earliest part – the time of your birth – furthest away, and the most recent part, the present, nearest to you. There's no right or wrong way to do this, so just point to let me know where in your imagination that road or path or stream appears to begin.* (The patient points.) *Thank you. Now, where is the present?* (The patient indicates the present.) *Thank you. Now … if the future were also a road or path or stream, how would that run?* (The patient points.) *Thank you.*

We consider it important to add the following as part of the set-up for later change work:

> *Of course, this is not a real thing. It's just the way the brain makes a map of how we use time. But sometimes the brain tends to act as if the map is real. And if it isn't detailed enough or doesn't suit our purposes, we might need to change it. Does that make sense?* (Make sure you have the patient's understanding and agreement before proceeding.)

Note: Before we proceed, we suggest you elicit your own time line for future use.

Time line variations

Almost as many different permutations of time lines exist as there are people. Some may place the past behind them, others to one side. Yet other people perceive the past in front of them, or encircling them, or as extremely short or even non-existent. Likewise, the future may be curved, sloping, wide, narrow, short, long, or, invisible. Two points should be borne in mind here:

1. The patient's organisation of his time line has subjective relevance (even though it may be outside his conscious awareness).
2. Whatever other characteristics might be revealed, he will be either associated into his time line (it seems to pass through his body) or dissociated from it (the time line passes from past to future separated by a distance from his body).

Cultural variations

Some writers suggest that different cultures have distinctive ways of coding time, and experiences show that this may be true – up to a point. Certainly, many people claim to detect (and sometimes suffer at the hands of) cultural time-keeping that differs significantly from their own. But, in practice, our own experience has been that where health problems exist, we can proceed using the same approach with patients from other cultures as we do within our own.

The time line as a diagnostic tool

In Medical NLP, the first application of the time line is as a diagnostic tool. Table 14.1 shows some observations made by ourselves and other practitioners.

The patterns are just some of the many possibilities you may encounter. In using the time-coding diagnostically:

1. Accept it as if it were a 'real thing', and ask yourself what effect this could have. (For example, if the past – particularly a traumatic past – were running continuously as a kind of internal movie in front of a subject, he would almost certainly be considerably disabled by the subliminal memories, or would 'keep running into' the same kind of experience.)
2. Always check with the patient. As an example, we suggest asking, "Now, if time were really running past without touching you, how much would you feel in control over your life? How would it be to step back into your own life?"

Table 14.1 Time line observations

Orientation	*Effect*
1. The time line is markedly separate from the patient's body	Time is "passing me by"; "things are out of reach"; "no control" over events
2. The past is directly in front of the patient	Extremely common in behavioural patterns that keep repeating; where the patient is adversely affected by, or reminded of, the past (including abuse and other traumatic experiences), or keeps "making the same mistake"
3. The future is behind the patient	Characterised by disorganisation; inability to plan; feelings of "hopelessness"; literally "no future" or confusion, when asked about anything beyond the present time
4. Extremely short or non-existent future	Often encountered in patients with a diagnosis, or fear, of terminal disease
5. Both the past and the future are in front of the patient	Sometimes associated with confusion between the past and future. (Patterns 3 and 6 are often seen in patients who have anxiety disorders arising from past traumas – that is, "since it happened in the past, it's going to happen in the future")
6. The time line runs from left to right in front of the patient	A frequently encountered arrangement (possibly related to hemispheric organisation and reading Western languages from left to right). Good for planning and organisation, but sometimes associated with a sense of detachment
7. The past or future is steeply inclined	The past or future has been or will be a tough climb
8. The time line encircles the patient	Often accompanied by feelings of being "trapped" and "running to stay in the same place"
9. The past is directly behind the patient's head	Amnesia; inability to "look back" at the past; failure to "learn from past mistakes"

The language of time

The patient's linguistic patterns

Pay special attention to the patient's temporal language. Note phrases such as, "I'm always putting things off" (suggesting that the patient's goals are not physically positioned on or in his representation of the future); "Time is passing me by" (suggesting dissociation); "I can't see a way forward" (the future is obscured); "I can't stay on track" (direction needs clarification); "I'm always short of time" (a truncated future); etc. These will provide you with clues as to how to proceed once the patient's time line has been reorganised.

The practitioner's linguistic patterns

Since we all process verb tenses differently (distinctions between different time frames being necessary in order to extract meaning from the communication), the Medical NLP practitioner uses temporal language to support a recoding of the patient's perception of his problem. A general rule is as follows:

- Draw resources from the future ("When you have found you are feeling better…");
- Place the problem in the past ("…and the problem you've been having has been sorted out …"); and,
- Anchor the solution-state in the present ("…what specifically do you find is different and better … now?").

Note: Use the Past Continuous Tense ("the problem you were having") rather than the Past Tense ("the problem you had") to avoid mismatching the patient and thereby risk losing engagement.

Reorganising the time line

We have two purposes in reorganising the time line when it seems to be dysfunctionally arranged – to provide a new, subjectively more appropriate or useful, frame for the patient's experience, and to access resources and make changes at different perceived times in the patient's life. Sometimes a simple reordering is enough to produce generative change, for example moving the past behind the patient, and opening up the future in front of him. We may speculate that 'experiencing' the past as 'behind' him changes his processing mode from a 'present, all-pervasive' problem to 'something that happened and is now over'.

A strong element of creativity and experimentation is necessary on the part of the practitioner, especially where complex and unusual configurations are encountered. We recall one patient (a fellow practitioner suffering from 'burnout') who visualised her future time line as "like a huge funnel, sloping down towards me, with massive amounts of 'stuff' pouring down at me like an avalanche". She described feeling "absolutely engulfed by everything"*. Rearrangement required several steps – including reversing the flow of tasks yet to be tackled so they moved away from, and not towards, her – and considerable experimentation before she began to regain a sense of control.

Changes are always made with the consent and cooperation of the patient. "Let's try something …" is a more respectful and productive approach than "Do this!" Some patients experience a strong kinesthetic when rearranging a time line; if this fails to settle down, rearrange it until it feels comfortable.

An individual's time line should be presented as neither right nor wrong, but simply as useful or not useful. Among the many possibilities available, we regard the arrangement shown in Figure 14.1 as the most compatible with both remedial and generative change.

Tips for reorganising the time line

All instructions may be prefaced by suggestions such as, "I want you to imagine you can actually take hold of the very start of your time line and begin to swing it around…", etc. Add the reassurance, "All your experiences, learnings and memories will stay in their proper sequence, as we …" etc.

* No surprise there, then.

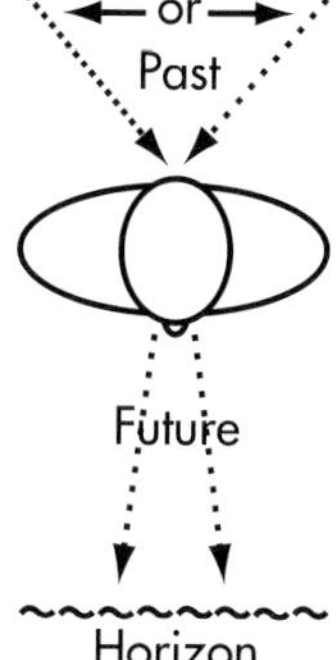

Fig 14.1 Time line arrangement (seen from above). The past time line now runs diagonally from behind towards the patient's head, either from the left or the right (depending on his preference), while the future is directly in front, opening up and extending over his imaginary horizon.

1. Reassociate the time line into the patient (if dissociated), metaphorically placing him back 'in' his own life (have him pull the time line towards him until it "clicks into place");
2. Have the patient swing the beginning of the past around until it runs diagonally towards either his left or right shoulder. A useful suggestion is, "You know how those people who somehow just bounce back from problems always say, 'Just put it behind you and move on'? Well, this is your chance to put it behind you – but if you need to look back at the past, it's there…";
3. Arrange the future running directly out in front of him, encouraging him to extend it out "over the horizon" ("This suggests a long life with lots of time still ahead");
4. Have the patient widen out the future time line ("So you have lots of room to put all your options, choices, opportunities", etc); then,
5. Throw the entire future time line into bright sunlight ("People sometimes talk about having 'a bright future'. Make it as bright as that …").

The final step in this process is to place the internal representation the patient made of his direction, outcome or goal on the future time line, "just a few steps in front of where you are now". Suggest, "This is the direction in which you want to move. Make sure it's bright and compelling –

something that really pulls you into it – and, we'll come back to it a little later."

Now, summarise for the patient:

> *So, what you've done here is to put everything that's happened behind you in the past so you can start to let it go. Of course, you can look back at it, if you need to, but it won't be distracting you* ("in your face"; "on top of you"; or any other metaphoric description the patient has given about his problem-state) *any more. And it's good to know that whatever has happened has already happened and is over with, and where you are now is in the present, with a very long, wide and bright future pulling you into it … isn't it?"*

The purpose of eliciting and reorganising the patient's time line may be regarded as expanding his internal map of reality. Even if we choose to regard this simply as a metaphor, the presupposition that problem states began – and can potentially conclude – in the 'past', and that a 'different' future can be envisaged, is a more hopeful model than the fear-ridden one with which he has been operating: that the problem is present-tense, all-pervasive and likely to extend indefinitely into the future.

EXERCISES

Elicit your own time line and reorientate it as suggested in Figure 14.1 above. Notice how it feels.

1. Place a well-formed outcome that you created on to your time line, a little in front of you. Ensure that it is richly detailed in all sensory modalities.
2. Explore how your life would be different were you to be strongly drawn into this outcome. Use all your senses to create a full representation.
3. List all the resources you have and all those you would need in order to turn this outcome into your personal reality.

15

Medical NLP Algorithms for Change: steps to transformation

If you've come this far and are prepared to entertain the possibility that people have internal maps of reality that are different from your own, congratulations.

If you have come this far and feel it is possible to recognise that your own map may be neither better nor worse – just different – and are prepared to co-create a new cartography, you have broken through one of the most impermeable barriers we know. This is the one that separates 'right us' from 'wrong them', the attitude that drives the delusion of superiority characteristic of the worst excesses of scientism, religion and politics, but which, once breached, has the potential to change ourselves and the world around us in ways almost beyond comprehension.

For, as a species, we create maps, and then ally ourselves with those whose maps correspond most closely to our own[147]. Logic has little to do with it. Our willingness to act for those who comply, and to ostracise or punish those who do not, often depends on power granted by some external 'authority', whether it is those who pay us, those who control the statistics or those who promise us eternal life.

Our intention in this book is not to overturn a 'paradigm', discard scientific method or introduce yet another 'alternative' medicine. It is to suggest that we learn to relate to, and work with, the uniqueness of the individual in front of us, in terms of his model, and not just to impose our own. Contrary to some opinion, we do recommend following scientific method. We urge practitioners to work systematically: gathering data, forming a testable hypothesis, and then altering it, if necessary. The difference is that we apply it to each person who consults us rather than relying exclusively on the theology of statistical 'proof'.

In this chapter, we will introduce several algorithms (step-wise approaches) for change. These are not to be confused with recipes or prescriptions. They are intended to provide a framework within which you can explore more creative, big-picture, whole brain (heuristic) approaches.

If we are careful to avoid premature cognitive commitment, Medical NLP's synthesis of algorithmic and heuristic thinking (nothing more than using 'both sides' of the brain, text *and* context) can lead to creative and effective outcomes that match the patient's unique needs. This can only come from exploring and respecting the patient's map. Even some Neuro-Linguistic Programmers advocate or claim "acuity" when, in practice, they are prescriptively imposing techniques on to their subjects with little consideration for, or understanding of, the subjects' uniqueness.

The ability to think heuristically and algorithmically is similar to what Ellen Langer has called Mindfulness[148]. In incorporating this approach into your practice, we anticipate that you will find newer and, we hope, even better, ways of becoming "the difference that makes a difference".

In this chapter, we will broaden our understanding and application of several core principles of NLP in order to integrate them into Medical NLP's three algorithms for change.

1. The power of association and dissociation

The word "dissociation" – like all nominalisations – is apt to cause problems. To many psychiatrists, it is a symptom of an often severe personality disorder, a breakdown of another nominalisation, the 'ego boundary'. To hypnotherapists, it describes the characteristic trance phenomenon of 'watching myself' thinking or carrying out suggestions. To practitioners of NLP, it is a deliberately induced state of 'stepping out' of an experience or memory and observing oneself from a bystander's point of view (Perceptual Position 3), usually resulting in a reduction in the intensity of an experience.

We have noted earlier that the patient's attempt to 'separate from', to not-have, his problem serves to keep in place a self-perpetuating causal loop. Negation can be represented linguistically, but not to our essentially non-linguistic right cortex. The more we try to not-have a symptom, thought or experience, the more the symptom or behaviour persists (whatever you do right at this moment, *don't think of the colour blue*).

Since the patient's attempt at dissociation is unsuccessful, he is tacitly seeking the practitioner's collusion in exorcising his negative kinesthetics. And much biomedicine is organised in precisely this way: to attempt to remove, chemically or surgically, the 'bad' experience.

The belief that medicine can – and should – somehow provide freedom from the ups and downs of life is pervasive. Increasingly, disappointments, losses, frustrations, and, challenges present themselves for medical solutions, fuelled by the promises of "cures" and "breakthroughs" by the media and the pharmaceutical industry. This medicalisation of everyday living has given rise to what Frank Furedi has dubbed the "therapy culture", which routinely defines people facing challenges as "vulnerable", "at risk", "emotionally scarred" or "damaged"[149].

The purpose of incorporating the principles and techniques presented in this book into the consultation process is not to 'fix' or 'cure' those who are faced with non-acute and non-organic problems, but to help them develop new skills to cope and grow from their experience.

The cliché that draws a distinction between temporarily helping a starving man by giving him a fish, or permanently resourcing him by teaching him how to fish, is apposite here. The word "doctor" derives from the Latin verb *docere*, to teach. Teachers educate, and "education", in turn, originally meant "to lead out". Ideally, the process of 'healing', should, at least in part, involve helping the patient to access, develop and draw out his own resources in order to be able to respond to those challenges, physical and emotional, that are unique in his world.

In Chapter 13 and elsewhere, we have pointed out that Medical NLP aims for 'successful' dissociation as *a prerequisite of any substantive change work*, rather than an end in itself. In order for the patient to be able to recode or re-experience his condition, he needs to be guided into an observer-state, effectively removed from his condition, but nonetheless allowing it to be present, temporarily free of the constraints of past or future concerns. This is where, with the guidance of the practitioner, the structure of his problem can be reorganised. After that, he may be reassociated into the more desirable state.

The first Medical NLP algorithm for change, therefore, is:

Dissociate – Restructure – Reassociate

This means simply that the patient 'steps out' of his problem, the change is effected 'over there', and the changed state, with all its sensory experience, is brought back 'into his body'. Many 'bespoke' techniques can be created using this algorithm.

2. Anchoring revisited

Anchoring, you will recall, involves linking a trigger (visual, auditory and/or kinesthetic) with a specific response. Thus far, we have used it to stabilise certain resources, largely to help the patient develop a health- and solution-oriented attitude to his situation (see Chapter 10). We are assuming you have practised setting and firing anchors with both patients and yourself.

Anchors, however, have much wider applications – and, indeed, are central to many, if not all, successful Medical NLP techniques.

Simple anchors

Imagine the possibilities for healing that open up when you simply connect the start (or some aspect) of a problem-state with a more resourceful response. Richard Bandler has described anchoring the sensation of an ambulatory blood-pressure harness monitor against an anxious patient's chest to feelings of deep calm and relaxation (thus, turning a 'reminder' of the problem into its 'cure'), and linking the smell and sight of roses with feelings of massive pleasure to short-circuit an allergic response[150].

Method

First create a powerful resource-state by stacking anchors. Then identify the start of the problem-state (or a moment before, if possible) and link this trigger to the resource-state. Repeat until the new sequence replaces the old. If you teach the patient to develop, set and fire anchors, you will substantially help him deal with his specific problem, as well as providing him with a strategy that will increase his overall sense of self-efficacy.

> ***Case history:*** *A student who reported becoming anxious when giving presentations as part of her college course sought help after being diagnosed with 'anxiety' and being offered either Cognitive Behavioural Therapy or medication. From our point of view, this was a classic case of a diagnosis made on the basis of text to the exclusion of context. It emerged that she became anxious only at college, and not in front of other groups, suggesting long-term therapy or medication was excessive. Instead, a state of calm confidence was elicited and anchored. She became rapidly adept at firing her anchor and later reported that giving presentations had ceased to be a problem*.*

Collapsing anchors

Similar affective states may be stacked to create complex, intense anchors. Dissimilar anchors will "collapse", resulting in a neutral state, or one that favours the more powerful of the two. This process can be used to 'extinguish' unwanted responses caused by a wide range of stimuli.

Method

1. Start by creating a strong, 'positive', stacked anchor. Do this systematically. Elicit past, strongly positive, experiences, associate the patient into each, and anchor on the same place. Test

* Coincidentally, we have actually seen a training video for new doctors with exactly this scenario. The diagnosis and suggested treatment were the same as for the patient referred to above. At no point did the trainers suggest that doctors should ask whether the problem existed in any context other than college. Therefore, the generic diagnosis of 'anxiety' was made. This is an example of the "representative heuristic" – and the consequences thereof.

thoroughly for effectiveness. We highly recommend including 'the ability to cope' as a component of the stack. Change state.

2. Elicit the unwanted response and anchor it *in a different place on the body*. Test and change state.
3. Fire both anchors simultaneously and observe the patient's response. Usually, he will display signs of confusion or disorientation. Hold the anchors until these minimal cues subside.
4. Release the negative anchor *first*, and then the positive anchor.
5. Change state and test the patient's response to the original negative stimulus.

Case history: *The patient presented with anxiety and disturbed sleep, complaining that the problem had started when she moved to an apartment near a railway line. Although she said the sound of passing trains was "not too bad", she found herself lying awake, becoming increasingly agitated, expecting one to come past. A strong, positive anchor of calm and relaxation was set. The negative response was anchored, and then both anchors were collapsed. The patient was given the task of "willing" trains to come along for exactly three days, and was told not to go to sleep on each of those nights until five trains had passed. She reported on her second consultation that she had "failed" to complete the task since she kept falling asleep before the second or third train*.*

Since almost all Medical NLP techniques involve collapsing anchors (this is explained further in Chapter 18), either directly or indirectly, the second algorithm for Change is:

Establish a Positive Anchor – Identify Negative Anchor(s) – Design a Technique around Collapsing Anchors

3. Chunking

The third core skill involves chunking up for both purpose/intention and down for process or procedure (strategy). Both states, present and

* This intervention combined collapsed anchors with "prescribing the symptom", a paradoxical technique developed by Milton Erickson.

desired, need to be chunked in each direction in order to apply this algorithm. By doing so, and, with appropriate framing, the practitioner simultaneously assists the patient to meet the positive intention of his problem and to develop a more appropriate strategy to achieve his desired state (See Chapter 5).

Chunking up for purpose and intention

The example is of a patient who seeks help for "drinking too much". Traditionally, a practitioner might ask when, how much and even why the patient drinks. Two questions we regard as potentially useful are, *When did you start?* and, *What caused you to start?* Take note of the answers, since these questions place the origins of the problem behaviour within the patient's model of time (see Chapter 14).

Ensure that the patient understands the concept of positive intention. It is often enough to include this during the normalisation stage of the consultation. Most patients respond with relief when we explain that symptoms and behaviours function protectively, and often "want something more for you, including getting you to pay attention to some need that may not yet have been met".

We can add the suggestion that, if the need is ignored, symptoms or behaviours sometimes change or become more intense. This both normalises changes in the frequency or intensity of symptoms, and presupposes that the patient can take more responsibility for his own well-being.

Chunking up for positive intention involves a series of questions, all of which are variations of, "What does drinking do for you?" The answer given ("It helps relax me"; "It gives me confidence"; etc) is acknowledged, and then chunked again.

"And, when you have (the patient's reply), what else does that give you that's even more positive?"

The patient's response ("It makes it easier for me to cope", etc) is acknowledged, and the chunking continues.

"And, when you have (the patient's last reply), what else does that give you that's even more positive?"

The process continues, starting each of your responses with the phrase, "**And**, when you have …", until the patient arrives at his core value, which will be expressed as a nominalisation, often with transcendent or spiritual overtones: *peace, fulfilment, comfort,* etc. Almost inevitably, the core value will represent a protective intention. *This must always be respected and the need met by whatever intervention you choose to apply.*

The practitioner then asks the patient to recall or create an example of his core value, guiding him into a sensory-rich experience. Anchor the core value.

Chunking down for sequence or strategy

With the core value of the positive intention elicited and anchored, the practitioner begins to chunk in the opposite direction, in order to establish the sequence (strategy) the patient has been using in order to start and maintain his behaviour.

As explained earlier, strategies are most easily elicited by first observing the patient's description of the behaviour, noting especially the respective sequences of eye accessing cues and sensory modalities used. Prompt with variations of these questions, *What's the very last thing that happens before you* (response or behaviour)? *And what happens then? And what happens next?* etc. Continue until the entire strategy has been elicited.

Since a strong neural network already supports the strategy of the problem-state, the new strategy should be adapted to fit the existing sequence as closely as possible. For example, should the patient's problem strategy involve, say, $A^d > K^{i-} > V^i >$, it may be easier to design a new A > K > V strategy that results in a positive, rather than a negative, outcome. For example (using an actual transcript):

> Patient: *After work, I think: "You deserve to relax; you've worked hard." And then I remember what it feels like to be completely free of all my worries, and I see it like being like a space where no-one else can get at me; the drink is like a barrier all around me. The problem is I know this way is harming me …*
>
> Practitioner's response: *So, when you realise you need to take time out to relax because you've worked so hard and can take some time out in another way that's healthier, which allows you to see yourself in a space where, just for the time being, nobody else can get to you, would you be*

interested in experimenting with it? (This opens the way to exploring and testing alternative strategic routines: yoga, meditation, listening to music, etc).

However, ensure that any two-point loops (see Chapter 5) are taken into consideration, and, if necessary, resolved*.

Mapping across

With both the core value and the strategy of the problem-state identified, the objective now is to map both across to a desired state (Figure 15.1). The intention is to collapse two meta-anchors – the problem-state (PS), and, the desired state (DS). For that reason, the desired state must be detailed, desirable and very clearly identifiable to the patient before attempting the transition.

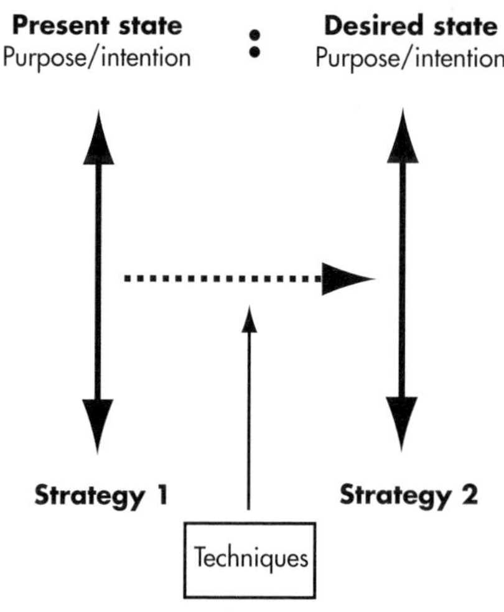

Fig 15.1 Mapping from problem-state (PS) to desired state (DS)

* A two-point loop may, of course, be a useful inclusion in a positive strategy. Richard Bandler's "the more … the more" pattern ("The more you start to worry about X, the more you remember you have the resources to cope") is an example of a linguistically installed positive two-point loop reinforcing a patient-centred locus of control.

Chunking, especially when identifying strategies, should be meticulous and detailed. It provides large amounts of information that can drive effective change. The third Medical NLP algorithm for change, therefore, is:

Chunk for Purpose/Intention and Strategy/Procedure

The patient's perspective

Not only is the patient the expert on how his condition manifests in his experience, but he also has intuitive resources regarding how well a proposed alternative to his problem-state will fit. This is where you should be particularly alert to his responses to your suggestions. To avoid failure and loss of confidence, it is important not to try to impose overt change without his understanding and complicity, and without fully meeting hitherto unmet needs.

Transition: creating acceptance

Once the purpose or intention of a problem has been established, it is often easiest to invite the patient's opinion on how to proceed.

Social psychologists (and salespeople) are aware that our commitment is often greater to our own opinions and decisions than to those suggested by others. (There are, however, exceptions to this 'rule'. Older patients and those particularly submissive to the practitioner's 'authority' may readily agree to your suggestions. We strongly recommend that you ensure the patient is fully congruent, whether he is making his own suggestions, or responding to yours.) Questions that may facilitate patient concordance include:

Now we understand your symptom (X) has really been wanting to protect you, how can we find a way that that protectiveness (X) can instead help you achieve your new outcome (Y)?

If you could have (positive intention Y) without having to have (symptom X), how interested would you be in doing that?

We know we need to do something differently if we want a different result. If we can find a different way to do things so that you had more of (negotiated outcome Z), would that be something you would want?

Once you are confident that you have the patient's full agreement, test for any suggestions or solutions that might spontaneously emerge:

> *That's good. Now, just before we begin* (allaying performance anxiety)*, if you could think of a way to do things differently, what would that be?*

Surprisingly, patients often volunteer a new strategy. If that occurs, consider it a gift, and proceed immediately to exploring the strategy for well-formedness. If it is semantically well formed and is likely to meet the elicited positive intention, proceed immediately to installing the strategy.

Installing a strategy

New strategies can be installed in several different ways. These include:

1. **Anchoring.** Elicit the steps in sequence. Anchor each in a different place on the body (the knuckles of one hand may be easiest and least invasive). Fire them repeatedly in sequence until the new strategy runs automatically when the trigger event or feeling is invoked.
2. **Role playing.** This involves practical rehearsal, with the practitioner taking the part of any 'significant other' in the patient's scenario.
3. **Mental rehearsal.** We explore this in greater detail in Chapter 18.
4. **Linguistically.** The 'language of influence' – informal hypnosis – is the subject of Chapter 16.

All four of these approaches may be employed during the same session. We encourage this approach, known as layering, using several appropriate techniques to ensure strong, new behaviours and responses.

Other approaches to consider

The Swish Pattern in essence collapses one anchor (the problem state (PS)) with a stronger, more desirable state (DS), so that the latter extinguishes the former, or, creates a 'neutral' state. Effective Swish Patterns require:

- a desired state that features at least two, preferably three, submodalities;
- movement from an associated state to a dissociated state (where ongoing behavioural changes, such as healthier eating habits, are intended), or from associated to associated (where a fixed state, such as 'being a non-smoker', is the objective); and,
- repetition – the swish should be repeated until the patient cannot easily recover the PS. The patient should open his eyes between repetitions to break state, and always start the next round with the PS, until the PS has been de-activated and the trigger automatically activates the new neuronal pathway to the desired state.

Method

The 'classic' Swish Pattern involves setting up the DS as a small, dark square in the bottom right-hand corner (K^i) of the patient's visual representation of the PS, and then rapidly expanding the DS while shrinking the PS, accompanied by a *'sw-i-i-sh'* sound from the practitioner to add an auditory component.

Other variations include:

- putting the DS far out on the patient's horizon line with the PS in whatever position it naturally occupies, and then rapidly reversing the positions of the two states; and,
- concealing the DS behind the PS, and then opening up a window in the centre of the PS and rapidly expanding it so the desired state pops through.

Note: Although the Swish Pattern as outlined above relies on strong visual qualities, both auditory and kinesthetic swishes can be designed, following the same principles. Where a kinesthetic lead is followed, remember the rule that negative feelings are experienced as contracted and localised, whereas positive feelings are expansive.

EXERCISES

1. Experiment with association and dissociation to become familiar with your own responses. When dissociated from an undesired experience or memory, how would you prefer it to be? Construct the appropriate desired state using all sensory modalities.
   - Chunk both the PS and the DS to establish purpose or intention as well as strategy for each.
   - Explore how you could satisfy the positive intention of the PS with a strategy that is more appropriate than that of the PS.
   - Practise anchoring, role-playing and mental rehearsal to install the new strategy, and test each one for effectiveness.
2. Practise the Swish Pattern until you have at least three different ways of doing it.

16

Hypnosis in Healing and Health: language and influence

Hypnosis is a process that nobody really understands, but about which everyone has an opinion. Despite the fact that it has a 200-year history as a valuable tool in the practice of Western medicine, many health professionals still regard it with suspicion and fear. The real problem, of course, is the word. As another nominalisation, "hypnosis" suggests some-'thing' that is implanted inside the patient to operate independently of his 'will'. This has prompted the most recent researchers to turn to neural scanning in order to find out where it lives and what it looks like when it's at home.

Predictably, changes in brain function have been found, most notably in the brainstem, thalamus and anterior cingulate, suggesting, in part at least, that the effect can be observed as affecting the level of executive functioning of the brain[151]. However, none of these studies explains how such a wide range of effects can take place under hypnosis, although they do agree that certain changes are characteristic of the state, for example, diminished peripheral awareness and increased focal attention; a significant suspension of the experience of linear space and time; and, a 'dislocation' between the somatosensory cortex and the higher brain centres that, somehow, gives the nervous system permission to create or ignore certain subjective experiences.

Of course, neural activity does not occur in isolation. It is contextual, and our experience is that the phenomenon we call hypnosis, in fact:

- is less rare and exotic than often thought;
- occurs naturally and spontaneously as part of a continuum of consciousness, rather than a discrete condition;
- developed as an evolutionary response to certain conditions; and,
- emerges as the function of a relationship of one kind or another.

Because we feel that at least part of the reservations of the medical profession result from the word itself and the image projected by the popular media, we will more frequently use the terms, “trance”, “trance-state”, “unconscious response”, “other-than-conscious processing”, and, “altered state” as synonyms, depending on the context.

Characteristics of trance

The trance state exhibits three important characteristics: focus, abstraction and association/dissociation.

Focus, as we have said, involves a reduction of peripheral data. Rather than scanning the internal or external environment, the subject deletes any information not consciously or unconsciously perceived as relevant to the issue at hand, whatever that happens to be.

Abstraction refers to the process of withdrawing from the external environment, moving progressively inward at the expense of competing data from the ‘outside’.

Dissociation occurs when the subject disidentifies with his physical and psychological boundaries, uncritically becoming merged (associated) with the experience contained within the boundary conditions of the current trance-state.

A state in which the subject has little or no overt contact with the external world is known in NLP as “down-time” trance.

Trance states are accompanied by various degrees of suggestibility, from the gentle exhortations of the hypnotist to “relax and let go”, to the phenomenon of post-hypnotic suggestion, the apparently automatic behaviour carried out after the subject emerges from the trance in which the suggestion has been implanted. We are not claiming that “suggestibility” exists as some-thing inside the subject. Rather, as we will discuss further below, it is a function of certain classes of relationship.

Signs of developing trance

It is comparatively easy to observe specific changes related to developing trance in the subject's physiology, especially when the practitioner's vision is wide and relaxed. The most common markers include:

- defocused or fixed gaze;
- flattening of the facial muscles;
- reduced muscle tonus;
- altered breathing rate;
- changing blink rate; and,
- slower, sometimes slurred, speech.

These minimal cues may emerge spontaneously as the subject becomes increasingly absorbed in his internal world, or in response to the practitioner's suggestions. 'Suggestions', in turn, may be direct or indirect (see *Inducing and amplifying trance*, page 221).

Everyday trance states

Trance can develop spontaneously. We are all deeply familiar with the process of becoming completely absorbed in a book or film, or of arriving at a destination without any conscious awareness of having driven there through busy traffic.

When that happens, we might not immediately realise that someone has spoken to us, or have been aware of the passage of time. Where film drama and well-crafted literature are involved, we enter a curious state of dual awareness: part of us is immersed in the challenges and emotions of the protagonists as if they were happening to us, while at the same time we are well aware that we are reading a novel or clutching the DVD remote control.

These state changes are accompanied by natural trance phenomena, such as analgesia (forgetting a headache while engaged in an interesting conversation); amnesia (forgetting to carry out a task agreed while involved in another absorbing experience); and, negative hallucination (experiencing something as 'absent', even when it is in plain sight of others).

The continuum of consciousness

The spectrum of consciousness extends from conditions in which conscious cognitive processing is significantly reduced, to heightened states of awareness, usually associated with 'peak' or 'religious experiences'. From the 'blackness' of the former to the heightened sensory virtual reality of the latter, an almost infinite range of possibilities exists. We drift in and out of a rich variety of altered states without noticing. Familiarity is what prevents us from noticing the shifts that come with changes in our sensory input; social demands; biological rhythms; and, emotional fluctuations.

Our 'default consciousness' is considered ordinary to us simply because no 'unordinary' quality comes into our awareness. We do not regard it as a trance state, even though our attention encompasses only what presents itself as 'important' at that particular moment. Our foci of attention are reduced, but still serve our immediate needs. When we simply 'are', we are in our most habitual altered state.

Thus, 'everyday' trances are unlikely to cause problems; indeed, if we define trance as involving focus, abstraction and association, we may well have created a number of varying trance states appropriate to the different roles we are required to play during each day.

However, when trance hijacks our freedom to involve ourselves in experiences other than those contained within itself, problems arise. Our default consciousness fades, along with our ability fully to function within it, as we become increasingly absorbed in the characteristics of the problem-trance.

The function of trance

Trance experience has been a favoured pursuit of our species since the beginning of time. From the states of altered awareness induced by driving tribal drums and the ingestion of sacred organic substances, to the addiction to the 'buzz' of contemporary club music and recreational drugs, humans have been inexorably drawn towards heightening or changing their experience of 'reality'. But, what predisposes us to state-alteration in the first place?

One theory – and this is probably the most useful model in the context of this book – is that trance evolved as a protective mechanism for where physical fight or flight failed. The cascade of endorphins that accompanies both the 'freeze' and the trance state, so the theory goes, reduces (somewhat) the experience of being torn limb from limb. Many of the markers of trance occur in human beings in times of extreme crisis, including a loss of physical sensation and extreme distortion of the subjective sense of time.

Some researchers believe that Multiple Personality Disorder (MPD), characterised by several different and discrete 'personalities', is the product of trauma-induced trance-formation. Certainly, 'deep' trance, with its rigidity of limbs, slow, shallow breathing and absence of reaction to external stimuli, has, on the surface, much in common with the "playing possum" response observed throughout the natural world.

These behaviour patterns also seem to have much in common with unwanted feelings, responses and behaviours that patients often claim "just happen", no matter how illogical they seem or how much they want to suppress them. Another shared characteristic is that of trance logic, the tendency to 'explain' the symptom in terms that may seem utterly absurd to the observer. This parallels Michael Gazzaniga's "interpreter"[152], suggesting that the experience of trance occurs wordlessly in the right cortex, while the left struggles to make sense of the behaviour.

A further argument to support the 'protective mechanism' theory emerges from studies of childhood trauma, some cases of which are believed to create states dissociated from the hostile environment and associated into a 'safe' fantasy world or alternative 'identity'. According to some neurobiologists – who call these trances "imprints" – such experiences are 'fixed' in our neurophysiological structure by chemical washes, presumably creating a kind of template of situations to be avoided in the future (see Chapter 2).

Several factors appear to be instrumental in creating and amplifying trance, including heightened emotion (e.g. sudden trauma); repetition; a sense of reduced control; and, sustained allostatic load.

Our contention, in advancing this model, is that many 'functional' disorders share key characteristics with trance, and that part of the Medical NLP practitioner's role is to disassemble the problem trance, while creating more resourceful responses based on widened, rather than constricted, perception and cognitive processing.

Relational trances

Trance itself is a product of relationship – whether it is the relationship between hypnotist and subject; subject and object of absorption (a movie or book); or, the patient and his problem.

Bonded disconnection (see page 135) is a particularly insidious trance-deepener. The more focus, absorption and association are applied to attempting to negate the problem, the more deeply entrenched it is likely to become. As Korzybski pointed out, the quality of the Inferences made about the experience can feed back to higher levels to deepen allostatic load. This inevitably occurs when the problem is framed as 'other' than 'ourselves'.

Attempts to make changes at this level of separation are unlikely to be successful. We know from experience that adopting the 'one-up' role of advisor or coach has minimal impact on the structure and process of complex 'functional' problems – and we recommend that you avoid this, unless absolutely necessary (such as instructing the patient how to take his medication). Avoid, too, the trap of entering into a symmetrical argument with the patient in the hope that your superior logic will prevail. This approach runs counter to the *Ko Mei* principles of Medical NLP and risks placing the practitioner as 'other' to the patient, thereby reducing his ability to influence.

Effective influence is, by nature, en-*trancing*. The etymological origin of the word "trance" is the present participle of the Latin verb *transire*, to "go" or "cross over". The sheer number of English words deriving from this compound verb (transit, transition, transitory, transfer, etc) reflects the multi-ordinality of the word "trance" itself.

We may think of 'going into trance' as crossing over the boundaries of conscious and unconscious, external and internal, left hemisphere and right hemisphere, body and mind. We might also consider the 'effectiveness' of trance as a mutually agreed breaching of the boundaries between 'you' and 'me'. In trance, the boundary conditions between patient and practitioner become increasingly permeable, so that 'your' thoughts may merge seamlessly with 'mine', your 'suggestions' become my 'decisions'. Needless to say, it is especially important to be ethical and respectful as these distinctions are breached.

Chapter 16

The family trance

Patients and their problems do not exist separately from the system in which they live, and the most immediate system we should consider is the family. It is fairly self-evident that one member's chronic illness may disrupt the lives of siblings, parents or children. This, in turn, can worsen the patient's condition, particularly if there exists an atmosphere – real or imagined – of resentment or blame.

Two other issues need to be examined to facilitate healing and health:

1. the role that the patient or the patient's problem plays in the family dynamics; and,
2. the effect recovery might have on the system as a whole.

The practitioner should explore any 'gains' the condition may bring, either to the patient or to his primary caregiver(s). In chunking for positive intentions, it may emerge that the symptom acts to prompt other family members to provide the nurturing the patient desires.

Such a strategy, albeit an unconscious one, may be effective, but at a price – for example, a depletion of the family's energy, patience and financial reserves. Equally, the caregivers may be meeting their own needs for significance and meaning within the relationship; they are 'needed', and therefore important.

Another possibility – most frequently encountered in children who present with behavioural disorders or problems such as bed-wetting and soiling – is that the condition acts to distract the parents, or other members of the family, from problems perceived as potentially more threatening to the patient's safety than the condition itself. Some patients, adults included, appear somehow to have the capacity to create or maintain an otherwise distressing condition for some perceived "greater good".

Case history: *The patient, a 34-year-old married man with two children, presented with "work-related stress". Although he had one of the worst cases of weeping eczema the practitioner had ever seen, he initially made no mention of his skin condition.*

When the practitioner referred to it, the patient shrugged and said that even though his condition had not responded to treatment, it was "under control". He explained that his widowed mother came to his home every day to clean and dress the eruptions. He admitted that his relationship with her was conflicted and that he resented her "fussing", but felt he could not ask his mother to stop caring for him because "I'm the only person she's got left in her life". Some months later, the patient called in considerable distress, saying his mother had died instantly in a road accident.

When the patient arrived for his appointment, the practitioner was stunned. The patient's skin appeared new and pink and without blemish. When the practitioner had the opportunity to ask about any treatment he had received, the patient seemed slightly embarrassed. He said, "It's the strangest thing. I was unbelievably shocked and guilty when I heard about my mother's death. I felt somehow I hadn't done enough for her. But, within a few hours, the itching stopped, and a few days later I noticed that the eczema was drying up. It disappeared in less than a week."

The possibility that the patient's problem was caused, or at least, maintained, by a need to provide his mother with a 'purpose' in life cannot easily be dismissed. However, rather than implying that some gain or benefit may be causing or maintaining the problem, which we regard as presumptuous and disrespectful, it is preferable to open the subject of family dynamics in the following manner:

Now, because this problem has been going on for some time, the roles of all the people around you will change when you start to get better. Even though they may have been upset that you have been ill, there could be the chance that in some way they will feel they are not needed or appreciated any more. How would you suggest you could make them still feel important even as you're getting better?

The intention here is to encourage the patient to begin to alter his role as a passive recipient of care to an active agent of his own recovery, while ensuring that the system within which he lives regains balance. When we asked one little girl the question suggested above, she smiled in delight and responded immediately, "I'll ask my Daddy to help me with my homework – even if sometimes I know the answers."

CHAPTER 16

Conflicting trances

Conflicting responses and behaviours are commonly encountered in many 'functional' disorders. These are usually signalled by linguistic markers, such as, "On the one hand I … and on the other …"; and, "Part of me wants to (X), but another part …" .

If conflicting trances are seen to have been set up at different stages in the subject's development, each with the positive intention of meeting a specific need, deconstruction and integration is both practical and effective. We will discuss approaches to resolving conflicting trances in the Chapter 18, but, for the moment, we advise practitioners to begin to approach each state as discrete and functioning in some way (at some time in the patient's life) as a protective mechanism, even though they are presently experienced as functioning in opposition to each other.

Chunking to core values and positive intentions often allows us to resolve conflict.

Case history: *The patient, a new father who had been diagnosed with Obsessive Compulsive Disorder, reported that "part" of him wanted to be a good and responsible parent, whereas "the other part" was convinced that if he did not carry out certain rituals, his family would die. His obsessive behaviour, though, was causing problems with his wife and, he believed, was also affecting his baby son.*

After the practitioner helped the patient to reduce the level and automaticity of his sympathetic arousal, they arrived at the understanding that both "parts" wanted safety and security for him and his family, but were pursuing it in mutually destructive ways. Together, the patient and practitioner worked to resolve the conflict (see Chapter 18), and the patient returned home to "see what happens".

On his second consultation, some weeks later, the patient reported that his obsessive behaviour had "just gone away" – except for one ritual that he needed to discuss. He said he felt compelled each night to kiss his fingers four times and place them gently on his sleeping son's cheek.

The practitioner asked whether he felt that this ritual helped him and his wife to sleep better at night. The patient said, "I'm pretty sure it does." The practitioner then suggested that the ritual might even help his baby grow up secure in his father's love and protection, and the problem was permanently laid to rest.

Two other forms of interpersonal trance may be encountered. These are what we call the "couple trance" and the "cultural trance".

Where problems in relating are concerned, the couple trance may often be found to exist as a self-reinforcing loop, in which certain actions of one person trigger a response in the other, which, in turn, sets off another round – and so it continues[153]. In designing interventions, the practitioner should take this two-point loop into consideration.

Cultural trance refers to the unquestioned acceptance of the rules and injunctions of one's cultural or religious group, and the conflicts that this might engender. Problems often occur simply because the 'rules' imparted by the group are 'self-sealing' – that is, they discourage new information that might challenge the belief. The practitioner should be particularly careful not directly to challenge the belief-system, nor attempt to impose his own world-view.

Case history: *The patient, a young man who was about to be married, presented with erectile dysfunction. Although he was due to get married, he was shocked while changing after a work-out at his local gym to "catch himself" looking at the bodies of other men. Coming from a deeply conservative and religious family, he "just knew" this was "wrong" and that he deserved to be punished.*

He spontaneously shifted into a significantly altered state when asked to pay attention to the memory of the experience of looking at other men – to "simply watch yourself and notice what happens". This is controlled dissociation, a valuable approach to disassembling trance states. Anxious not to pre-judge whether or not the patient had homosexual inclinations, the practitioner then invited him to "go inside and ask" what "other meanings" this behaviour might have (the presupposition here was that there might be meanings other than the one that was limiting him).

The man remained silent for some minutes, then emerged from his state of absorption, visibly relaxed and smiling. He confided that he had never seen another man's naked body and wanted to see how he "shaped up" by comparison.

Apparently, he had decided that he had shaped up well enough, and called back several months later to report that he was happily married and sexually fully functional again.

'Undoing' trance

It may seem paradoxical that we can induce trance to 'undo' trance, until we recognise and accept that neuronal networks have the potential to reorganise themselves when their boundary conditions are breached and new information is introduced and accepted. Psychiatrist Dr Susan Vaughan believes that effective change-by-communication directly alters neuronal networks[154], while Nobel prizewinner Eric Kandel, one of the world's leading experts in neuroplasticity, suggests that information (words) may even alter the way our genes express themselves via a rearrangement of the connections between the nerve cells of our brains[155].

As the subject dissociates from external triggers and reduces the flow of data competing for his attention, he relaxes and moves further away from higher-order levels of verbal abstraction and deeper into the non-verbal levels of Object and Event experience. Put more simply, he 'does' less, and 'is' more. By becoming a relaxed, permissive observer of his own internal functions, he effectively removes the two strongest bulwarks of trance: physiological tension and semantic evaluation. Without either words to tell his story or a pattern of muscle tension to help maintain the state, the boundary conditions of a specific trance can begin to disassemble.

We (the authors) contend that moving closer to the silent, purely experiential level is a necessary precursor to restructuring experience; we are still surprised how often patients spontaneously self-regulate when they master this ability simply to 'let go and let it be'. As we explain in the exercise section at the end of this chapter, this is a core Medical NLP skill that has many useful applications.

Patients who understand and master this process have a powerful tool to support them in dealing with bouts of chronic pain, depression, anxiety, compulsive behaviour, etc. Arthur J. Deikman notes that the ability to shift attentional awareness into what he calls the observing self "reduces the intensity of affect, of obsessive thinking, and of automatic response patterns, thus providing the opportunity for modification and control, for increased mastery"[156].

Inducing and amplifying trance

One of the misconceptions that still dominate is that people cannot be hypnotised "against their will". While it may be true that when the subject is fully aware that the hypnotist is "trying to put me under", he will be able to counteract suggestions to relax and focus, it is entirely possible to facilitate the development of trance without ever using words such as "hypnosis", "trance" and "relax".

As we have stated elsewhere, states are contagious; we seem to be equipped with a tendency to entrain one to another. 'Suggesting' that the patient enter an altered state therefore can be accomplished by:

1. Entraining the patient by entering an altered state yourself. This is a skill elevated to high art by Richard Bandler. "If you want someone to relax, or go into any other state," he says, "go there first." However, we should add that, while the ability to enter a trance state in which you can still function in full conscious awareness – called "up-time" trance – is an extremely useful and energy-preserving state, it does require practice. We have observed more than one student attempting to lead a partner into trance only to succumb himself.
2. Slowing and pacing both your breathing and your word-groups to match the patient's out-breath. Heart Rate Variability (HRV) shows us that the sympathetic nervous system is activated on the in-breath, and the parasympathetic nervous system on the out-breath. We are therefore 'chaining' together a succession of 'mini-breaks' to create one contiguous state of relaxation and inwardly turning attention.
3. Reinforcing each sign of developing trance by gently acknowledging it with a nod, an encouraging smile or a repeated phrase, such as, "That's right."
4. Following a series of linked factual statements (truisms) with a recommendation or suggestion that directs the subject towards trance – for example, "So, you've had the tests and we've looked

at the results and seen they are negative (all verifiably true) and so now you can relax and I'll show you how you can learn to reduce stress more effectively..."

As trance develops, it may be wise to reassure the patient that it's "okay to close your eyes for a few moments to relax if that feels more comfortable. I'll let you know when it's time to come back into the room."

The fallacy of the "deep" trance

The representation of trance as a place into which we fall, sink or float down – the 'deeper' the better, if we wish to 'fix' a particularly recalcitrant condition – may be a useful metaphor to use with patients. However, 'levels' of trance are artificial measures created in research laboratories and bear little relation to real-world transformational work.

The assumption that a 'deep' trance is a prerequisite of major shifts in perception and capability is misplaced. Deep, somnambulatory trance often leaves the subject slow and unresponsive, while a state barely perceptively different from the subject's default consciousness is often enough to permit effective work to be carried out. A certain level of skill and sensory acuity is required by practitioners to recognise the developing trance state and to exploit it effectively.

The practitioner's role

In many ways, our role as practitioners is to help 'de-hypnotise' the patient who is in the grip of bonded disconnection, by changing his relationship to his problem.

Even in the face of strong 'resistance', this may be accomplished in any number of ways. We have already given several examples of this, including the tried-and-tested, "When you have (accomplished the desired state), what would be different and better?" Another example might be to ask the patient simply, "Why *should* you change?", or, even, "Why *shouldn't* you change?" The purpose of overcoming 'resistance' is *always* to satisfy patient needs and *never* to dominate or control.

However, we do, on occasion, gently provoke the patient to argue for change, rather than – as is often the case – to present every argument for why he has to stay the same.

Do not be surprised if the patient seems disoriented when you change tack this way. Paul Watzlawick suggests that this kind of shift in logical typing undermines the patient's "game", which is entirely based on the (often unconscious) presupposition that the practitioner's role is to *make* him change.[157]

A number of possibilities to create bespoke approaches quite naturally occur when we understand that, while structure and process can be changed and outcomes designed, these have the greatest potential for success when we have helped the patient to change his relationship with his problem – and possibly with others in his familial or cultural environment.

Trance, NLP and concordance

Very little distinction can be made between trance and NLP processes and techniques. By definition, when the subject turns inwardly to focus on certain processes and procedures, he may be said to be 'in trance'.

Equally, concordance and adherence – two qualities necessary to effective treatment outcomes – may be thought of as a form of trance. Andre Weitzenhoffer, a researcher and prolific writer on the subject of hypnosis, often remarked that spontaneous responses to suggestions in the waking state were indistinguishable from those elicited by hypnosis. Few practitioners will have considered trance as a significant factor in good clinical practice. We suggest they do.

EXERCISES

I. **Non-evaluative self-observation.** You will undoubtedly recognise this pattern from earlier discussions in this book:

1. Scan your body internally for any pain or tension. If you have a specific 'negative' emotion or worry that dominates your attention, notice how and where it manifests itself as a kinesthetic.

2. Give the kinesthetic permission to be there as it is and, in your imagination, step back, out of your body, and simply observe what is happening purely as a physical experience.
3. Describe out loud (if possible) the characteristics (submodalities) of the experience, being careful to avoid semantic evaluations, such as "painful", "worrying", "awful", etc.
4. Stay aware of changes as they occur, and describe them (again in purely physical terms), as the experience resolves itself.

Patients must be guided through this process, possibly several times, so they fully understand it and can have the confidence to apply it on their own.

Note: We often use this to depotentiate the response to a specific problem, and then follow it with the appropriate intervention (see Chapter 17).

II. Creating trance-inducing language patterns. By definition, "induction" means "inwardly turning". In creating trance-inducing statements, we reverse the inference-to-fact process referred to in Chapter 6. This progressively leads the subject (or oneself) from external, verifiable 'reality' into a more internal state of absorption.

1. Make **three factual** statements followed by **one** statement **inferring** comfort, relaxation, etc. (For example: "You are sitting back in the chair, your feet on the ground, your hands in your lap, and you can allow yourself to relax, just a little more…").
2. Follow this by **two factual** statements and **two inferential** statements.
3. Follow this, in turn, by **one factual** statement and **three inferential** statements. From this point on, all statements can be overtly 'hypnotic'.

Note: This pattern can be used to practise self-hypnosis. Factual statements may be sights, sounds or sensations in and around you.

When you wish to end the trance, simply tell the subject (or, yourself) slowly and comfortably to come back into the room, wide awake.

17

From 'Functional' to Functioning: restructuring dysfunctional states

Patients suffering from chronic and 'functional' disorders are stuck – literally and metaphorically. The experience of being trapped by a body and mind that no longer perform naturally or follow orders can be overwhelmingly debilitating. With many of the conditions eluding diagnosis and effective treatment, the frustration experienced by the patient often infects the practitioner, with demoralising results.

'Literal' stuckness is easily demonstrated. If the submodalities of either patient or practitioner are examined, we will almost certainly see that they lack movement. Their representations of the problem lack process and action. Their sensory representations are still, restricted, or loop continuously in a self-maintaining cycle of failure. The successful resolution of a problem will always be accompanied by a shift from 'still' to 'moving'. Healing, whether or not it involves a "cure", is a return to "flow".

We are often asked by hopeful newcomers to Medical NLP for "the" cure for depression (or anxiety, chronic pain, Post-Traumatic Stress Disorder, etc). Our reply is always, "It depends on the patient." The presupposition that the prescriptive approach of Western medicine can be applied to all patients suffering from superficially similar disorders misses the essential point. Medical NLP holds that the patient who has the condition is the key to relieving the condition that has the patient.

Therefore, even though in this chapter we review the underlying structure and process of three components of commonly encountered complex, chronic conditions – depression, anxiety and pain – these are not intended to be applied prescriptively. Rather, we urge you to remember always to return to basics – structure, process, purpose and intention – and then to develop approaches out of the principles and techniques outlined earlier in this book. In the following chapter, we will present a number of patterns that can be used as templates for further interventions. Avoid being too constrained by formal diagnoses.

Although all clinical guidelines categorise conditions and make specific recommendations, these are *evaluative* statements and cannot accurately reflect the fullness of the patient's experience. Do not confuse text with context, the patient with his symptom, the diagnosis with the disease itself. Therefore, the headings we give to the following sections are intended as general, not definitive, descriptors.

Note: Since we regard allostatic load as an underlying cause or component of all 'functional' disorders, we suggest encouraging patients to adopt a regular programme designed to evoke the Relaxation Response, the psychophysiological counter-balance to the fight-or-flight response (see Appendix A). The Relaxation Response has been demonstrated to have a regulatory effect on many disorders classed as 'functional' or 'somatoform', possibly by restoring hemispheric balance[158,159,160].

Depression

Considerable damage has been done to both the patient and the healer's 'art' by the current belief that depression is a purely biochemical disorder. As we have mentioned elsewhere, diagnostic criteria increasingly exclude the events and experiences surrounding the patient's condition, and seek, instead, to tackle the symptom itself. We have no verb in English to describe the process of 'depress-ing', but we urge you to remember that it is not a 'thing', but a behaviour or response.

The structure of depression

Patients suffering from feelings of depression often:

- are orientated to the past, rather than the present or future;
- adopt a specific, 'downcast' physiology;
- think 'globally' (that is, are unaware of exceptions to their experience);
- worsen their condition by trying to dissociate (and failing);
- are running a two-point loop ($K^{i-} > A^{d-} > K^{i-} > A^{d-} >$, etc); and,
- have still, dark, depressing submodalities.

Developing interventions

Consider:

- time line adjustment;
- changing physiology;
- dissociation (coach into an observer position);
- eliciting exceptions to their problem-state (anchor);
- negotiating a well-formed outcome (anchor);
- helping to create an exit point (imagining moving to a 'different' future) to the auditory–digital-kinesthetic loop (change submodalities, apply the Swish Pattern, collapsing anchors, installing a new strategy); and,
- conditioning and reinforcing new behaviour (see Chapter 18).

We also suggest that the practitioner explores and addresses the following lifestyle issues:

- daily structure;
- diet and exercise; and,
- social support.

Not only do these suffer when a patient becomes depressed, but a serious disruption of any or all of them may actually *trigger* a depressive response.

Anxiety

Anxiety should always be regarded (and reframed) as a protective response that is either overactive or de-contextualised. Anxious patients are usually trapped in:

- a two-point loop that runs from past (sensitising experience) to future (visions of the event recurring), ignoring present 'reality';
- the continued experience of an associated, physiological response to representation (re-presentation) of the feared event;
- overwhelming submodalities of feared event; and,
- diminished and constricted submodalities of coping abilities.

Developing interventions

Consider:

- time line change (place the sensitising incident, trauma, etc in the past);
- dissociating and orientating to present experience (coach into an observer state and observe physiology from a "safe distance", allowing spontaneous submodality changes to promote psychophysical dissipation);
- 'edit' submodalities;
- condition and reinforce new behaviour (see Chapter 18).

Note: Post-Traumatic Stress Disorder has a similar structure to anxiety disorders and panic attacks, and may be approached as suggested above. We do emphasise the need to incorporate coping strategies into all outcomes to increase the patient's sense of self-efficacy and to inoculate against a sense of 'failure' should the response (or something like it) occur at a later date.

Case history: *Lenny, a 27-year-old biker, had been diagnosed with Post-Traumatic Stress Disorder after being knocked off his motorcycle by a bus. He was amnesiac for events immediately following the accident, and suffered recurring flashbacks and panic attacks, nightmares and pains unrelated to the physical injuries he had received. He reported that his recollection of the accident was confined to a continuous loop ("the bus, being knocked off, blackness, the bus, being knocked off, blackness"), which he described as "like a computer game, except you can't get out of the level you're stuck on."*

After reframing Lenny's responses as "protective", albeit somewhat excessive, and coming to an agreement that he would seek an important *lesson to be learned from his experience (satisfying the positive intention), the practitioner helped him create a more detailed scenario, based entirely on witness reports of events following the moment of impact. Lenny was then invited to cut his repeating loop and insert the new sequence*. He refused to do it as an entire sequence, and said "part of him" was prepared to do this only one frame at a time. Sensitive to his need to re-access his trauma in small, safe steps, the practitioner sat back and waited.*

When Lenny completed this, he associated back into the new representation, and was surprised to experience his memory returning intact. He felt he had learned two important lessons from the crash – that he needed to ride defensively (aware of the potential erratic behaviour of others), and that "I'm not immortal". His level of anxiety continued to drop, and he pronounced himself ready to get back on his bike and ride home. He subsequently made a number of successful journeys, including one past the site of his accident, and has not reported back with any further problems since.

Pain

Pain is one of the greatest, most enduring, mysteries of medical science and the human condition. While it is broadly described as "an unpleasant sensory and emotional experience associated with actual or potential tissue damage"[161], chronic pain, as experienced by millions of sufferers, continues to resist the most advanced pharmacological and remedial treatment available. It is also one of the most widely reported reasons for primary care attendance. According to a World Health Organisation 15-country study, pain is the main reason for 22% of patients seeking medical assistance[162].

Chronic pain can affect all areas of a patient's life. A recent report in the *In Practice* series outlined the problem. "Chronic pain detrimentally

* Lenny had mentioned earlier that he worked in a recording studio, and was therefore familiar with the process of editing and sequencing. The practitioner identified this as a resource, and used both his interest in computer games and his professional knowledge to design a metaphor for change. This is what we mean by 'utilisation' (see Chapter 12)

affects all aspects of physical health, not only those directly related to the underlying cause. It is associated with significant disability, unemployment and loss of other physical roles. These produce social and financial problems, which include reduced earning capacity, family disharmony and isolation."[163]

Other psychological consequences include reduced self-esteem, anxiety and sleep disturbance. Recent research has suggested a higher mortality, particularly from cancer, among people with widespread pain.[164]

Running parallel to the challenge faced by the victim of chronic pain is the fact that the medical care system is severely taxed by the demands placed on it. As the *In Practice* report adds, "It stimulates a huge number of prescriptions, investigations and referrals, causes frustration in its resistance to treatment, and leaves patients and doctors with low expectations of successful outcomes."

The categorisation of pain continues to challenge the medical profession. Some sub-groups of "medically unexplained" pain include:

- **pain without injury** (for example, tension headache and trigeminal neuralgia – studies show few discernible indicators of injury or abnormality);
- **pain 'disproportionate' to the severity of the injury** (for example, the passing of a kidney stone);
- **pain after the healing of an injury** (for example, whiplash, phantom limb syndrome)[165,166]

Victims in any of these three categories are often frustrated and depressed by the failure of the medical profession to diagnose and treat what is to them a very real and distressing problem. Suggestions that the sufferer may benefit from counselling or psychiatric intervention improves the situation for few people. The inference, that their pain is not 'real', may not be verbalised by the attending clinician, but it often sensed by the patient.

What makes pain different?

The failure of most cognitive approaches to medically unexplained pain may derive from the failure to recognise how it differs from other affective disorders.

Emotions such as fear, lust, rage and attachment may all be responsive to rational challenge, as with the cognitive behavioural therapies, since each of them has both an identifiable affect centre in the brain and an easily identifiable external 'cause'. We fear something specific that has happened or might happen, or desire something or someone relatively easily identifiable. A subject-object (internal-external) relationship exists, and that relationship is the focus of treatment.

However, no affect centre for medically unexplained pain has been identified, and a specific, easily identifiable, external 'cause' is usually absent[167]. Therefore, no subject-object relationship exists, and the pain 'just is'. Treatment that suggests the patient's problem is the way he is thinking about the pain, rather than the pain itself, is, understandably, a frequent cause of added distress. The pain is real.

Medical NLP approaches the problem somewhat differently. Before proceeding with any intervention, it is necessary to elicit a *representation* of the pain at the Object level, and then externalise it so there can be a relationship with which to work.

Revealing the glyph

At various points in the book, we have suggested using questions such as, "What's it like?"; "What else is it like?"; and, "How does it happen?" in order to elicit the structure and process of an experience. We are looking for sensory-based descriptions (size, shape, colour, movement, etc), rather than evaluative statements such as "awful", "burning", "bad", etc.

The patient will often report his experience as a three-dimensional object, for example "a sharp knife", "a hot red ball", "a bright burning ribbon, like a magnesium strip". In Medical NLP, such a representation is called a "glyph" (from "hieroglyph", meaning a carved object that represents more than itself), and, for therapeutic purposes, it is treated as 'real'. This creates a subject-object relationship that the practitioner now seeks to restructure by exploring submodality changes, especially those involving the restoration of movement. (See Chapter 18 for approaches to working with the glyph.)

Patients suffering from chronic pain are often:

- in high limbic arousal;

- disorientated in time (past experience and future anxieties compounding present experience);
- trapped in bonded disconnection (intensifying their experience by trying to not-have it), and generalising their experience (convinced that one or more episodes denotes the inevitability of further 'attacks'); and,
- deleting the visual and auditory components of their experience and inattentive towards exceptions to or changes in their experience (deletion).

Developing interventions

Useful approaches include:

- establishing a regular programme to invoke the Relaxation Response (see Appendix A);
- reorganising the time line to separate out clearly past, present and future pain*;
- resolving or depotentiating the cause (if a single event) or history (using Visual-Kinesthetic Dissociation, etc (see Chapter 18);
- dissociating (moving to a 'safe place' and observing the 'self' from a distance is a commonly applied 'hypnotic' technique in pain control, especially involving acute or episodic bouts, such as dental surgery or childbirth);
- observing and dissipating (coaching into an observer state and observe physiology from a 'safe distance', allowing spontaneous submodality changes to promote psychophysical dissipation).

> ***Case study:*** *Sean, a 28-year-old male whose foot had been blown off by a landmine 25 years before, presented with low back and leg pain having had lumbar discectomy six years previously. Drug and physical therapies had failed. He was insistent that the explosion was not in any way*

* Milton Erickson, who experienced a lifetime of chronic pain, based many of his interventions on reducing the subjective experience by marking out 'past' and 'future' as non-existent, thereby suggesting that the patient had only 'present pain' to contend with.

a problem, and that he was simply seeking to find relief from his chronic pain, which he rated as 7 on the Subjective Measure of Comfort Scale (SMCS).

While he was talking, the practitioner paced and led him into a more relaxed state, before briefly introducing him to a technique to activate the Relaxation Response (see Appendix A). When describing the pain, he used metaphors, such as a "pestle" being pushed into and moved up and down the lumbar scar. He experienced the pain as "burning, red pressure".

The practitioner invited him to transfer the image to a PC monitor. The patient exhibited considerable V^r *and* V^c *eye movement behind closed lids (characteristic of vivid visualisation), and then reported that he had been successful. The monitor – an old, green and black model – was situated in his lower, left visual field. He repeated the process, but this time created a more desirable state. He chose "the best screen available", large and flat, on which he projected himself as healthy, active and pain-free, using vibrant colours. He reported a feeling of comfort spreading through his body.*

Under the guidance of the practitioner, Sean repeatedly "swished" from the small, dark screen to the larger one, until he could no longer easily recover the trigger image. He reported that his level of pain had reduced to 3 on the SMC Scale. The practitioner continued the consultation, using a variety of embedded suggestions of comfort and coping abilities to help the patient build a model of future experience and behaviour.

At the second consultation, two weeks later, Sean reported that the effect had faded and that his own attempts to practise the Swish Pattern had failed. The practitioner responded by suggesting that trying to overcome pain might increase its intensity, and coached the patient into sitting back, dissociating and "simply observing".

The kinesthetic spontaneously began to expand and move, and changed colour to "flame" (a submodality shift to visual). The flame moved up Sean's body and back, finally separating out and moving away, to become a source of warmth "like the sun". He finished the consultation in a smiling, relaxed state, engaged and interested in the process. He was keen to continue practising these methods at home, if required.

Cross-lateralisation

Anecdotal evidence suggesting a strong relationship between hemispheric lateralisation and a wide range of chronic disorders is gaining increasing support from researchers in various fields. Simply put, homolateralised brain activity (abnormally favouring one hemisphere over another) has been implicated in conditions as wide-ranging as dyslexia, certain 'learning disorders', Obsessive Compulsive Disorder, depression, medically unexplained pain, anxiety, psychosis and even immunological disorders[168]. For this reason, we (the authors) often use 'whole-brain' exercises adjunctively with other interventions.

The body-brain system operates bidirectionally (brain function influencing body function and vice versa) and is cross-lateralised (each hemisphere directing and being directed by the opposite side of the body). It follows that interventions that reduce homolateralisation and increase whole-brain activity deserve attention. A number of Medical NLP approaches have been developed and/or adapted from this premise. These include breathing, meditative and physical techniques. These are further discussed in Appendix B.

18

Repatterning and Future-Pacing: making and maintaining change

More than 30 years ago, the creators and developers of NLP could only speculate how many of the techniques they were using empirically could actually work. How was it possible that some people could free themselves from a long-standing phobia, allergy or trauma – sometimes in a matter of a few minutes?

Up until then, psychological change, we were led to believe, was possible, but only with considerable time and effort. Even today, the "brief" cognitive therapies require upwards of eight sessions, and success often needs to be boosted with psychotropic drugs. However, research from the frontiers of brain science reveals that the belief that neuronal function can only be affected pharmacologically and/or with considerable psychological effort is questionable. The key is the capability of the brain called neuroplasticity.

A few decades back, it was widely believed that the brain was a closed, machine-like system, functioning only within the boundaries of its genetic heritage. The neuronal patterns we started out with were the neuronal patterns we died with, give or take the ones we lost along the way to the ravages of time.

But the brain, as we are looking into it in the 21st century, is a very different affair. We know now that it co-creates our 'reality' according to past experiences and present events. We can recognise how its moods and memories resonate in every cell of our bodies. We are beginning to realise that it mediates the way our bodies store and communicate the emotional assaults we experience[169]. And that its extraordinary ability to invent internal realities can have as big an impact on our health and well-being as an external trauma or a germ or a gene. We even have come to suspect, through the new science of epigenetics, that it helps us hold our DNA in trust for later generations – for, if we drink, or smoke, or stress too much, we may pass the consequences on to our descendants for centuries to come.

Above all – and this is probably the brain's most extraordinary quality – it is the only organism that we know of anywhere in the universe that has the capacity to evolve itself. By an experience, an act of imagination or learning, we can create a psychophysical reality that is more (or less) capable, resourceful and healthier than the one we had a day, or a month or a year before[170]. Repatterning, in the Medical NLP model, may be seen as a protocol that is aimed first at the neurological/experiential stratum, and then at the levels of behaviour and its evaluation.

This takes place in two main stages: the first, deconstructing and replacing the dysfunctional pattern with a more useful and appropriate response or behaviour, and the second, applying conditioning techniques (future-pacing) to accustom the patient, both cognitively and neurologically, to the changes as he is likely to apply in his post-treatment life.

In order to understand better how the techniques we present below are structured, it should be recalled that most Medical NLP techniques rely on:

- dissociation, repatterning and reassociation; and,
- collapsed anchors.

Future-pacing and why it works

For many years, 'visualisation' and other imaginal techniques were regarded as likely to have minimal effect on real-world functioning. Its popularity among followers of 'New Age' complementary therapies increased suspicion among many mainstream scientists, even though there were indications that it could be an effective supplementary approach to enhancing sports performance[171]. This, too, is changing – and for good reason. It works.

> Think of the number three for a moment. Imagine it written up on a surface inside your head. As you do that, your visual cortex lights up exactly as if you were seeing the same digit. Now, imagine picking up a heavy barbell and begin to perform a series of curls – the same exercise you might do with free weights at a gym. Hear your personal trainer urging you on. Imagine (without actually moving your body), that your bicep is beginning to tire; lactic acid is burning like hot wires. The weight seems to be getting heavier.

Astonishingly, experiments show that if you did this regularly enough with full absorption, your muscles would actually strengthen – only 8% less than if you had actually done the exercise[172].

For some years now, scientists, including V. S. Ramachandran, have used a device called a "mirror box" to treat problems such as phantom limb pain, reflex sympathetic dystrophy pain (chronic pain persisting long after an injury has healed) and "learned" pain. The mirror box works by reflecting an image of a healthy limb onto its wasted or absent counterpart. The illusion 'rewires' the patient's neurology to facilitate improvement or recovery from his physical condition.

A problem encountered with mirror box therapy is that the longer the pain has persisted, the less effective treatment is likely to be. However, Australian scientist, G. L. Moseley demonstrated that patients who were taught to simply *imagine* moving their injured limb reduced or completely eliminated their pain[173].

Future-pacing – a form of conditioning – then, incorporates the imaginal capabilities of the mind, together with practical application of the new behaviour pattern, wherever possible. It is important, when designing an intervention, that the patient's response to both *thinking* about the problem, as well as his actual real-world experience, is tested (using the SMC Scale, if appropriate).

After intervention and future-pacing, patients should be encouraged to resume their normal (or their new) activities as soon as possible and report back for readjustment or reinforcement, if required. (A useful injunction is, "I'd like you to go back and notice specifically what's different and better so we can talk about that next time.")

Despite our simplified model of internal processing outlined in Chapter 5, we do not mean to suggest that each sense is entirely localised in its own area of the brain. The work of Harvard Medical School's Alvaro Pascual-Leone has confirmed considerable cortical overlap between senses and has demonstrated that various "operators" organise sensory data from different sources in order to create experience. These operators are in constant competition to process signals effectively, depending on both the significance and the context of the signal[174].

Designing a future-pace

Rule 1: Ensure that it is fully represented in all sensory modalities, in as much detail as possible.

Rule 2: It should meet all the requirements of well-formedness. It must also be attractive and relevant to the patient and his model – not that of the practitioner.

Rule 3: A future-pace for an *ongoing* response or behaviour (for example, exercising three times a week, or following a specific eating plan) should be dissociated. This is thought to prompt the brain to continually move to 'close the gap', facilitating maintenance.

Rule 4: A new state (for example, being a non-smoker) should be represented as associated, in order to 'lock in' a discrete condition with clear boundary conditions.

Rule 5: The new state, response or behaviour should be placed on the patient's time line. If necessary, create a means of metaphorically locking it in place.

Rule 6: After the patient has been future-paced, he should be fully reassociated, together with his new pattern(s), using suggestions to "float back above your future road or pathway, bringing into the present all the experiences, learnings and resources from your new future, and drop down into your own body so that you can fully own and apply everything you've learned now as you get ready to move on from here into the future…" etc (note the hypnotic language).

Before applying any of the patterns below, ensure that:

1. the patient's time line has been adjusted, with past events (including the problem) 'behind' him, but not hidden; and,
2. the agreed outcome/direction is well formed in all sensory modalities and placed on his future time line, a little in front of him.

Note: All interventions are designed to be completed within a single session. Do not attempt to carry a pattern over from one consultation to the next. Patterns should be executed rapidly to ensure pattern recognition by the brain. Repeat until automated.

Remember to apply the Subjective Measure of Comfort Scale before and after each intervention.

The patterns

Accessing and working with the glyph

Glyph-work is an important tool of Medical NLP. It is simple, effective and, often, quite remarkable in its effectiveness.

If we steer the patient away from linear description and value judgements (Inferences) towards a purely felt sense (non-evaluative self-observation), the symptom may be experienced as a three-dimensional 'form', which in Medical NLP we call a glyph (see Chapter 17). A pain, for example, may be "like a wire, burning very hot, white, like phosphorous"; anxiety may be "like a dark, cold hole" in the stomach. Pain is often experienced as red or black.

The glyph corresponds to the Object level of Korzybski's Structural Differential. Richard Bandler's observation that 'experience' had characteristics (submodalities) was, in the opinion of the authors, little short of revolutionary. Until then (and even now), cognitive therapists had attempted to effect change only at the language level, unaware that the Event occurring within the subject's nervous system is perceived with form and substance in the form of a metaphoric shape, before it can be translated into words.

Neurological function at the Object and Event levels appears to be more fluid than that at the level of Inference (largely because the way we speak or think about our experience helps to maintain its structure).

Glyphs are marked by the following characteristics. They:

- have submodalities. It is often unnecessary to elicit them; the subject will usually describe them with surprising ease and specificity;
- are described as if existing as tangible 'objects' with existence independent of the subject;
- are usually perceived as painful and threatening;
- all involve a kinesthetic of movement – although the movement is either blocked or looping (no resolution). *The patient is always physically resisting the possibility of movement in order to try to dissociate from the experience.* It is our contention that this resistance to 'what is' causes as much, if not more, psychic and physical pain than the condition itself; and,
- are always localised. 'Bad' feelings have distinct boundary conditions and are contracted in nature. 'Good' feelings, such as excitement, joy, love and orgasm, are expansive and unbounded (moving outwards, often beyond the perceived confines of the body).

Resolving the glyph

It is sometimes possible to resolve a problem by working with the glyph alone, especially where no particularly traumatising event is perceived as, or is actually, responsible for the response.

Paradoxically, one of the conditions for resolution involves moving out of resistance to the experience. Resistance is painful. Resistance (at this stage) is the only response the patient has at his disposal. Apart from the physical tension required to resist an unwanted internal experience, the kind of Inferences made by the patient and others reviewing his problem have the potential for 'locking' the experience in place, or even making it worse.

It is a prerequisite that the patient acquire the skill for (temporarily) tolerating the symptom, and then learn how effectively to dissociate so that the structure and process can be changed. It cannot be changed if he is actively resisting, or trying unsuccessfully to dissociate from, it.

Method for resolving the glyph

1. Create meaning. Explain the purpose or intention behind the symptom while reassuring the patient that it is responding excessively or out of context (reframe);
2. Create acceptance. Encourage the patient to accept the experience: "Just for the moment, allow it to be there. Don't try to change it. Simply let it be the way it is";
3. Dissociate: "Now, either take a step back or put it out in front of you so you can observe it, almost as if it's happening to someone else. Just be the observer and watch the way it is";
4. Elicit submodalities – for example, ask, "What's it like?"; "What's it doing?"; "What's happening?" Ensure that what the patient describes is structural, rather than evaluative or inferential. If he seems stuck, prompt (but do not lead) with gentle questions such as, "If it had a colour, what colour would it be?"; "What shape is it?"; "Are the edges hard or soft, distinct or fuzzy?", etc. Test especially for a sense of movement. Movement will usually be stalled or looped;
5. Promote change. Create a spirit of experimentation while you do this. Non-evaluative observation, without direct intervention, is our preference. Give permission for the glyph to change itself, but do not directly try to change it. Discourage the subject from being similarly interventionist. Be curious; encourage the subject to notice how change "happens" spontaneously when we stop resisting it.
6. If the subject seems stuck, prompt gently and with as little direction as possible – for example, "I wonder what would happen if the colour became a bit less intense?"; "Ask the (ball, knife etc) what needs to happen", etc;
7. When the patient reports a positive change (allowing the glyph to change *always* leads to positive, relaxed, expansive feelings), have him reassociate with it, checking that the internal kinesthetic has been positively transformed. Suggest that he allows the feeling to "expand and flow through every, organ, every muscle, nerve and cell", etc; and,

8. Then have the patient mentally project himself into the future, noting how his feelings, behaviours and responses will be different. Do the final step at least three times and test to see whether the old response can still be accessed. If it can, return to Step 5.

Glyphs may also be swished – but ensure that all its submodalities are turned down or projected into the distance until they disappear. Only then can they be brought back in their new form.

Simple scramble pattern

Method

The scramble pattern may be used alone to change simple behaviours and responses, or adjunctively, with other patterns, to disrupt more complex constellations of problems. The principle is simply to interrupt a sequence by repeatedly 'scrambling' its component parts. A scrambled pattern should always be replaced with an alternative response to reduce the possibility of relapse.

1. Identify and number four or five distinct steps in the patient's process (for example: **1.** notice people watching, **2.** begin to breathe erratically, **3.** feel your cheeks becoming warm, **4.** wonder whether they are noticing, **5.** begin to blush).
2. Starting with the original sequence, coach the patient into experiencing each step, using its number as a cue.
3. Begin to call out the numbers in different orders, increasing the speed as you go.
4. After six to eight cycles, stop and test.
5. If the unwanted response is not extinguished, repeat, ensuring that the patient is fully associated into each step as you call out its number.

Full sensory scramble

Method

1. Have the patient associate into and hold the negative kinesthetic as strongly as possible.

2. Using a pen or your finger, have the patient follow with his eyes (without moving his head) through all eye-accessing positions in rapid succession. Ensure he tries to maintain the kinesthetic at its highest level throughout.
3. Increase the speed, and randomise the movements.
4. Continue for 60–90 seconds, change state, and then test.
5. Repeat, if necessary, until the negative kinesthetic has been substantially reduced.
6. Future-pace.

Visual-Kinesthetic Dissociation (Fast Phobia Cure)

This is the earliest, and one of the most commonly applied, techniques developed by the founders of NLP. It can be used to treat simple phobias, including 'social phobia', fear of public speaking, etc. It can also be incorporated in more complex protocols, as shown below. This version incorporates a final step (essentially a future-pace) as standard.

Note: Where the patient may have an extreme response to accessing thoughts about the trigger event or object, it is important to ensure he is "double-dissociated" (that is, he is watching his dissociated self carrying out the procedure, rather than watching the procedure himself). Instruct him to "step out of, or float up from, your body, so you are watching yourself from a safe distance, watching the events. You don't have to watch the events yourself."

Ensure the patient is fully relaxed, and anchor the state in case you need to bring him back into a 'safe place'.

1. Have the patient imagine sitting in a movie theatre, with a small, white screen placed in front of him and a little above eye level. On the screen is a small, still, monochrome picture of a moment or two before the sensitising event that led to his phobic response (**Safe Place 1**).
2. Instruct him to imagine creating a movie containing "all the experiences, responses and feelings you have had about this problem". Reassure him that the movie, when it is run, will be small, distant and in black-and-white, and when it is complete, the screen will 'white out' (**Safe Place 2**).

3. Have him float out of his body and up, into a position from which he can both observe himself and control the running of his movie.
4. Instruct him to switch on the projector and run the sequence from **Safe Place 1** to **Safe Place 2** very rapidly, allowing the screen to white out when it is finished.
5. Have him float down into his body and then step up into the white screen at the end of his movie.
6. Turn on all the colours and sounds, and have him rewind the movie, experiencing events and sounds, associated, in reverse order until he emerges in **Safe Place 1.**
7. Have him return to his seat and repeat steps 3 through 7, from three to five times, before testing. Notice that the final step is always run through from end to beginning (**Safe Place 2** to **Safe Place 1**).

When the phobic response has been substantially reduced (to a 1 or a 2 on the SMC Scale), you can begin the second part of the intervention.

1. Future-pace as follows. Sitting back in his seat, the patient expands the screen until it extends to the edges of his peripheral visual field.
2. Have him create a full-colour, richly detailed movie of him coping resourcefully in the situation that previously triggered his phobic response. Suggest he incorporates a soundtrack comprising music that he finds particularly uplifting.
3. When he is satisfied with the movie and its soundtrack, have him run it (dissociated) from beginning to end, two or three times, each time starting at the beginning.
4. Then, have him step into the movie (associated) and run it 'as if' he were actually experiencing this reality now. With his permission, you may also hold the safety anchor you set at the beginning of the intervention.
5. Suggest he takes a few moments to run the resource movie several times, making sure he always starts at the beginning, until he is satisfied that everything he sees, hears, and, now, feels will support him in coping positively from now on. Reinforce with

presuppositions and embedded commands to take on this new pattern as a permanent response.

V-K Dissociation is a powerful and useful technique. However, we caution against its indiscriminate application. Sometimes phobias serve an important purpose and disruption, without taking ecology into consideration, could be detrimental to the subject, as the example below illustrates.

Case history: *The subject, a leading consultant gynaecologist, volunteered on one of our training courses with a disabling phobia of spiders. He believed his fear arose from waking up on two occasions to find large spiders on his pillow when he was a child in Africa. However, when the trainer probed further, the subject recalled a further incident in which his baby sister was bitten and went into anaphylactic shock. He became markedly distressed at recalling his helplessness at being powerless to help his sister.*

The trainer asked how that experience might have served a positive purpose in his later life, and the subject promptly replied, "I can cure anaphylactic shock in babies", suggesting his childhood feelings of helplessness had contributed to his choosing to be a doctor. Mindful that a simple 'blow-out' of the phobia might impact the subject's career, the trainer abandoned his plan to demonstrate the V-K Dissociation Pattern, and elected instead to apply a different intervention to resolve traumatic events, described below, in order to preserve all ecological considerations, while still resolving the disabling fear of spiders.

The advanced Medical NLP Swish Pattern

The version of the Swish Pattern outlined below is unique to Medical NLP and has the added value of automatically placing the Problem-State (PS) on to the patient's past time line.

Method

1. Check that the PS is in the position it naturally occurs in, in the patient's internal representation.
2. Place the desired state (DS) directly behind him (Figure 18.1).

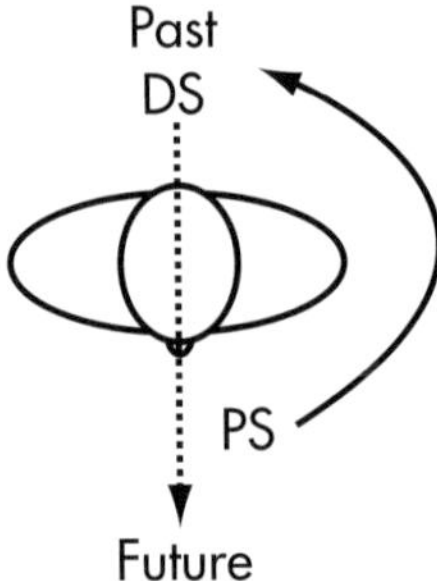

Fig 18.1 Medical NLP Swish Pattern. The desired state (DS) is placed behind the subject (seen from above), and the problem-state (PS) trigger in front. The PS trigger is swished around the subject as the DS is brought through the subject's body with an accompanying, strong kinesthetic.

3. Simultaneously, send the PS around him onto his past time line, while bringing the DS directly through his body into the position previously occupied by the PS. As this happens encourage him to create a strong kinesthetic of the DS moving through his body.

Other variations include:

1. putting the DS far out on the patient's horizon line with the PS in whatever position it naturally occupies, and then rapidly reversing the positions of the two states; and,
2. concealing the DS behind the PS, and then opening up a window in the centre of the PS and rapidly expanding it so that the DS pops through.

Note: Although the Swish Pattern as outlined above relies on a visual lead, both auditory and kinesthetic swishes can be designed, following the same principles.

Resolving internal conflict

Internal conflict is often marked linguistically ("Part of me wants to X, but another part wants Y", or, "On the one hand I X, but on the other I Y"). Sometimes the patient will 'mark out' different parts, gesturing to one side of his body and then to the other. We suspect this may reflect opposing hemispheric activity.

Method

1. Explain that the parts are often set up at different times in the patient's life and have therefore developed differing approaches to trying to meet his perceived needs, even though both are motivated by a shared positive intention.
2. Externalise each part, together with all its characteristics (dissociation). This may be accomplished by having the patient extend both hands, palms uppermost, and 'place' one part in each. Suggest, "Each hand now holds a part with all its beliefs, behaviours and qualities." Have the patient code the totality of each part with a distinctive colour.
3. Chunk each in turn to find shared positive intention (see Chapter 11).
4. Point out that, since both parts have a shared positive intention, they can cooperate in creating a range of possible new responses that will allow the patient to have more appropriate responses. (For example, if part A wants 'freedom' and part B 'security', both might want 'peace and contentment' as a core value. Ask, "How can the security-seeking part benefit from being a bit freer, less rigid? And how would the freedom-loving part benefit from ensuring you have a degree of security and safety in whatever you're doing?"
5. When the patient has found the 'middle ground', have him fix his attention on the space between his hands and begin to float them together, eventually blending the two colours to represent the new 'third' state. Reassure both parts that the intention is not to eliminate them (they might be needed in a specific context), but to widen their range of responses.
6. Have the patient bring his hands towards his body and imagine the new colour and all its qualities flowing into his body and life (reassociation). Give lots of hypnotic suggestions presupposing more choices and a wider range of responses.
7. Future-pace new potential responses, and test this by having the patient think of how he could respond to situations that previously caused him problems.

Resolving traumatic events

Important note: The treatment of serious traumatic events, such as severe physical or sexual abuse, should not be attempted without adequate training. See the Resources section for specialised workshop training.

Trauma – often long-forgotten, and including childhood abuse and neglect – is coming under increasing suspicion as a major factor for the later development of a wide range of medically unexplained conditions, including many causing chronic pain[175]. Compelling neurophysiological evidence is emerging that the patient suffering from extreme 'overwhelm' can become locked into a self-perpetuating cycle of psychological arousal, undischarged 'freeze' state and actual physiological changes.

Because of the downregulation of the frontal cortex, the patient's inability logically to process the 'reality' of the threat profoundly affects his capacity to break out of the condition. One significant effect is that his response to 'time' becomes dislocated. In the words of behavioural neurologist Robert C. Scaer, he is "locked in the past, incapable of experiencing the present, and blind to the future". The future, he adds, "holds no other possibilities than existential threat"[176].

The treatment of 'functional' disorders caused, or exacerbated by, trauma (if they are diagnosed) is currently heavily slewed towards symptomatic relief by pharmacological means (blocking the kinesthetic) and/or some form of 'talking cure', often encouraging the patient to challenge or deny the debilitating effect of his thoughts and feelings.

Both these approaches, in one way or another, deny the somatic 'reality' of the patient's experience. And, in seeking to have the patient do the same, they not only inadvertently disregard the patient's somatic experience as a 'doorway' to his internal map, but attempt to brick up an opening to integration, healing and health. The ability to perceive, find meaning in and act upon the felt sense has been demonstrated to have powerful clinical application in a wide range of medical conditions, including migraine, vertigo, hypertension, and immune disorders, such as multiple sclerosis, arthritis and cancer[177].

The patterns below seek to integrate what we know so far about the patient's relation to time, his ability to reconnect with the frontal cortex, the importance of meaning and metaphor and, above all, the validity of his somatic response.

The Affect Bridge

Affect Bridging is a technique designed to identify events perceived as causal. We do not automatically accept these revelations as 'real', but regard them as part of the patient's model, and therefore potentially useful in restructuring the maladaptive behaviour or response.

Note: We advise caution in setting up an Affect Bridge to avoid associating the patient into a deeply disturbing event. Therefore, our instructions should always include suggestions that he "go back as your adult self, and observe from a safe place, as if on a television or movie screen". This minimises the risk of full abreaction and possible re-traumatisation.

Method

1. Have the patient fully experience the somatic response to the problem state and anchor when the experience is at its height.
2. Hold the anchor and instruct the patient to "follow the feeling back to the first time you felt this way".
3. Release the anchor as soon as the patient identifies the source and, if necessary, have him dissociate as described in the note above.

> ***Case study:*** *The patient, aged 27, had problems eating anything but soft food, such as scrambled eggs and porridge. His gag response was anchored and bridged back to a long-forgotten incident in which, as a small child, he had choked and lost consciousness while eating bananas and custard. (This is a simple, clear example of the symptom – gagging – acting as a solution to, or protection from, the patient's underlying problem. See Chapter 11.)*

Changing responses to past experiences

The severity of traumatisation is often associated with the subject's perceived loss of control at the time of the trauma. Therefore, this pattern depends on accessing and stacking strong coping resources. Although the number of steps involved may seem daunting at first, there is a logical structure which, when mastered, allows for improvisation and adaptation.

1. Have the subject identify the traumatic event. Do not immerse yourself or him in unnecessary detail. Reassure him that "while we can't change what happened, we *can* change our response to what happened" (this paces the patient's belief or experience about the gravity of the experience, while opening him to hope about his ability to change).
2. Return him to his present, 'more adult', associated self and explore the resources by which the 'past self' would have been able better to cope had he had them at the time of the trauma. Have the subject convert the resources into a symbol – for example, a colour or a light.
3. 'Send' the resources back down the past time line to the younger self, and then have the subject move rapidly over the past time line to associate into the body of the younger self in time to receive the resources "from the future". Test by asking the subject how he would feel differently or better with these resources. Have him "keep those feelings" and return to his present, adult self.
4. Send the adult self back as an observer to watch and report on how the traumatising incident would have played out differently when the subject had the means better to cope.
5. If any anger, frustration, fear, etc persists, especially where a significant other was responsible for the trauma, give the subject permission "in the privacy of your own mind" to say, do or feel whatever was not said, done or felt at the time. You may observe considerable activity, physical and emotional, during this phase. Remain engaged and wait until the process is complete. Dissipation of the freeze state may express itself as "silent abreaction" (usually gentle weeping) – a positive development, calmly to be supported.
6. Have the adult self associate into the scenario and reassure the younger self that he is safe and will survive, overcome and flourish now.
7. Have the subject step out and associate into his younger self and receive that information he or she was lacking at the time.
8. The subject then steps back out into his adult self, and reassociates with his newly resourced younger self by drawing him back into his (adult) body.

9. Using hypnotic language, such as, "Now, with all the resources you have given your younger self, combined with the greater knowledge and experience of your adult self to protect it, rapidly travel back up the past towards the present, allowing your unconscious to transform, recode and reorganise all your past experiences in the light of these new understandings." Use multiple injunctions to reinforce the effect. This is known as "layering" your work.
10. When the subject reaches the present, he stops and watches himself moving into the future. Encourage him to notice and report how his responses, behaviours and feelings are now in the light of the 'new' past experiences.
11. Have him travel right to the end of the future time line, and then float up and back, and reassociate into his body, integrating all the resources and experiences from both past and future for use from the present moment on.
12. Repeat this several times, floating back to before the traumatic event (with all the positive resources), up the past time line to the present, and then as in step 11.
13. Anchor in the full-sensory representation of present comfort and optimism and future self-efficacy.
14. Test for responses to past event. If some distress persists, repeat the process or layer work with other principles, such as V-K Dissociation, reframing, collapsing anchors, etc.

Note: This pattern may be used "content-free" – that is, without explicit knowledge or revelation of the original traumatic event. If the patient shows reluctance, acknowledge his need for privacy, and simply proceed with reference to "the original situation or event".

Metaphoric transformation

Metaphoric transformation resembles the previous pattern, with one important exception: the use of patient-generated metaphors and memories to drive change. Do not necessarily expect to 'understand' how the metaphor is relevant to the patient's subjective experience; by definition, it represents something much more extensive and encompassing than its surface appearance.

Method

1. Have the patient fully associate into the kinesthetic of the problem state. Prepare him by explaining the principle of "unconscious association" – that is, that the brain makes many connections and will present those which are particularly relevant at this time.
2. Ask him for his earliest memory. Note that we are not asking him to speculate on the 'cause' of his problem, but simply to move back into the very earliest memory he can retrieve.
3. When he does that, suggest his unconscious mind has presented a specific memory as a metaphor, either to identify the 'cause' of the problem, or to suggest a solution. Ask, "If you could, or, if you needed to, how would you prefer to remember this in a way that will help you deal differently and better with the problem you have been having?"
4. Assist the patient in designing a new, more useful memory.
5. Anchor his responses, and then follow steps 9 through 14 as outlined in the previous pattern.

> ***Case history:*** *The patient, in his early 40s, presented with symptoms of extreme allostatic load, and revealed that he had been "compulsively" unfaithful to his wife. When she found out, their relationship came under extreme strain. He suggested he was drawn to other women as "a kind of mother substitute", since he had grown up with a punitive mother and no father. His earliest memory was of being trapped inside with his mother, trying desperately to get out to the safety of his grandmother's house. The door was locked.*
>
> *When asked how he would like to change the memory, he said instantly, "I don't want to leave my mother. I just want to know the door can open." He made the change to the memory, completed the intervention, and, at the time of writing, more than a year later, reported no urge to be unfaithful and was happy in his marriage.*

The Alternative Reality Pattern

This, somewhat esoteric sounding, pattern emerged from an extended conversation with a physicist – who was suffering from a knee injury that had resisted treatment – about the theories of alternative realities and the unreliability of memory. The former proposes an infinite number of potential realities, only one of which materialises when a specific action is taken, and the latter is based on recent research suggesting that memories are 'reconstructed' each time we access them. The pattern has subsequently proved useful in a wide range of situations, both as a stand-alone intervention and adjunctively with other treatments.

When introducing the concept of alternative realities, it may be useful to refer to several popular films, such as *Sliding Doors* and *The Matrix*, which explore the theme.

Method

1. Set up in parallel formation several 'potential' past time lines, including one that incorporates the accident or incident perceived as having caused the problem (Figure 18.2).

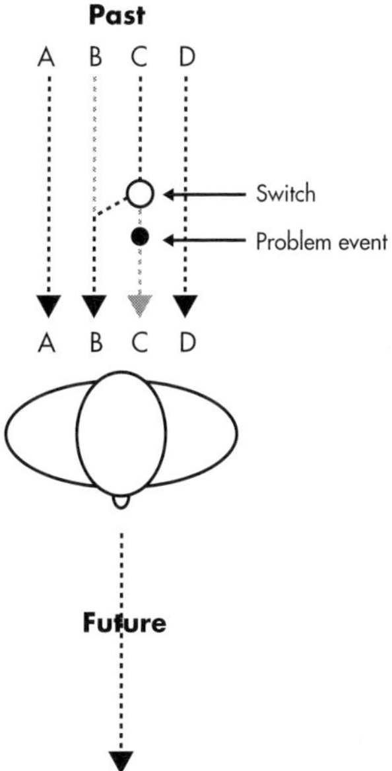

Fig 18.2 The Alternative Reality Pattern (seen from above). Instead of running from C to C and into the future, this pattern diverts the past at the switch, just before the problem event, to the 'alternative reality': C to B.

2. Have the patient float up and over the causal incident and back down on to that time line some considerable distance before the event.
3. Set up a 'switch' (the analogy of the rail switches used to divert trains onto another line is useful) just before the problem event.
4. Select an alternative line that events can switch to instead of following the old route through the problem event and beyond. Elicit as much detail as possible about the chosen alternative reality.
5. Have the patient move rapidly up the old reality, then switch to the new version, and on. Follow steps 10 through 14 as outlined in the two previous patterns.
6. Repeat this at least five times, and then test.

Dealing with multiple conditions

Patients will sometimes present with several loosely related problems. The practitioner's options are as follows:

- Have the patient arrange the problems in order of importance and suggest starting with the most important one, leaving the others for further consultations. This requires a clinical assessment that may not actually meet the patient's needs.
- Suggest you both explore all the problems for any underlying or common factors. This process utilises chunking and reframing.

Method

1. Write a brief description of each problem in its own column.
2. Chunk each in turn for its positive intention. Ensure this is a core issue – that is, that the patient is unable to proceed any further.
3. Find the commonalities that all the problems share. Chunk and/or reframe until a single, shared intention is identified.
4. Select the appropriate intervention and apply.
5. Test to ensure that changes are reflected in each problem area (that is, whether the core change generalises out into all).
6. Future-pace each outcome individually and test again to ensure the appropriate changes have been made.

Case history: *The patient was clinically obese, and his knee pain was so intense that he could only walk with sticks. He complained that he was bored, had lost all interest in life and, while he knew he had to change his diet, was unable to find the motivation to do so. He also felt his wife was becoming increasingly distant, and he worried that she might leave him.*

Together, the practitioner and the patient agreed that: (1) his eating was seeking to buffer him against his general feelings of malaise (2), his lack of motivation protected him from failure, and (3), his wife's apparent withdrawal could mean she didn't want to add to his problems. All three intentions were reframed in positive terms: (1), feeling good (2), succeeding in his efforts, and (3), re-engaging with his wife.

In exploring for commonalities, the practitioner asked, "When you've become slimmer and fitter, what will you be doing that these problems have prevented you from even considering until now?" The man looked down at the floor and began to cry softly. He said, "We used to take lovely walks in the countryside. I really want to do that again."

When the man had dissipated enough distress to allow him to resume, the practitioner redirected the patient towards a plan that would gradually reduce his intake of food and increase his activity. He was instructed to seek out his wife's help, both in maintaining his lifestyle changes, and in planning walks in the country.

The patient started to leave in buoyant mood, excited about "getting my life back again" and anxious to speak to his wife. When he was at the door, the practitioner called him back – to hand him the sticks he'd forgotten at the side of his chair.

The patterns in this chapter and elsewhere in the book represent only a small number of possibilities. We encourage you to experiment with your own combinations, based always on the needs of the patient. Readers can discuss their findings and explore other possibilities by visiting the website www.magicinpractice.com.

19

Communicating for Life: the way forward

This final chapter draws together the Medical NLP Consultation Process into a coherent whole, discusses ways of increasing patient adherence and points the way forward. We hope, by incorporating even some of the principles and techniques we have discussed, that you will have the means to equip the patient for future challenges, so that the symptoms that brought him to you in the first place will have served their purpose - to prompt him to reorganise at a higher, more complex and more effective level of functioning.

The three phases of the Medical NLP Consultation Process (Table 19.1) function as a map by which the practitioner can locate his present position and then move to whichever other area may become necessary. He should not be constrained by the structure; like all sufficiently detailed maps, it should be used as a guide only. Navigating through the landscape in partnership with the patient, and with curiosity, flexibility, and "attitude", is the crux of the healing journey.

The way forward

The clinical effectiveness of all but a few treatments depends on two factors: how well the patient remembers information and instructions, and how closely he adheres to them. Recall and adherence are automatically improved when practitioners follow some of the principles and techniques referred to elsewhere in this book (for example, providing ori-

Table 19.1 The three-part Medical NLP Consultation Process

Phase	*Purpose*	*Tools*
1. Engagement	Managing first impressions	Engagement
	Rapid engagement	Technique
	Achieving concordance	Yes-sets + negative framing
		Anchoring
2. Alignment	The uninterrupted story	Shaping
	Gathering quality data	Feedback
	Entering the patient's world	Priming
	Accessing and stabilising resources	Framing and reframing
	Patterns, metaphors and meaning	Outcome elicitation
	Negotiating outcomes	Patient-generated metaphors
3. Reorientation	Developing and applying interventions	Submodalities
	Increasing patient self-efficacy	Glyphs
	Future-pacing and testing	Medical NLP change algorithms
		Hypnosis
		Conditioning and future-pacing

entating statements, entering and working from within the patient's model, and discussing and agreeing treatment programmes and well-formed outcomes). Further suggestions follow below.

Recall

Research consistently shows that the patient forgets between 40% and 80% of medical information provided by health-care professionals, sometimes within minutes of leaving the consultation. The more details provided, the fewer are remembered.[178] Furthermore, almost half the information given is incorrectly recalled.[179]

Improving recall

- Do not exceed the patient's conscious processing chunk size (remember the Law of Seven Plus or Minus Two).
- The practitioner's explanatory frameworks must match those of the patient.[180]

- Seek feedback from the patient in his own words. By repeating instructions, patient recall is increased by 30%[181].
- Present information in a form that matches the patient's sensory preferences, but also offer versions in other modalities. Spoken (auditory) instructions alone are the least effective[182]. Written instructions (visually presented) have been shown to increase recall[183], but difficulties occur among non-native speakers or those with low education or literacy. Graphics, such as cartoons and pictographs, are particularly useful adjunctive means of conveying information to patients, increasing both recall and adherence by up to 80%[184].

Adherence

Fewer than half of all patients follow treatment plans and instructions. Britain's National Audit Office reports that wasted drugs alone could be costing the country up to £100 million a year[185], whereas in the United States, the cost has been estimated at more than $100 billion[186].

Adherence is a function of many processes. These include:

- the quality of the relationship (the 'emotional resonance') between practitioner and patient;
- effective communication;
- understanding of, and respect for, the patient's real reason for seeking help (not necessarily immediately evident); and,
- semantically well-formed outcomes, with clearly defined steps.

Remember: if *both* practitioner and patient cannot put the requirements into specific, sensory-based (factual) words, they are unlikely to be carried out.

Increasing recall and adherence

One of the important messages of this book is that *patients do not necessarily know* ***how*** *to get better* – or, to put it differently, they may lack the solution-oriented neurological pathways necessary for change. Also, it is important that new neural paths need to be activated, preferably several times (conditioning), in order to function.

New pathways and a mechanism to set them in motion may be installed as follows:

1. Divide instructions into several (three to five) distinct steps.
2. Outline each step clearly, then
3. ask a question that can be answered only after the patient has mentally run through the necessary steps.

Take, for example, balance-assisting exercise instructions given to a patient diagnosed with labyrinthitis (inner ear disturbance):

Step 1: *Take a look at the instruction sheet.*

Step 2: *As you can see, the exercises are simple …*

Step 3: *and you need to do them regularly five times a day…*

Step 4: *for the next four weeks so you can start feeling better.*

Question: *Now, when do you think would be the best times of day for you to do them all?*

After the question has been asked, be sure you allow the patient time to consider his response.

Two important factors to remember

Both recall and adherence are directly affected by two factors: attentional narrowing and state-dependent learning.

Attentional narrowing occurs when stress and anxiety trigger sympathetic arousal – a common result of carelessly delivered diagnosis, prognosis and treatment options. The central message of a communication ("You have X disease") can severely occlude supporting information, impairing both memory and recall[187].

State dependency is an equally common phenomenon whereby information acquired in a particular psychosocialphysiological context (environment, mood, degree of sympathetic arousal, etc) can only be fully retrieved when that state is reactivated. Thus, if the patient's anxiety levels rise during the consultation, he is unlikely to remember instructions and advice in a more relaxed environment at home[188].

It is important, therefore, to remember to *recognise and reduce the patient's allostatic load* ***before*** *you proceed.*

We began this book by wondering how it could be that, at this highly advanced stage of our development, we could find ourselves so profoundly disabled by such a wide range of physical and emotional disorders that appear to have no medical explanation. One of our suggestions was that scientific inquiry, responsible for so many other extraordinary achievements, continues to approach the human body-mind as an assemblage of almost unconnected parts rather than a deeply complex and highly organised dynamic system.

The purpose of *Magic in Practice*, therefore, was to outline a three-part holistic consultation process that developed and maintained a 'healing relationship' between patient and practitioner, respected the patient as a 'whole person', and helped him re-learn more resourceful patterns for physical and psychological well-being. In doing this, we required a mongrel approach. We foraged in many different fields for fragments we could model and use to create a more coherent picture, not simply of how people become ill, but how they can get better.

We were guided in this by the organising principles of Neuro-Linguistic Programming, as co-created and developed by Dr Richard Bandler. We have acquired from his guidance and inspiration the compulsion to be curious, experimental, flexible and (we have been told) argumentative. We hope, in the pages that have preceded this, we have been able to drive home the message that what is most important about any consultation is the patient and the result he gets. More than science, more than research, more than targets, audits or statistical proof, it is the patient and the uniqueness of his experience that matters most. And it is your relationship with him that can open him to new understanding, behaviour and change.

Appendix A

The Relaxation Response

The "Relaxation Response" is a term coined by Harvard Medical School's Herbert Benson to describe a state that differs significantly from the three states of waking, sleeping and dreaming on which research into consciousness had thus far focused. The state – also known as "restful alertness" – is marked by dramatically reduced metabolic function, measurably deeper even than deep sleep, coupled with an inner 'wakefulness'.

While considered by some psychologists to be related to a form of relaxed, non-verbal and receptive mode of mental functioning known as primary-process thinking, Benson, and later researchers, including Milton Erickson's research partner, Ernst Rossi, came to regard it as a discrete 'fourth state' of consciousness, naturally occurring, but previously unrecognised in Western culture. As Rossi elaborates in *The 20-Minute Break*, we appear to have evolved with the potential to benefit from recognising and responding to natural mind-body cycles, now known as ultradian rhythms, which occur every 90–120 minutes[189].

Benson and his colleagues – inspired by research into the Indian technique of Transcendental Meditation®, newly imported into the West – began to investigate the effect of regular practice of the Relaxation Response. Their early research indicated effectiveness in the treatment of hypertension, cardiac irregularities, headaches, anxiety disorders, premenstrual syndrome, and mild and moderate depression[190]. Later studies showed benefits to patients suffering from back pain, arthritis, gastrointestinal disorders, including irritable bowel syndrome, angina, infertility and chemotherapy-induced nausea[191].

Several researchers believe that the distinctive mix of alpha and theta brainwaves demonstrated during practice of the technique marks specific neurological changes related to psychophysiological self-regulation[192]. Part of its effect is believed to result from the dissipation of accumulated stress, or entropy, thus increasing emotional and physical resilience to day-to-day stressors.

The Relaxation Response differs significantly from more familiar 'relaxation exercises' in that it appears to act cumulatively on the functioning of the 'alarm system' of the brain, most notably by downregulating activity in the reticular formation and thalamus.

Two important characteristics of the Relaxation Response are its essential passivity and its reiterative nature – that is, rather than relying on an external prompt, such as recorded instructions, it repeatedly 'feeds back' into the subject's current level of awareness, progressively deepening his state. Several variations of the technique have proved effective, but the essential components include:

- set times to practise undisturbed (preferably twice a day, for approximately 15 minutes each); and,
- a word or short phrase that acts as an 'anchoring' device (the meaning of the word is less important than its sound. Open vowel sounds, such as those in words like *peace, calm* and *relax*, seem to be more suitable than those with hard consonants).

Method

1. Sit comfortably, close your eyes and wait for 20 or 30 seconds for the body to begin to quieten its activity.
2. Silently repeat the word, in time to each out-breath. Do not deliberately change your natural rate or depth of breathing; simply use the exhale to provide a natural rhythm.
3. Adopt an entirely passive attitude towards thoughts that occur. Do not try to resist them or to force your attention to stay with the word.

4. However, when you 'come to' and realise you have been thinking of something else, gently return to the repetition of the word.
5. When the time is up (feel free to check your watch or a clock), let go of returning to the word, wait for another half-minute or so, and then slowly open your eyes.

Note: Even though you might experience many thoughts, especially when you begin the practice, your heart rate, breathing and metabolism will slow down automatically. Therefore, avoid getting up too abruptly when the session is over. Also, do not practise for longer than 20 minutes to avoid excessive stress release.

We suggest the practitioner guide the patient through the process to ensure full understanding, rather than simply giving instructions. Be sure to emphasise the necessity for regularity of practice.

Alternative methods

For those with visual or kinesthetic sensory preferences, the technique can be adjusted as follows.

Visual

The subject picks a simple coloured shape that he gently holds in his inner attentional field. Each time he becomes aware that he has drifted off onto thoughts or other distractions, he gently brings his attention back to the shape.

Kinesthetic

The subject places his attention on his nostrils and simply notices the sensation of his breath as it moves in and out. He may silently count each out-breath if he so wishes.

Visual-Auditory-Kinesthetic method

The subject begins at 1, imagining he is breathing in an image of the number itself, seeing and feeling it gently settle in his lower abdomen as he breathes out. He then breathes in 2, visualising it settling gently on the number 1 as he breathes out. His goal should be to reach 10, stacking each number, one on top of the other, before starting again.

Appendix B
Cross-lateral Exercises

Cross-lateralisation may be used adjunctively to help patients suffering from anxiety, depression, immune disorders, brain injuries, childhood behavioural disorders, and other conditions in which homolateralisation (reduced activity of one hemisphere) is suspected. The challenge level of the exercises should be increased progressively to force neural connectivity.

Alternate nostril breathing

Sit comfortably. Place one forefinger on the forehead between the eyebrows, position your thumb on one nostril, and your second finger on the other.

Close one nostril, breathe out, then breathe in through the open nostril, then close it and open the other. Breathe out, then in. Close that nostril and repeat the process for 5–10 minutes.

Note: Ensure that each cycle of breathing begins on the out breath so that the cross-over takes place after the in-breath.

Basic cross-marching

Stand with the hands at the sides, and then, while looking slightly up, begin to march in place, ensuring that each hand crosses the body's mid-line to touch the opposite knee.

Complete 10–40 repetitions several times a day.

Cross-marching with eye movements

Follow the instructions for the previous exercise while moving the eyes in large circular movements in both directions, without moving the head.

The challenge level of both cross-marching exercises can be increased by adding an auditory component (counting out loud, reciting the alphabet, etc). When this becomes easy, increase the challenge further: recite the alphabet backwards, count down from 100 in sevens, etc.

Nose-to-ear exercise

Sit comfortably in an upright position. Start with both hands resting on the knees (centre position), and then simultaneously touch the tip of nose with the left hand and the left ear with the right hand. Return the hands to the centre position, and then the reverse the movement: the tip of the nose with the right hand, and the right ear with the left hand. Repeat 10 to 12 times.

Note: Cross-lateralisation may be used even where the patient is immobilised or unconscious. Two people need to work together, gently lifting one knee and moving the opposite hand to touch it, etc.

Resources

Magic in Practice *reader support site*

Readers of this book may visit the support site, www.magicinpractice.com for further information, downloadable material and advice. This is a unique opportunity to interact directly with the authors and other practitioners interested in Medical NLP. In order to enter the site, you will be asked to provide your name and e-mail information, and will then be prompted for a password. The password for readers of this edition of *Magic in Practice* is: **communicate.**

Training in Medical NLP

For further information about Society of Medical NLP Health Practitioner and Master Practitioner licence trainings in the United Kingdom, visit www.medicalnlp.com. *Please note that only the Society of Medical NLP is authorised to provide Society of Medical NLP Health Practitioner, and Society of Medical NLP Master Health Practitioner certification to health professionals. If you wish to verify a claimed association with the Society, e-mail info@medicalnlp.com with your inquiry.*

Choosing an NLP licence course

If you plan to attend any other NLP course and would like advice on choosing one that matches your needs, visit www.medicalnlp.com for a free, downloadable consumer guide.

Trainings by Dr Richard Bandler

For Dr Bandler's itinerary, visit www.richardbandler.com. See also www.paulmckenna.com for London courses featuring Dr Bandler.

NLP news and international seminars

For NLP news and international seminars: www.purenlp.com. Sign up for John Lavalle's regular newsletter.

General Semantics

The Institute of General Semantics, founded in 1938 by Alfred Korzybski, provides information, trainings and materials on all aspects of General Semantics, or, the study of language-as-behaviour. Visit http://time-binding.org

References

Preface

1 Clarke A (1961) Clarke's third law. In *Profiles of the Future.* London: Weidenfeld & Nicolson.
2 Olde Hartman TC, Lucassen PL, van de Lisdonk EH et al (2004) Chronic functional somatic symptoms: a single syndrome? *British Journal of General Practice* **54:** 922–7.
3 Starfield B (2000) Is US health really the best in the world? *Journal of the American Medical Association* **284**(4): 483–5; Null G, Dean C (2003) *Death by Medicine.* New York: Nutrition Institute of America.
4 National Audit Office report (3 November 2005). Available from: www.nao.org.uk/publications/nao_reports/05-06/0506456.pdf
5 BMA Health Policy and Economic Research Unit (2000) *Work-related Stress Among Senior Doctors: Review of Research.* London: BMA Health Policy and Economic Research Unit.
6 See www.cfah.org
7 Adapted from Bakal D (1999) *Minding the Body.* New York: Guildford Press.
8 Bandler R, Grinder J (1975) *The Structure of Magic.* Palo Alto, CA: Science and Behavior Books.
9 Antonovsky A (1979) *Health, Stress and Coping.* San Francisco: Jossey-Bass.
10 Dixon M, Sweeney K (2000) *The Human Effect in Medicine.* Oxfordshire: Radcliffe Medical Press.

11 Lambert MJ (1992) Psychotherapy outcome research: implications for integrative and eclectic therapists. In Norcoss C, Goldfriend M (eds) *Handbook of Psychotherapy Integration*, Ch. 3. New York: Basic Books.

12 Kelso JA Scott (1995) *Dynamic Patterns – the Self-Organisation of Brain and Behaviour*. Cambridge, MA: MIT Press.

13 Lipton B (2005) *The Biology of Belief.* California: Elite Books.

14 McEwen B (2002) *The End of Stress as We Know It.* Washington DC: Joseph Henry Press.

15 Dixon M, Sweeney K (2000) *The Human Effect in Medicine.* Oxfordshire: Radcliffe Medical Press; Horvath AO (1995) The therapeutic relationship. *In Session* **1,** 7–17; Krupnick JL et al (1996) The role of the therapeutic alliance in psychotherapy pharmacotherapy outcome: findings in the National Institute of Mental Health Treatment of Depression Collaborative Research Project. *Journal of Consulting and Clinical Psychology* **64,** 532–39.

16 Ambady N et al (2002) Surgeons' tone of voice: a clue to malpractice history. *Surgery* **132**(1): 5–9; Levinson W et al (1997) Physician-patient communication: the relationship with malpractice claims among primary care physicians and surgeons. *Journal of the American Medical Association* **277**(7): 553–9.

17 Zajicek G (1995) The placebo effect is the healing force of nature. *Cancer Journal* **8**(2) 44-45.

18 Brody H (1997) *The Placebo Response.* New York: HarperCollins.

19 Kirsch I, Saperstein G (1998) Listening to Prozac but hearing placebo: a meta-analysis of antidepressant medication. *Prevention and Treatment* (online journal): htpp://content.apa.org/journals/pre/1/1/2

20 Thompson WG (2005) *The Placebo Effect and Health.* New York: Prometheus Books; Horvath AO (1995) The therapeutic relationship. *In Session* **1,** 7–17.

21 Balint M (2000) *The Doctor, His Patient and the Illness.* London: Churchill Livingstone.

Chapter 1

22 Human Givens: Radical Psychology Today (Spring 2002) *How We Are* **9**(1): 7.

23 Starfield B (2000) Is US health really the best in the world? *Journal of the American Medical Association* **284**(4): 483–5; Null G, Dean C (2003) *Death by Medicine*. New York: Nutrition Institute of America.

24 National Audit Office report (3 November 2005). Available from: www.nao.org.uk/publications/nao_reports/05-06/0506456.pdf

25 Greenberg PE, Sisitsky T, Kessler RC et al (1999) The economic burden of anxiety disorders. *Journal of Clinical Psychiatry* **60**(7): 427–35.

26 http://www.scmh.org.uk/80256FBD004F6342/vWeb/pckHAL6FBJPF

27 Galsziou P, Chalmers I, Rawlins M, McCulloch P (2007) When are randomised trials unnecessary? Picking signal from noise. *British Medical Journal* **334:** 349–51.

28 Thomas KB (1987) General practice consultations: is there any point in being positive? *British Medical Journal* **294:** 1200–2.

29 Duncan BL, Miller SD, Sparks JA (2004) *A Revolutionary Way to Improve Effectiveness Through Client-directed, Outcome Informed Therapy*. San Francisco: Jossey-Bass.

30 Vase L et al (2003) The contribution of suggestion, desire and expectation to placebo effects in Irritable bowel syndrome patients: an empirical investigation. *Pain* **105**(1–2): 17–25.

31 Segerstrom SC, Miller GE (2004) Psychological stress and the human immune system: a meta-analytical study of 30 years of inquiry. *Psychological Bulletin* **130**(4): 601–30; Kopp MS, Rethélyi J (2004) Where psychology meets physiology: chronic stress and premature mortality – the Central-Eastern European health paradox. *Brain Research Bulletin* **62:** 351–67.

32 Bandler R (1993) *Time for a Change*. Capitola, CA: Meta Publications.

33 Benedetti F, Amanzio M, Vighetti S, Asteggiano G (2006) The biochemical and neuroendocrine bases of the hyperalgesic nocebo effect. *Journal of Neuroscience* **26:** 12014–22.

34 Kurtz A, Silverman J (1991) *The Medical Interview: The Three Function Approach*. St Louis, MO: Mosby-Year Book Inc.

35 Usherwood T (1999) *Understanding the Consultation: Evidence, Theory and Practice*. Philadelphia: OUP Buckingham.

36 Dixon M, Sweeney K (2000) *The Human Effect in Medicine*. Oxfordshire: Radcliffe Medical Press; Horvath AO (1995) The therapeutic relationship. *In Session* **1:** 7–17; Krupnick JL et al (1996)

The role of the therapeutic alliance in psychotherapy pharmacotherapy outcome: findings in the National Institute of Mental Health Treatment of Depression Collaborative Research Project. *Journal of Consulting and Clinical Psychology* **64:** 532–9.

37 Bandura A (1977) Self efficacy: towards a unifying theory of behavioural change. *Psychological Review* **84:** 191–215.

38 Lipton B (2004) *The Biology of Belief.* Santa Rosa, CA: Elite Books.

Chapter 2

39 Rosendal M, Olsen F, Fink P (2005) Management of medically unexplained symptoms. *British Medical Journal* **330:** 4–5.

40 Wessley S, Nimnuan C, Sharpe M (1999) Functional somatic syndromes; one or many? *Lancet* **354:** 936–9.

41 Olde Hartman T, Lucasseen P, Van de Lisdonk E, Bor H, Van de Weel C (2004) Chronic functional somatic symptoms: a single syndrome? *British Journal of General Practice* **54:** 922–7.

42 Banyard P (1996) *Applying Psychology to Health.* London: Hodder & Stoughton.

43 Selye H (1936) A syndrome produced by diverse nocuous agents. *Nature.* **July** (138): 32

44 Buchanan TW, Lovallo WR (2001) Enhanced memory for emotional material following stress-level cortisol treatment in humans. *Psychoneuroendocrinology.* **April** (3): 307–17.

45 For a highly readable, yet scientifically grounded, account of recent developments in this field, we suggest endocrinologist Bruce McEwen's book, *The End of Stress As We Know It* (2002). Washington DC: Joseph Henry Press.

46 Sterling P, Eyer J (1988). Allostasis: A new paradigm to explain arousal pathology. In: Fisher S, Reason J (Eds.), *Handbook of Life Stress, Cognition and Health.* New York: John Wiley & Sons.

47 Nesse RM, Williams GC (1966). *Why We get Sick: The New Science of Darwinian Medicine.* New York: Vintage Books.

48 Klieger R, Miller J (1978) Decreased heart rate variability and its association with increased mortality after acute myocardial infarction. *American Journal of Cardiology* **59:** 256–62.

49 Zeigarnik B (1927) Das Behalten erledigter und unerledigter Handlungen. *Psychologische Forschung* **9:** 1–85.

50 For a comprehensive review of the literature on this subject, see Rothschild B (2000) *The Body Remembers: The Psychophysiology of Trauma and Trauma Treatment.* New York: WW Norton & Company.

51 Leader D, Corfield D (2007) *Why Do People Get Ill?* London: Hamish Hamilton.

52 Avenanti A, Bueti D, Galati G, Aglioti SM (2005) Transcranial magnetic stimulation highlights the sensorimotor side of empathy for pain. *Nature Neuroscience* **8**: 955–60.

53 Ax AA (1964) Goals and methods of psychophysiology. *Psychophysiology* **1:** 8–25.

54 Dobbs D (2006) A revealing reflection. *Scientific American Mind* **April/May:** 22–7.

55 Stern D (2002) Attachment: from early childhood through the lifespan. Conference presentation, audio recording 609–17. Los Angeles: Lifespan Institute.

56 Hatfield E, Cacioppo JT, Rapson RL (1994) *Emotional Contagion: Studies in Emotional and Social Interaction.* Cambridge, UK: Cambridge University Press.

57 Yue G, Cole KJ (1992) Strength increases from the motor program: comparison of training with maximal voluntary and imagined muscle contractions. *Journal of Neurophysiology* **67**(5): 114–23.

58 Egolf B, Lasker J, Wolf S, Potvin L (1992) The Roseto effect: a 50-year comparison of mortality rates. *American Journal of Public Health* **82**(8): 1089–92.

59 Anderson NB, Anderson PE (2003) *Emotional Longevity*. New York: Viking Penguin.

60 House JS, Robbins C, Metzner HL (1982) The association of social relationships and activities with mortality: prospective evidence from the Tecumseh Community Health Study. *American Journal of Epidemiology* **116:** 123–40.

61 Berkman LF, Leo-Summers L, Horwitz RI (1992) Emotional support and survival following myocardial infarction: a prospective, population-based study of the elderly. *Annals of Internal Medicine* **117:** 1003–9.

62 Leserman J et al (2000) Impact of stressful life events, depression, social support, coping and cortisol. *American Journal of Psychiatry* **157:** 1221–28.

63 Cohen S et al (1997) Social ties and susceptibility to the common cold. *Journal of the American Medical Association* **277:** 1940–4.

64 Seeman M, Lewis S (1995) Powerlessness, health and mortality: a longitudinal study of older men and mature women. *Social Science in Medicine* **41:** 517–25.

65 Wolff C, Friedman S, Hofer M, Mason J (1964) Relationship between psychological defences and mean urinary 17-hydroxycorticosteroid excretion rates. *Psychosomatic Medicine* **26:** 576–91.

66 Chapman C (1989) Giving the patient control of opioid analgesic administration. In Hill C, Field W (eds) *Advances in Pain Research and Therapy*, vol. II. Philadelphia, PA Lippincott Williams and Wilkins.

67 Rodin J (1986) Ageing and health: effects of the sense of control. *Science* **233:** 1271–6.

68 Melin B, Lunberg U, Soderlund J, Grandqvist M (1999) Psychological and physiological stress reactions of male and female assembly workers: a comparison between two different forms of work organisation. *Journal of Organisational Psychology* **20:** 47–61.

69 Sapolsky R (2004) *Why Zebras Don't Get Ulcers: The Guide to Stress, Stress-Related Diseases, and Coping*, 3rd ed. New York: Henry Holt.

70 Peterson C, Seligman M, Vaillant G (1988) Pessimistic explanatory style is a risk factory for physical illness: a 35-year longitudinal study. *Journal of Personality and Social Psychology* **55:** 23–27.

71 Kubzansky L et al (2001) Is the glass half empty or half full? A prospective study of optimism and coronary heart disease in the normative ageing study. *Psychosomatic Medicine* **63:** 910–16.

72 McCullough M et al (2000) Religious involvement and mortality: a meta-analytical review. *Health Psychology* **19:** 211–22.

73 Frankl V (2004) *Man's Search for Meaning*. London: Rider & Co.

Chapter 4

74 Freud S (1977) *Introductory Lectures on Psychoanalysis.* (formerly titled *General Introduction to Psychoanalysis.*) The Standard edition (James Strachey, translator and editor) New York: WW Norton.

75 Pinker S (New Ed 1995) *The Language Instinct: The New Science of Language and Mind*. London: Penguin Books Ltd

76 House JS, Landis KR, Umberson D (1988) Social relations and health. *Science* **241:** 540–5; Hafen Q, Karren KJ, Frandsen KJ, Smith NL (1996) *Mind/Body Health: The Effects of Attitudes, Emotions and Relationships*, Boston: Allyn & Bacon; The GUSTO Investigators (1993) An international randomised trial comparing rour thrombolytic studies for acute myocardial infarction. *New England Journal of Medicine* **329:** 673–82.

77 Bargh JA, Chartrand TL (1999) The unbearable automaticity of being. *American Psychologist* **54**(7): 462–79.

78 Pert CB, Ruff MR (1985) Neuropeptides and their receptors: a psychosomatic network. *Journal of Immunology* **135**(2): 820–6.

79 Rosencranz MA et al (2005) Neural circuitry underlying the interaction between emotion and asthma symptom exacerbation. *PNAS* **102**(37): 13319–24.

80 Pert C (2006) *Everything You Need to Know to Feel Good*. Carlsbad, CA: Hay House.

81 Thaler Singer M, Lalich J (1996) *Cults in Our Midst*. Hoboken, NJ: Jossey Bass/Wiley.

82 Korzybski A (1933 (1994)). *Science and Sanity: An Introduction to Non-Aristotelian Systems and General Semantics*. Englewood, NJ: Institute of General Semantics.

83 Miller GA (1956) The magical number seven, plus or minus two: some limits on our capacity for processing information. *Psychological Review* **63:** 81–97.

84 McGuire IC (1996) Remembering what the doctor said: organisation and older adults' memory. *Experimental Ageing Research* **22:** 403–28.

Chapter 6

85 Libet B (1992) The neural time factor in perception, volition, and free will. *Revue de Métaphysique et de Morale* **97:** 255–72.

86 Wegner DM (2002) *The Illusion of Conscious Will*. Cambridge, MA: Bradford Books.

87 Bolles E (1991) *A Second Way of Knowing: The Riddle of Human Perception*. New York: Prentice-Hall.

88 *Oxford Concise Medical Dictionary* (2000), 5th edn. Oxford: Oxford University Press.

89 Wahl PW, Savage PJ, Psaty BM, Orchard TJ, Robbins JA, Tracy RP (1998) Diabetes in older adults: comparison of 1997 American Diabetes Association classification of diabetes mellitus with 1985 WHO classification. *Lancet* **352:** 1012–15.

90 Report of the Expert Committee on the Diagnosis and Classification of Diabetes Mellitus. *Diabetes Care* 1997; **20:** 1183–97.

Chapter 7

91 Gladwell M (2005) *Blink*. London: Allen & Lane.

92 Ekman P, Frieson WV (2003) *Unmasking the Face*. Cambridge, MA: Major Books.

93 Ambady N, Rosenthal R (1993) Half a minute: predicting teacher evaluations from thin slices of nonverbal behaviour and physical attractiveness. *Journal of Personality and Social Psychology* **64**(3): 431–41.

94 Korsch BM, Gozzi EK, Francis V (1968) Gaps in doctor-patient communication. *Pediatrics* **42:** 855–71.

95 Damasio A (1994) *Descartes' Error*. New York: GP Putnam's Sons.

96 Allen J, Burkin A (2000) Interview by Berkley Rice: How plaintiffs' lawyers pick their targets. *Medical Economics* **77:** 94–96, 99, 103–104 passim.

97 Dixon M, Sweeney K (2000) *The Human Effect in Medicine*. Oxfordshire: Radcliffe Medical Press; Horvath AO (1995) The therapeutic relationship. *In Session* **1:** 7–17; Krupnick JL et al (1996) The role of the therapeutic alliance in psychotherapy pharmacotherapy outcome: findings in the National Institute of Mental Health Treatment of Depression Collaborative Research Project. *Journal of Consulting and Clinical Psychology* **64:** 53–9.

98 Laver J (1991) *The Gift of Speech*. Edinburgh: Edinburgh University Press.

99 Pear TH (1931) *Voice and Personality*. London: Chapman & Hall.

100 Linville SE (1998) Acoustic correlates of perceived versus actual sexual orientation in men's speech. *Folia Phoniatrica et Logoapedia* **50:** 35–48.

101 Karpf A (2006) *The Human Voice – the Story of a Remarkable Talent.* London: Bloomsbury.

102 Langer E (1990) *Mindfulness.* Cambridge, MA: Da Capo Press.

Chapter 8

103 Ornstein R (1997) *The Right Mind; Making Sense of the Hemispheres.* Orlando FL: Harcourt Brace.

104 Beckman HB, Frankel RM (1984) The effect of physician behaviour on the collection of data. *Annals of Internal Medicine* **101:** 692–6.

105 Musashi M (2005) *The Book of Five Rings* (trans. Cleary T). Boston, MA: Shambhala Publications.

106 Tversky A, Kahneman D (1973). Availability: a heuristic for judging frequency and probability. *Cognitive Psychology* **5:** 207–32.

107 Rosenhan R (1973). On being sane in insane places. *Science* **179:** 250–8.

Chapter 9

108 Motluk A (2006) How many things can you do at once? Our flawed talent for multitasking. *New Scientist* **7 April:** 28–31.

109 Gazzaniga M (1998) *The Mind's Past.* Berkley, CA: University of California Press.

110 Evans P, Hucklebridge F, Clow A (2000) *Cerebral Laterisation and the Immune System, in Mind, Immunity and Health.* London: Free Association Books.

111 Pink D (2005) *A Whole New Mind; Why Right-Brainers Will Rule the Future.* New York: Riverhead Books.

112 Platt FW, McMath JC (1979) Clinical hypocompetence: the interview. *Annals of Internal Medicine* **91**(6): 898–902.

113 Desmond J, Copeland L (2000) *Communicating with Today's Patient.* San Francisco: Jossey-Bass.

114 Realni T, Kalet A, Sparling J (1995) Interruptions in the medical interaction. *Archives of Family Medicine* **4:** 1028–33.
115 Burack R, Carpenter R (1983) The predictive value of the presenting complaint. *Journal of Family Practice* **16**(4): 749–54.
116 Miller S, Hubble M, Duncan B (1996) *Handbook of Solution Focused Brief Therapy*. San Francisco: Jossey-Bass.

Chapter 10

117 Brody H (2000). The Placebo Response. New York, NY: Cliff Street Books
118 Thomas, K B (1987), General practice consultations: is there any point in being positive? *British Medical Journal* **294:** 1200–02.
119 Vase L et al (2003) The contribution of suggestion, desire and expectation to placebo effects in irritable bowel syndrome patients: an empirical investigation. *Pain* **105**(1–2): 17–25.
120 Lipton B (2005) *The Biology of Belief*. Santa Rosa, CA: Mountain of Love Productions.
121 Balint M (2000) *The Doctor, His Patient and The Illness*. London: Churchill Livingstone.
122 Searle J (1995) The Mystery of Consciousness. *New York Review of Books*. **2 November** and **16 November**: 60–61.
123 Hoyle F (1983) *The Intelligent Universe*. New York: Holt, Rinehart & Winston.
124 Schroth M (1970) The effect of informative feedback on problem solving. *Child Development* **41**(3): 831–7.

Chapter 11

125 Kopp S (1977) *Back to One*. Palo Alto, CA: Science & Behavior Books.
126 Lakoff G, Johnson M (1980) *Metaphors We Live By*. Chicago, IL: University of Chicago Press.
127 Lakoff G, Johnson M (1999) *Philosophy in the Flesh*. New York: Basic Books.

Chapter 12

128 Wolf IJ (ed.) (1965) *Aphorisms and Facetiae of Bela Schick*. Baltimore: Waverly Press/Knoll Pharmaceutical.

129 Robinson R, West R (1992) A comparison of computer and questionnaire methods of history-taking in a genito-urinary clinic. *Psychology and Health* **6:** 77–84.

130 Engel G (1977) The need for a new medical model: a challenge for biomedicine. *Science* **196:** 129–36.

131 Duncan BL, Miller SD, Sparks JA (2004) *A Revolutionary Way to Improve Effectiveness Through Client-directed, Outcome Informed Therapy*. San Francisco: Jossey-Bass.

132 Vase L et al (2003) The contribution of suggestion, desire and expectation to placebo effects in irritable bowel syndrome patients: an empirical investigation. *Pain* **105**(1–2): 17–25.

133 Bandler R, Grinder J (1982) *Reframing*. Moab, UT: Real People Press.

134 Littlewood R, Lipsedge M (1989) *Aliens and Alienists*, 2nd ed. London: Unwin Hyman.

135 Kubler-Ross E (1969) *On Death and Dying*. New York: Macmillan.

Chapter 13

136 The Disease-Illness Model (1984) of McWhinney et al, University of Western Ontario, suggested the “transformed clinical method” also known as “patient-centred clinical interviewing”, to differentiate it from the more traditional “doctor-centred” method.

137 de Shazer S (1994) *Words Were Originally Magic*. New York: Norton.

Chapter 14

138 In Clark RW (1984) *Einstein: The Life and Times*. New York: Avon.

139 Friedman M, Rosenman R (1974) *Type A Behaviour and Your Heart*. New York: Alfred A Knopf.

140 Csikszentmihalyi M (1991) *Flow: The Psychology of Optimal Experience*. Copenhagen: SOS Free Stock.

141 Whitrow G (1972) *The Nature of Time.* London: Thames & Hudson.
142 Ornstein R (1969) *On the Experience of Time,* New York: Penguin.
143 Dossey L (1982) *Space, Time and Medicine.* Boston MA: Shambhala.
144 Nishiyama K, Johnson J (1997) Karoshi-death from overwork: occupational health consequences of the Japanese production management. *International Journal of Health Services.* Available from: www.workhealth.org/whatsnew/lpkarosh.html
145 Siu R (1974) *Chi, A Neo-Taoist Approach to Life.* Cambridge, MA: MIT Press.
146 Benson H (1990) *The Relaxation Response.* New York: Avon Books.

Chapter 15

147 For an extensive review of research into our human tendency to act out of the rules of group thinking, we know of no better book than David Berreby's *Us and Them – Understanding Your Tribal Mind* (2005) London: Hutchinson.
148 Langer E (1989) *Mindfulness.* Reading, MA: Addison-Wesley.
149 Furedi F (2004) *Therapy Culture: Cultivating Vulnerability in an Uncertain Age.* London: Routledge.
150 Conversation with the author (GT).

Chapter 16

151 Rainville P, Price D (2003) Hypnosis phenomenology and neurobiology of consciousness. *International Journal of Clinical and Experimental Hypnosis* **51**(2): 105–29; Ray WJ, De Pascalis V (2003) Temporal aspects of hypnotic processes. *International Journal of Clinical and Experimental Hypnosis* **51**(2): 147–65; Szechtman H, Woody E, Bowers K, Nahmias C (1998) Where the imaginal appears real: a positron emission tomography study of auditory hallucinations. *Proceedings of the National Academy of Sciences of the United States of America* **95:** 1956–60.
152 Gazzaniga M (1998) *The Mind's Past.* Berkley, CA: University of California Press.

153 Kershaw CJ (1992) *The Couple's Hypnotic Dance*. New York: Brunner/Mazel.

154 Vaughan AC (1997) *The Talking Cure: The Science behind Psychotherapy*. New York: Grosset/Putnam.

155 Kandel ER (1998) A new intellectual framework for psychiatry. *American Journal of Psychiatry* **155**(4): 457–69.

156 Deikman J (1982) *The Observing Self: Mysticism and Psychotherapy*. Boston, MA: Beacon Press.

157 Watzlawick P (1974) *Change: Principles of Problem Formation and Problem Resolution*. New York: WW Norton.

Chapter 17

158 Ornstein R (1972) *The Psychology of Consciousness*. San Francisco: WH Freeman.

159 Benson H (1996) *Timeless Healing*. New York: Scribner.

160 Jacobs GD, Benson H (eds) (1992) *The Wellness Book*. New York: Fireside.

161 Perskey H (1979) Pain terms: a list of definitions and notes on usage recommendations by the IASP subcommittee on taxonomy. *Pain* **6:** 249–52.

162 Gureje O, Von Korff M, Simon GE, Gater R (1998) Persistent pain and well-being. A World Health Organisation study in primary care. *JAMA* **280**: 147–51.

163 Smith Blair H (September 2002) Chronic pain: a primary care condition. *In Practice (ARC)* **9:** 1–5.

164 Mcfarlane M, McBeth J, Silman AJ (2001) Widespread body pain and mortality: prospective population based study. *BMJ* **323:** 662–4.

165 Melzack R, Wall PD (1982) *The Challenge of Pain* London: Penguin.

166 Loeser JD (1994) Tic douloureaux and atypical face pain In Wall PD, Melzack R (eds) *Textbook of Pain*, 3rd edn. Edinburgh: Churchill Livingstone.

167 Scarry E (1985) *The Body in Pain*. New York: Oxford University Press.

168 Evans P, Hucklebridge F, Clow A (2000) *Mind, Immunity and Health: The Science of Psychoneuroimmunology*. London: Free Association Books.

Chapter 18

169 Ogden P, Minton K, Pain C (2006) *Trauma and the Body*. New York: Norton.

170 For an easily accessible and impressive account of recent developments in research into neuroplasticity, we recommend Norman Doidge's book, *The Brain that Changes Itself* (New York: Viking Penguin, 2007).

171 Feltz DL, Landers DM (1983) The effects of mental practice on motor skill learning and performance: a meta-analysis. *Journal of Sports Psychology* **5:** 25–57.

172 Yue Guang, Cole K (1992) Strength increases from the motor program: comparison of training with maximal voluntary and imagined muscle contractions. *Journal of Neurophysiology* **67**(5): 1114–23.

173 Moseley GL (2004) Graded motor imagery is effective for long-standing complex regional pain syndrome: a randomised, controlled trial. *Pain* **108:** 192–8.

174 Pascual-Leone A, Hamilton R (2001) The metamodal organisation of the brain. *Progress in Brain Research* **134:** 427–45.

175 Henningsen P, Zipfel S, Herzog W (2007) Management of functional somatic syndromes. *Lancet* **369:** 946–55.

176 Scaer RC (2001) *The Body Bears the Burden: Trauma, Dissociation and Disease*. New York: Haworth Medical Press.

177 Bakal D (1999) *Minding the Body: Clinical Uses of Somatic Awareness*. New York: Guilford Press.

Chapter 19

178 McGuire LC (1996) Remembering what the doctor said: organisation and older adults' memory for medical information. *Experimental Aging Research* **22:** 403–28.

179 Anderson JL, Dodman S, Kopelman M, Fleming A (1979) Patient information recall in a rheumatology clinic. *Rheumatology Rehabilitation* **18:** 245–55.

180 Tuckett D, Boulton M, Olson C, Williams A (1985) *Meetings Between Experts*. London: Tavistock.

181 Bertakis KD (1977) The communication of information from physician to patient: a method for increasing patient retention and satisfaction. *Journal of Family Practice* **5:** 217–22.
182 Thomson AM, Cunningham SJ, Hunt NP (2001) A comparison of information retention at an initial orthodontic consultation. *European Journal of Orthodontics* **23:** 169–78.
183 Blinder D, Rotenberg L, Peleg M, Taicher S (2001) Patient compliance to instructions after oral procedures. *International Journal of Oral and Maxillofacial Surgery* **30:** 216–19.
184 Houts PS, Bachrach R, Witmer JT et al (1998) Using pictographs to enhance recall of spoken medical instructions. *Patient Education and Counseling* **35:** 83–8.
185 Available from: www.nao.org.uk/publications/nao_reports/06-07/0607454.pdf
186 Berg JS et al (1993) Medication compliance: a healthcare problem. *Annals of Pharmacotherapy* **27:** 1–24.
187 Ley P (1979) Memory for medical information. *British Journal of Social and Clinical Psychology* **18:** 245–55.
188 Schramke CJ, Bauer RM (1997) State-dependent learning in older and younger adults. *Psychology of Aging* **12:** 255–62.

Appendix A

189 Rossi EL, Nimmons D (1991) *The 20-Minute Break: Using the New Science of Ultradian Rhythms*. Los Angeles: Jeremy O Tracher.
190 For a summary of related research, see Benson H, Klipper MZ (1975) *The Relaxation Response*. New York: HarperTorch.
191 Benson H, Stuart E (eds) (1992) *The Wellness Book*. New York: Fireside.

Glossary

Abreaction: The sudden and violent release of repressed emotion (cf. *Silent Abreaction*). Abreaction is to be discouraged to avoid re-anchoring the subject to his distress.

Affect bridging: The linking by anchoring or other means of feeling or response with its original cause.

Alignment: The stage where one enters the patient's model in the Medical NLP Consultation Model.

Allostasis: The process of achieving stability through psychological, physical or behavioural flexibility.

Allostatic Load: Chronic psychological, physical or emotional stress, preventing Allostasis.

Analogue: Data presented in continuously variable form, rather than in discrete packages (c.f. *Digital*). The changing volume of speech is Analogue, while the words used are Digital.

Anchor: A stimulus or trigger paired with a specific response. Anchors may be set deliberately or inadvertently, openly, or covertly.

Anchor collapsing: When two different anchors fire simultaneously, the end result is a mixed or neutral state. Neither original anchor will remain intact.

Anniversary Effect: The tendency of some patients to experience recurrence of symptoms at significant times of their lives.

Associated: Experiencing through your own senses (seeing through your own eyes, hearing with your own ears, feeling with your own feelings).

Auditory: Representational system pertaining to sense of hearing.

Away-From: Motivational pattern marked by avoidance of an unwanted experience, rather than by accomplishing a desired outcome (Towards).

Biomedical: Biological or physiological process in relation to the field of medicine.

Bonded Disconnection: Paradoxical attempt to 'not-have' a symptom or feeling that in practice reinforces the unwanted experience.

Brainwashing: Changing the thoughts, beliefs, behaviours and responses of a subject without his knowledge and/or consent.

Bridging: Connecting two previously unconnected qualities or states, conversationally or by deliberately anchoring.

Burnout: (See *Compassion Fatigue*).

Calibration: Establishing the relevance of non-verbal responses by testing.

Cartesian Dualism: Also known as the "Mind-Body Split"; suggests mind and body operate independently of each other.

Cause-and-Effect: Real or perceived causal relationship involving two or more events.

Chronopathic: Problems caused by the subject's perception/experience of Time.

Chunking: Altering experience and perception by focusing on large or smaller units of information.

Compassion Fatigue: Term used interchangeably with "Burnout" to describe the adverse effects on the practitioner of over-involvement in the patient's problems. Negative physical and emotional response to stresses experienced in the caring professions.

Conditioning: Used in two senses by Medical NLP: 1. Classical Conditioning, as defined by Behaviourism, and 2. repetition or practice to help the subject create new neural patterns.

Congruence: The alignment of beliefs and other internal experience with behaviour.

Consciousness: Everything that is in current awareness.

Content: The 'story', including perceived 'cause', associated with a problem; the product of reflection, interrogation and psychoanalysis.

Description: The first verbal level in the Structural Differential that follows the Object Level. The patient's symptoms.

Digital: Data presented in discrete packages, rather than in continuously variable form (c.f. **Analogue**). Words, for example, are Digital, whereas the changing volume in which they are spoken is Analogue.

Dissipation: The biological discharge of entropy. A requirement for maintaining allostasis.

Dissociation: Experiencing an event as if separated from the self.

Ecology/ecological: Used in NLP to emphasise that all interventions and new behaviours should be 'fit for purpose' and will not cause problems in other contexts of the person's life.

Emotional Contagion: The tendency to express and feel transferred emotions similar to those of others.

Engagement: 'Connecting with' the patient; gaining rapport, concordance, etc.

Entropy: The result or waste products of the degradation of energy. Used in Medical NLP to refer to undischarged emotional overload; the as-yet unmetabolised chemical residue of systemic stress.

Epigenetics : Effect of psychosocial crises on genetic information. May be hereditary.

Evaluation: Judgements, opinions, inferences (essentially unverifiable) drawn from information.

Event: Pre-verbal level of Korzybski's Structural Differential referring to disturbance of the subject's neurology. The Event or process is *not* within the subject's conscious awareness.

Evidence-Based Medicine: Use of currently available "best evidence" in making decisions about patient care. Largely dependant on Randomised Controlled Trial for acceptance.

Exit Point: A point in a strategy that allows the subject to know when to stop the processing.

Expectancy: The positive (or negative) anticipation of both patient and practitioner regarding the efficacy of treatment.

Explanatory Styles: Term used by Martin Seligman et al to describe subjects' world-view.

Eye-Accessing Cues: Unconscious eye movements reflecting the Representational Systems used by the individual to process information.

Fact-Evaluation Spectrum: Process allowing the speaker or listener to differentiate between sensory-specific data and opinion.

Faith Effect: The ability to elicit changes in health or well-being associated with a sense of connectedness or a strong spiritual belief.

Felt Sense: Subjective, internal, non-verbal bodily awareness or sensation linked to a specific experience. (See also: *Kinesthetic* and *Somatic Marker*)

Flooding: Overwhelming exposure to anxiety-provoking stimulus while preventing or inhibiting the flight component.

Frame: Construct of how a situation or event is perceived. **Reframing** allows changing parameters within the construct, e.g. changing content or context.

Functional Disorder: Condition for which no pathological cause has been identified.

Functional Magnetic Resonance Imaging (fMRI): A process applying Magnetic Resonance Imaging (see *Magnetic Resonance Imaging*) to render haemodynamic responses of neuronal activity.

Future-Pace: The act of imagining the event having taken place in the future.

Gene Expression: The process by which the inheritable information from a gene is manifested as a protein, enzyme or RNA sequence.

General Adaptation Syndrome (GAS): Term used by Hans Selye to describe the process of adaptation to long term stressors.

General Semantics (Alfred Korzybski): A field pertaining to the study of the relationship of language with neurological function (not to be confused with "semantics").

Glyph: A kinesthetic experienced and treated as a three-dimensional 'object' – e.g. a "red ball" of pain.

Heart Rate Variability (HRV): Diagnostic tool in cardiology and obstetrics (and Medical NLP), which provides a reliable measure of the functioning of the Autonomic Nervous System (ANS) This, in turn, reflects the overall psychophysical status of the subject.

Homolateralisation: Physical or emotional behaviour which results from overdependence on one brain hemisphere over the other.

Host-Resistance: Measure of an individual's or group's resistance to illness.

Hyperchronic: Problems caused by the subjective sensation of time moving too rapidly – e.g. stress.

Hypochronic: Problems caused by subjective sensation of time 'dragging' – e.g. depression.

Hypnosis: A method or practice of inducing 'suggestiblility' in a subject, sometimes considered to be a normal extension of human consciousness.

Hypnotic Phenomena: See *Trance Phenomena.*

Imaginal: Sensory-rich internal creation of an experience or behaviour with the intention of creating corresponding neural networks.

Inference: Term used in General Semantics to refer to the evaluation of an experience.

Ko Mei: Derived from the Indo-European roots of the word "communication", a term used in Medical NLP to denote the process of communication as a *coming together in order to effect change.*

Layering: Using two or more different techniques towards a given outcome to increase likelihood of success.

Limbic Arousal: Increased activity of the limbic system leading to generation of emotions such as rage, elation, fear.

Linear Time: The progression of time experienced sequentially

Linguistic Relativity (Also **Sapir-Whorf Hypothesis**)**:** The effect on experience of the language used.

Magnetic Resonance Imaging (MRI): An imaging technique involving powerful magnetic fields rendered by computer software in 3-dimensional images.

Medical NLP: The proprietary development and application of NLP principles and techniques specifically within the field of health care.

Meta Model™: A linguistic model developed by Richard Bandler and John Grinder exploring the transformation of meaning to expression, or Deep Structure to Surface Structure.

Meta-Psychology: An explanation of how 'psychology' works.

Meta-State: A state that creates another state – e.g. anxiety that one will have an anxiety attack, fear of fear.

Mirror Neurons: Neurons which excite when a subject observes an event or action 'as if' he were experiencing the event or action himself. Believed to be the neurophysiological foundation of empathy.

Modalities: Referring to our five senses, especially when describing how subject experience is 'created'.

Modelling: A process described by Richard Bandler as the act of "creating a calculus which describes a given system".

Molecular: Pertaining to molecules - i.e. stable, neutral groups of at least two atoms linked by strong chemical bonds.

Negative Frame: A linguistic pattern (e.g. - "isn't it?"; "wouldn't it?"; "can't it?") usually employed to increase agreement.

Neuroplasticity: The ability of brain architecture to be changed by experience.

NLP: The study of the structure of subjective experience.

Nominalisation: Verb transformed into a noun; a 'process' represented as a 'thing'.

Normalisation: Process whereby the practitioner behaves as if events are normal or accepts them to be normal within the context and framework of the subject's own belief-system or cultural reference.

Object Level: The second pre-verbal level of Korzybski's Structural Differential. At this level the Event or process is within the subject's conscious awareness.

Orientating Statement: Information given by physician to patient informing him of what is happening, or is about to happen.

Outcomes: Specific results negotiated and worked towards as a function of the consultation process.

Pacing: Matching aspects of the subject's behaviour or responses to facilitate rapport.

Predicates: Words used to describe which representational system someone is using.

Preframing: Setting in advance the boundary conditions of an experience or event.

Premature Cognitive Closure: Tendency to make decision and initiate action before all available information has been processed.

Presupposition: Information assumed, but not overtly stated, to be present in order for a statement to be understood.

Primary Process Thinking: A form of relaxed, non-verbal and receptive mode of mental functioning.

Priming: The use of words covertly to trigger a specific psychological response from the listener. (See also *Scrambled Sentence Test*)

Process: Strategies or schemas applied in the execution of a feeling, behaviour or response.

Psychological Modulators: Experiences and conditions affecting psychological well-being.

Psychotropic: The action of a drug on the central nervous system whereby it alters brain function.

Randomised Control Trial (RCT): Statistical tool for measuring a predefined effect of a single drug or medical procedure on a standardised, defined subject population.

Reframing: Changing the meaning of an experience, behaviour, or event, by changing its context or interpretation.

Reification: Process of treating an abstraction as a concrete or material object.

Relaxation Response: Antithesis to the fight-or-flight response; invoked by certain meditative techniques.

Reorientation: Third phase in the Medical NLP Consultation Process in which techniques are applied to bring about change.

Representational Systems: Senses through which the brain receives information about the environment – e.g. visual, auditory, kinesthetic.

Resistance: Reason given by some psychologists for why their patients don't respond to treatment.

Restful Alertness: A state experienced during meditation characterised by reduced metabolic activity coupled with wakefulness.

Safety Netting: Giving instructions to a patient as to what action to take in the event of his condition worsening or persisting.

Salutogenesis/Salutogenic: Directed towards achieving healing and health (c.f. *Pathogenic/Pathogenesis*).

Scrambled Sentence Test: Psychological test involving the rearrangement of a group of words in order to extract meaning and affect behaviour; may involve *Priming*.

Secondary Traumatisation: (See *Burnout, Compassion Fatigue* and *Vicarious Traumatisation*).

Shaping/Behavioural Shaping: Indirectly guiding and reinforcing 'useful' or desirable behaviour, while ignoring or correcting that which is not desired.

Signal-to-Noise Ratio (SNR or S/N): Derived from engineering, SNR refers to the relationship between meaningful information (the Signal) and background confusion (the Noise).

Silent Abreaction: The gentle, controlled release of repressed emotion. Dissipation of entropy (see also *Abreaction* and *Entropy*).

Single-Cause Hypothesis: The belief that each illness is caused by a single pathological agent.

Solution Frame: Construct aimed at orientating the subject towards moving towards solutions rather than away from problems.

Solution-orientated thinking: Seeking solutions rather than spending all available time on analysing problems. Useful in medicine where all 'causes' of a problem have been eliminated.

Somatic Marker: Term coined by Antonio Damasio to refer to the internal sensation accompanying a particular emotional experience. (See also *Kinesthetic* and *Felt Sense*)

Somatoform: Expressed physically by the body.

Split/Splitting: The division of experience into smaller component parts in order to render it more manageable.

Stacked/stacking anchors: Two or more different responses set to be activated by the same stimulus. Most commonly, stacking is used to create a particularly powerful resource state.

State: The integrated sum of mental, physical and emotional conditions from which the subject is acting.

Strategy: Sequence of internal processes resulting in a specific feeling or behaviour.

Stress-Enhanced Memory: Memory 'fixed' by traumatic events (believed to be a function of increased serum cortisol).

Structural Differential: A model created by Alfred Korzybski to demonstrate the process of verbal abstraction used in an attempt to describe subjective experience.

Structure: The way in which a specific behaviour functions, as opposed to the reasons it exists (*Content*).

Submodalities: The unique characteristics of the sensory modalities used to create subjective experience – e.g. when we think of a holiday as a picture (Modality – Visual), is the picture in colour or black and white (submodality of the Visual modality).

Sympathetic Arousal: Arousal of the Sympathetic Nervous System (SNS), giving rise to the fight-or-flight response.

Symptom-Solution Linkage: A technique in Medical NLP in which a new, resourceful response is attached to the trigger of an older, less resourceful, one.

Systematic Desensitisation: A technique used in behavioural psychology to treat phobias by gradual exposure to the object of fear.

Thought-changing: Term used in psychology in place of the more colloquial "brain-washing".

Time Distortion: Subjective temporal experience that differs from 'objective' clock time.

Time Line: Subjective construct which metaphorically organises the individual's past, present and future experience spatially.

Towards: Motivational pattern marked by seeking to accomplish or achieve a particular goal.

Trance: An altered state of consciousness usually marked by reduced awareness of external events and increased focus on specific thoughts or feelings. Often accompanied by increased 'suggestibility', and used interchangeably with *Hypnosis.*

Trance Logic: Explanations advanced by the subject to explain behaviour induced by post-hypnotic suggestion. These often appear laughable or bizarre to unhypnotised observers.

Trance Phenomena: Behaviours usually associated with deep hypnosis (e.g. Amnesia, Arm Levitation, Hallucination etc).

Transcranial Magnetic Stimulation (TCMS): The utilisation of variable magnetic fields to modulate and map neuronal brain activity.

Transderivational Search: Attributing meaning to the statement of another from within one's own experience.

Two-point Loop: A self-maintaining repetitive sequence within a strategy.

Ultradian Rhythms: Biorhythms which occur in 90- to 120-minute cycles.

Unconscious: Everything that is outside present awareness.

Unconscious Association: Connections between present and past experience made by the brain on an other-than-conscious level.

Up-Time Trance: Altered, or hypnotic, state in which the subject maintains contact with the 'external world'.

Verifiable Data: Sensory-based information (c.f. **Inference**).

Vicarious Traumatisation: The detrimental effect to the practitioner of exposure to accounts of the client's traumatic experience.

Index

Index